PRAISE FOR *STRATEGIC LOGISTICS MANAGEMENT*

'This book covers various aspects of logistics management succinctly and elucidates how they can bring competitive advantage to organizations in dynamic business environment. Viewing various aspects of logistics through the lenses of organizational theories brings interesting perspectives. Emerging issues like resilience and circularity have also been covered. This book encompasses the existing body of knowledge of logistics management in a very lucid way.'
Dr Abhijit Majumdar, Chair Professor (Decision Science), Indian Institute of Technology Delhi, India

'*Strategic Logistics Management* by Erik Sandberg is a must-read for professionals seeking to understand the true strategic power of logistics. Sandberg masterfully bridges the gap between traditional logistics and cutting-edge strategic management theory, demonstrating how companies can outperform competitors through superior logistics capabilities. With a balance of theoretical insight and practical application, this book offers invaluable tools for scholars and business leaders alike.'
Dr Carlos Mena, Daimler Endowed Professor of Supply Chain Management, Portland State University, USA

'This book will become a standard work for understanding how important logistics management is to run businesses in times of hypercompetition, not least the complex world in which the retail industry lives. Its approach, starting with understanding logistics management and then how to think strategically in order to put it into practice makes the book a must for company management, not least in retail management.

After reading the book, I can only agree with Erik about what he writes in the preface:

"In particular, it provides a comprehensive overview of the intersection between strategic management theory on the one hand and logistics and supply chain management practice on the other."'
Arne B Andersson, Senior E-Commerce Adviser, Swedish Trade (Svensk Handel), Sweden

‘It is refreshing to see a supply chain textbook with a strategic management focus and a practical business model perspective, involving stakeholders across the supply chain. These insights will be valuable for both academia and industry.’
Prof Dr Helen Rogers, Research Professor, Technische Hochschule Nürnberg/Ohm University, Germany

‘Logistics and supply chain management have now moved to centre stage in those organisations that seek to gain competitive advantage in a world of constant change and increasing uncertainty. The author of this insightful book has recognized the need for a systematic and structured approach to the development of a strategy that leverages logistics and supply chain management competencies and provides practical guidance on how this can be achieved.’
Martin Christopher, Emeritus Professor of Marketing and Logistics, Cranfield University, UK

‘Highly relieving to see a textbook (re-)focusing on logistics management which in recent years has almost been engrossed in the all-encompassing term of supply chain management (SCM). By approaching logistics management from the corporate strategy literature, we are – among other things - reminded about the big, global companies where logistics is a fundamental part of their business models, such as Ikea and Amazon. We had almost forgotten about the basis of SCM, namely the materials and information flows.’
Britta Gammelgaard, Professor, Supply Chain Management, University of South Denmark, Denmark

Strategic Logistics Management

Contemporary principles and practice

Erik Sandberg

KoganPage

Publisher's note

Every possible effort has been made to ensure that the information contained in this book is accurate at the time of going to press, and the publishers and authors cannot accept responsibility for any errors or omissions, however caused. No responsibility for loss or damage occasioned to any person acting, or refraining from action, as a result of the material in this publication can be accepted by the editor, the publisher or the authors.

First published in Great Britain and the United States in 2025 by Kogan Page Limited

2nd Floor, 45 Gee Street
London
EC1V 3RS
United Kingdom

8 W 38th Street, Suite 902
New York, NY 10018
USA

www.koganpage.com

Kogan Page books are printed on paper from sustainable forests.

ISBNs
Hardback 978 1 3986 1807 7
Paperback 978 1 3986 1804 6
Ebook 978 1 3986 1805 3

British Library Cataloguing-in-Publication Data

A CIP record for this book is available from the British Library.

Library of Congress Cataloging-in-Publication Data

Names: Sandberg, Erik (Professor of logistics), author.
Title: Strategic logistics management / Erik Sandberg.
Description: London ; New York, NY : Kogan Page, 2025. | Includes bibliographical references and index.
Identifiers: LCCN 2024044019 (print) | LCCN 2024044020 (ebook) | ISBN 9781398618046 (paperback) | ISBN 9781398618077 (hardback) | ISBN 9781398618053 (ebook)
Subjects: LCSH: Business logistics–Management. | Strategic planning.
Classification: LCC HD38.5 .S256 2025 (print) | LCC HD38.5 (ebook) | DDC 658.7–dc23/eng/20241018
LC record available at https://lccn.loc.gov/2024044019
LC ebook record available at https://lccn.loc.gov/2024044020

Typeset by Integra Software Services, Pondicherry
Print production managed by Jellyfish
Printed and bound by CPI Group (UK) Ltd, Croydon, CR0 4YY

CONTENTS

LIST OF FIGURES AND TABLES

Figures

Tables

PREFACE

Practitioners as well as scholars increasingly claim logistics management to be strategically relevant and a ground for a company's sustainable competitive advantage. In addition to being 'market-oriented' or 'product-oriented' with respect to its strategic intentions, a company can also be *logistics-oriented.* In such a company logistics management plays a critical role not just for production, purchasing, or any other function, but for the company as a whole. The performance of logistics activities such as transportation, storing and handling are not only acknowledged in terms of operational costs, delivery service or lead times, but also in terms of profitability, growth, and value creation for the entire company.

Accordingly, the strategic relevance of logistics management has been acknowledged in many existing textbooks, and terms such as 'strategic' or 'competitive' are often included in their titles. So far, however, these have mainly discussed the strategic relevance of logistics management from the logistics and supply chain management domain itself.

The premise of this book is to complement existing textbooks and explore the strategic relevance of logistics management by going outside the traditional logistics and supply chain management domain and apply strategic management theory. Overall, strategic management theory aims at explaining why some companies are able to outperform others over time. Strategic management theory hence provides a more 'objective' ground for how to understand and judge the strategic relevance of logistics management.

The book consists of two parts, targeting *understanding* and respectively *managing* strategic logistics management. The *understanding*-part consists of three chapters, taking stance in the market positioning-, resource-based-, and dynamic capabilities-perspectives. Based on the fundamentals of each perspective, the linkages between logistics management and a company's sustainable competitive advantage are systematically explored and illuminated in this part of the book. Together, the three perspectives cover a variety of strategic management theories that have been developed since the 1980s. As such, this part of the book provides the reader with the necessary 'glasses' for how to understand and analyse the role of logistics management in a company's sustainable competitive advantage. The *managing*-part then follows, presenting some of the main contemporary themes related to strategic logistics management, including logistics development, paradoxes, supply chain resilience, logistics-based business models, and circular supply chains. These topics are addressed in one chapter each where they are discussed from the strategic management perspectives presented in the first part of the book.

This book is mainly thought to be used in advanced logistics and supply chain management courses and modules at university level. Another target group for the book is senior-level practitioners in the field of logistics and supply chain management, for instance in conjunction with executive education. For both these targeted groups, this book offers new insights with respect to understanding as well as managing logistics management. In particular, it provides a comprehensive overview of the intersection between strategic management theory on the one hand, and logistics and supply chain management practices on the other. It presents a useful ground and new arguments for how to understand the role of logistics management when strategizing. Furthermore, it covers some of the most pressing managerial themes relevant in a contemporary logistics management context.

ACKNOWLEDGEMENTS

To write this book would not have been possible without inspiration and help from people around me including colleagues and friends. In particular I am grateful for the many discussions and joint writing processes I have had with professors Mats Abrahamsson, Rudrajeet Pal and Henrik Pålsson. I am also grateful to the team at Kogan Page that have supported me throughout the publishing process. Finally, a big thank you goes to my family that has supported me during the writing process. It took some time but it is now done!

ABBREVIATIONS

CE	Circular Economy
CPFR	Collaborative Planning, Forecasting, and Replenishment
CSCM	Circular Supply Chain Management
DCs	Dynamic Capabilities
ECR	Efficient Consumer Response
ELD	Experimental Logistics Development
IDCs	Interorganizational Dynamic Capabilities
KPI	Key Performance Indicator
PMS	Performance Measurement System
RBV	Resource-based View of the Firm
SCM	Supply Chain Management
SCO	Supply Chain Orientation
SCOR model	The Supply Chain Operations Reference Model
SKU	Stock Keeping Unit
VMI	Vendor Managed Inventory

WALKTHROUGH OF TEXTBOOK FEATURES AND ONLINE RESOURCES

There are several learning features described below, designed to assist readers in their learning and understanding.

Chapter outlines

Highlight the main issues and topics that will be covered in each chapter.

> A premise of this chapter is that a crucial task for strategic logistics management is to consider these conflicts of interest in a more structured and comprehensive manner than what has usually been emphasized in a logistics context…
>
> Section 6.1 introduces paradoxical thinking as a lens for how to understand the nature of conflicts of interest.

Case studies / Real-world examples

A range of case studies / real-world examples from different industries illustrates how key ideas and theories are operating in practice to help you to place the concepts discussed in real-life context.

Discussion questions

At the end of each chapter, these discussion questions can be used in tutorials or small study groups to stimulate debate and critical thinking.

1 Provide examples of trade-offs that are commonly discussed in a logistics and supply chain management context.

Study questions

Questions and activities throughout the text encourage you to reflect on what you have learnt and to apply your knowledge and skills in practice.

1 What does a supply chain orientation mean?

2 Explain briefly the financial logics of economies of scale, scope and integration.

Chapter summaries

Draw together the main threads of the chapter and summarize the key points.

Grounded in systems thinking, at the very heart of strategic logistics management is the need to constantly manage competing interests and goals that arise within and between companies in a supply chain. The existence of these conflicts of interest is a well-known fact in a logistics management context, typically addressed as trade-offs. This chapter has introduced paradox theory as a lens for a further, more thorough exploration of conflicts of interest in a logistics and SCM context.

Glossary

A detailed glossary is included at the end of the book for quick reference to key terms and definitions in the book.

List of abbreviations

This is included to provide you with quick and easy reference to any abbreviations used throughout the book.

References

Detailed references provide quick and easy access to the research and underpinning sources behind the chapter.

Online resources

Online resources include lecturer slides, an instructor's manual and additional comments on the study questions.

Downloadable resources are available at **www.koganpage.com/slm**

PART ONE
Understanding Strategic Logistics

The strategic importance of logistics management 01

For many companies the ability to plan, organize and manage logistics activities such as transportation, storing and handling is increasingly becoming a source for a sustainable competitive advantage. Instead of developing a strategy based on, for example their products or market presence, the strategy of these companies hinges upon a superior logistics performance. The company's strategic intentions with respect to various functional areas such as marketing, purchasing and production are still important, but what really is decisive for the company's overall success is the planning and organization of the physical flow of goods and related information-sharing across the company functions and in the supply chain towards suppliers and customers. In the very centre of these efforts stands logistics management.

This chapter outlines the meaning of such logistics-oriented companies (section 1.1), and discusses some of the trends that drive contemporary logistics development and the strategic relevance of logistics management (section 1.2). It also presents and defines key terms used in the book including logistics, logistics management, supply chain management and strategy (section 1.3), and some of the most recognized logistics strategies (section 1.4). Thereafter it provides an overview of the remainder of the book by introducing the content and themes in the chapters of the book (section 1.5).

1.1 Logistics-oriented companies

A fundamental starting point for this book is that, as indicated above, in addition to market-oriented or production-oriented companies, there are also companies that can be considered as *logistics-oriented*. Examples of such companies can be found in the manufacturing as well as in the retailing industry, spanning a wide spectrum of different sectors and niches. Some of the perhaps most common international examples of logistics-oriented companies are Wal-Mart, IKEA, Zara (Inditex), Apple, Nestlé, Hewlett Packard, Tesco, Amazon and Lidl. They all, in some form, use logistics as a means to enhance a sustainable competitive advantage, i.e. outperform competitors over time. Within these companies, logistics plays a vital role not just for production or purchasing, but for the company as a whole. The performance of logistics activities such as transportation, storing and handling are not only acknowledged in terms of costs, delivery service or lead times, but also in terms of profitability, growth and value creation for the entire company.

However, the actual design of logistics, as well as *how* logistics is strategically important, differs between the companies – this depends on the specific customers of the company and their demands.

For IKEA and Lidl, logistics means a superior cost control throughout the supply chain, with a focus on offering customers continually improved prices. For Zara (Inditex), logistics primarily contributes to a quick time-to-market, while Tesco can create competitive and efficient market channels by synchronizing information flows in the supply chain.

REAL-WORLD EXAMPLE Amazon: a logistics-oriented company

Amazon (i.e. Amazon.com Inc.) has, since the 1990s, developed from being an online book retailer in the US to a multinational e-commerce player, whose businesses spans delivery of software services and a vast variety of commodity products and groceries.

For Amazon, logistics plays a decisive role for the creation of a sustainable competitive advantage. Internally as well as externally throughout the supply chain, the physical flow of goods and related information is acknowledged as a crucial ingredient for operational efficiency and effectiveness, but also for its strategic impact on value creation and, ultimately, customer satisfaction. Due to its rapid growth and size, and the company's attention to consumer-centric delivery offerings, Amazon has for many years not only been able to rely upon external, existing third-party logistics providers and their services, but has also innovated and invested in many new logistics solutions internally to fulfil the company's strategic intentions. This means that logistics operations are part of Amazon's core business and are one of its key cornerstones, controlled and supported directly by top management.

Amazon's superior world-spanning logistics infrastructure in terms of, for example, transportation fleet and warehouses, is not only used for Amazon's own products, but is also essential for Amazon's business concept Fulfilment by Amazon (FBA), in which small and medium-sized retailers are offered leverage on Amazon's superior logistics infrastructure for storing, picking and packing, labelling, shipping and returns management when they sell products over Amazon's marketplace. The inclusion of these 'third-party sellers' on the marketplace is not only advantageous for Amazon's extraordinary product range (which is another essential part of Amazon's sustainable competitive advantage), and an additional revenue stream, but means also that Amazon's logistics operations can benefit from further economies of scale and scope, and improved utilization of, for example, transportation and storing capacities.

The logistics infrastructure is also fundamental to the success of Amazon Prime, the company's loyalty programme. Loyalty and customer satisfaction here are created by means of customer-centric, fast and comprehensive delivery services.

By supplementing the use of third-party logistics providers with their own logistics operations, these delivery services can:

1. be developed beyond the industry standards
2. be unique
3. function as a key signature for Amazon's customer offering

Another crucial element of Amazon being a logistics-oriented company, and closely aligned with the in-house logistics infrastructure and the competitive opportunities it brings (such as the FBA service and Amazon Prime) is Amazon's leading position when it comes to utilization of technology advancements. Amazon is well known as a forerunner when it comes to artificial intelligence (AI), machine learning, robotics, drones and automation. A common rationale for these applications is the continuous search for improved operational performance in the physical flow of goods. Amazon also has, thanks to its size and in-house control of logistics operations, the opportunity to experiment and test new technologies at scale.

The use of new technologies also means that Amazon has been able to collect and exploit vast amounts of data, including order history, logistics performance, consumer behaviour, weather forecasts, etc. This data is combined to optimize logistics performance throughout the supply chain. Advanced predictive analytics helps anticipate customer demand, adjust inventory levels, and optimize routing and delivery schedules. As such, this data-driven approach in logistics planning and execution ensures high efficiency and responsiveness to market changes.

SOURCES www.Amazon.com; Banker (2021); Manners-Bell and Lyon (2023)

1.2 Trends that drive the strategic relevance of logistics management

The strategic relevance of logistics is due to a number of contemporary trends in society (see Figure 1.1).

Figure 1.1 Trends that drive the strategic relevance of logistics

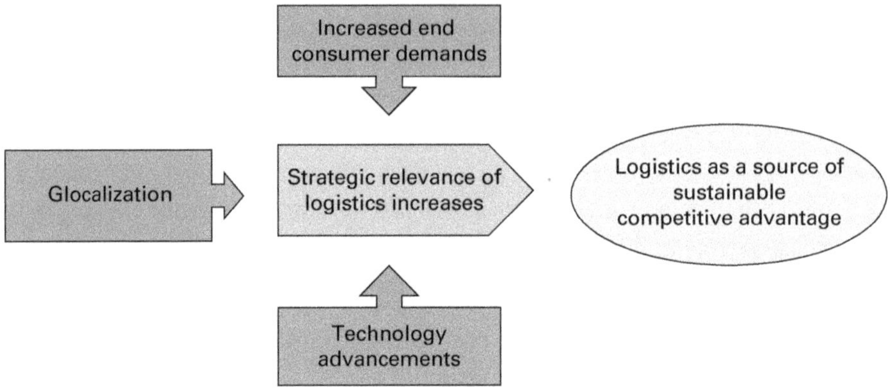

1.2.1 'Glocalization' – the design of global and local logistics flows

Many companies and their supply chains are today facing a development in which increased global, as well as local, supply chains should be navigated, i.e. there is a need to become 'glocal'. From a globalization point of view, many supply chains are today geographically dispersed. Products can be transported from one continent to another, and then all the way back, only to be sent on to a third continent where they are finally consumed. Despite recent years of protectionism, recognition of environmental impact of transports, and higher fuel and energy prices, there is (still) a continuous quest for cheaper and better products, and creation of economies of scale and scope that provide very strong arguments for a global trade. These arguments are also further accelerated by various market deregulations and global trade agreements.

In parallel with this globalization there has also been a development towards more local supply chain flows where, for instance, production is placed closer to customer markets as a means to decrease environmental impact and reduce complexity in the existing global supply chains. Automation and other technology developments mean that production in high-wage countries becomes more realistic from an economic point of view and hence causes changes in the supply chain structure. A redesign from global to more local (or regional) supply chains has also been shown to be a promising measure to cope with a volatile and unpredictable business environment. Supply chain disruptions caused by, for instance, climate changes and geopolitical instability often make more local supply chains more advantageous, where control can better be achieved, and lead times can be shorter.

The development towards more local supply chains, however, seldom means that the global supply chains can be completely removed. Rather, the supply chain structure of many companies ends up in a mix of global and local suppliers and customers, hence increasing the total supply chain complexity even further.

In summary, companies need to balance the pros and cons of globalization as well as localization, and design for 'glocalization'. In practice, this means more complex and diverse logistics operations where global operations must be combined with various local ones. For companies that are able to master these challenges better than rivals, superior glocal supply chain operations may constitute a foundation for a sustainable competitive advantage.

1.2.2 Increased end consumer demands

In most societies in the Western world, mainly characterized by an abundance of goods and services, the increased demands of customers have amplified the importance of logistics as a means to augment the core offering – typically a product or repair service. Today it is simply not always enough to have a superior, perhaps unique, product. It also increasingly needs to be made available to the buyer in the right place, in the right quantity, at the right time and at the right quality. This trend of convenience is perhaps most evident in the ongoing development towards more e-commerce and omnichannel business practices in the retail industry. In this context, logistics plays a crucial role as an 'order winner', as it becomes increasingly vital to offer fast and reliable deliveries as well as returns.

Another related end consumer demand, that also accentuates the strategic relevance of logistics, has to do with increased environmental and social concerns. When it comes to environmental impact, there is in general an increased awareness of the role logistics plays. For instance, the impact of transport on society's total CO_2 emissions is receiving increased attention, and the demands for reductions are becoming more evident. For logistics, this means, for example, an increased focus on how to organize and plan transports between goods owners and logistics service providers in the supply chain and identify the most appropriate transportation modes available. A societal focus on the environment also means that there is a growing demand for a more circular economy; which for logistics translates into an increased emphasis on return flows of various kinds, including both new and used products.

In addition to societal demands for economic and environmental sustainability, social aspects have also become increasingly important among end consumers. For instance, purchasing activities in developing countries and their impact on social sustainability are receiving greater attention. Beyond the working conditions of manufacturing itself, subsequent storage and transportation must also be considered. For companies in the Western world that are expected to ensure compliance with laws and regulations and, for example, that children are not exploited as labour, it is important not just to review the manufacturing activities but also the logistics activities that complement the actual production. Another essential aspect of social sustainability within logistics is ergonomically designed work processes to ensure the health and safety of staff are not compromised. Packaging is another example of something that can affect the health and safety of employees.

1.2.3 Technology advancements

Another trend that further amplifies the strategic relevance of logistics is technology advancements. Overall, new technology can be considered as an enabler for breaking new ground and finally realizing the essence of rather old fundamental logistics ideas, including, for instance, holistic thinking, optimized planning and collaborative information sharing throughout a supply chain. For example, the Internet of Things (IoT) and Big data with advanced analytics enable companies to monitor and analyse the entire supply chain in real-time. These potential new predictive insights and analyses allow companies to proactively address potential disruptions and optimize logistics operations in a way that was previously not possible.

As for the increased end consumer demands, an area where the technology advancements bring strategic relevance to logistics is e-commerce. Retail logistics operations, leveraging various technology advancements, are now at the heart of fulfilling the increased end consumer expectations on, for example, ability to track and trace services, fast deliveries and information. Indeed, embracing technology advancements in conjunction with the development of e-commerce logistics such as last-mile deliveries can yield a company a sustainable competitive advantage in the marketplace.

Furthermore, automation and robotics have transformed warehousing and distribution, enhancing both efficiency and accuracy. This technology-driven shift means companies can swiftly adapt to market changes and demands, positioning logistics as a tool for achieving strategic objectives of the company. In addition, as was mentioned above, automation constitutes an opportunity for companies to reorganize the global supply chain and again introduce, for instance, production and warehousing operations in high-wage countries.

In essence, technology advancements have elevated the strategic relevance of logistics. From a managerial point of view, it is important to note that the current technology advancements are now rapidly transforming the entire logistics and supply chain management landscape. The technologies are not just improving operational efficiency and effectiveness, but are also a fundamental driving force for strategic shifts, for instance enabling companies to be more customer-oriented, resilient, sustainable and competitive. Thus, various technological advancements have indeed been instrumental for logistics-oriented companies.

1.3 Definitions of logistics and supply chain management

Even though the term 'logistics' is an old concept used within the military, it was not until the 1960s that it began to be used in a business context. Within research and academia, it is even newer and has developed significantly in recent years. Perhaps the most cited definition of the term logistics comes from the global association Council of Supply Chain Management Professional's (CSCMP) website:

> The process of planning, implementing, and controlling procedures for the efficient and effective transportation and storage of goods including services, and related information from the point of origin to the point of consumption for the purpose of conforming to customer requirements. This definition includes inbound, outbound, internal, and external movements. (CSCMP, n.d.)

The management of logistics, i.e. logistics management as addressed in the title of this book, is by CSCMP defined in a similar manner as follows:

> Logistics management is that part of supply chain management that plans, implements, and controls the efficient, effective forward and reverses flow and storage of goods, services and related information between the point of origin and the point of consumption in order to meet customers' requirements. (CSCMP, n.d.)

In terms of activities included in a contemporary understanding of logistics, previously fragmented activities such as demand forecasting, purchasing, warehousing, packaging, transportation, distribution, and material handling have been increasingly combined under the umbrella term 'logistics', and logistics management therefore today incorporates the planning and responsibility for a long row of activities provided by a number of company functions.

Apart from the evolution of activities encompassed, the objective of logistics management has also evolved. From almost exclusively being about cost savings and reducing tied-up capital, logistics management today is also associated with terms like sustainability, value creation, revenue streams, competitiveness, and strategy (see Figure 1.2).

This development can be seen as a consequence of developments in the surrounding business environment and society. For example, the high interest rates of the 1970s made logistics an important tool for reducing tied-up capital. The 1980s shift towards flexible, customized production meant logistics also evolved in that direction. Today, society's focus on sustainability is reflected in the development of logistics. It is in light of this progression that this book becomes significant.

The more strategically important and relevant logistics has become, the more crucial it is to understand how logistics can contribute to a company's sustainable competitive advantage.

Figure 1.2 The evolution of the objectives of logistics management

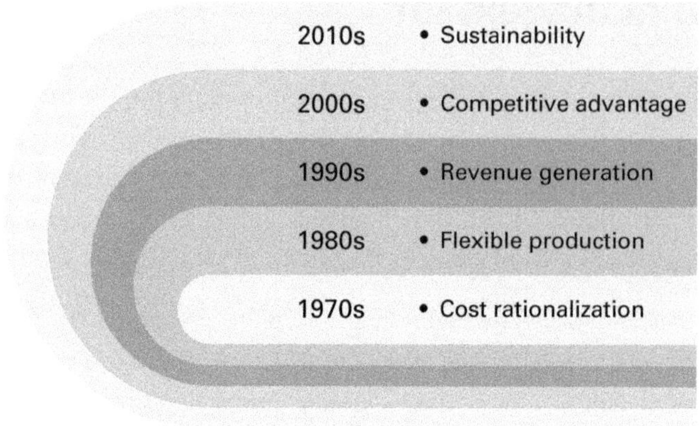

SOURCE Adapted from Sandberg and Abrahamsson (2019)

As the term 'logistics management' has evolved, and as is also indicated in the definition, the term 'supply chain management' is closely related to logistics management. The purpose of this book is to highlight primarily the strategic significance of logistics and logistics management, therefore, the book will mainly use logistics as its main term. However, since it is often difficult, and sometimes impossible, to distinguish logistics or logistics management from SCM, the book also indirectly sheds light on the strategic significance of SCM. It is therefore relevant to introduce SCM here shortly to the reader.

The term supply chain management was first coined in 1982 by logistics consultants Keith Oliver and Michael Webber (Christopher, 2016), who pointed out that many companies face a significant challenge in coordinating their increasingly long and complex supply chains with multiple objectives. As the term 'logistics' back then was very closely associated with internal warehousing and transportation, a new term was introduced to highlight the need for managing the external material flows also. SCM emphasized a systems perspective to be taken, and the importance of relationships with other players in the supply chain. Indeed, SCM continues to be a widely used term, and as for logistics, many definitions of the term have evolved over the years. A contemporary one is that of the CSCMP:

> Supply chain management encompasses the planning and management of all activities involved in sourcing and procurement, conversion, and all logistics management activities. Importantly, it also includes coordination and collaboration with channel partners, which can be suppliers, intermediaries, third party service providers, and customers. In essence, supply chain management integrates supply and demand management within and across companies. (CSCMP, n.d.)

Just like in the case of logistics management, the main message in SCM is that a company within a supply chain should strive for low costs and good service towards the end customers, which ultimately should lead to creating customer value. This should be achieved along the triple bottom-line perspective, where economic, environmental, as well as social performance are emphasized.

Sustainable low costs and good service are achieved in particular by means of coordination with other players in the supply chain. This coordination should be created through collaboration based on trust with customers and suppliers where a clear win-win thinking is fundamental. The processes in the supply chain – or perhaps rather the network of customers and suppliers – should be made visible and prioritized over individual functions, both internally and externally. The company's operations should not only be managed based on the best interests of the company itself, but rather from the entire supply chain's perspective, since companies in this chain are dependent on each other's performances. Indeed, as stated by Professor Martin Christopher, the real competition is not company against company, but rather supply chains against supply chains (Christopher, 2016).

In relation to this it is worth noting that SCM, as well as logistics management, needs to relate not just to a single supply chain that has *one* supplier and *one* customer. Instead, companies find themselves in a network of businesses that are all directly or indirectly connected to one another. A more accurate way to address SCM might thus be 'supply chain network management', acknowledging that a focal company is connected with several suppliers upstream as well as downstream. In fact, a focal company is very seldom involved in just one supply chain, but several. From a focal company's perspective, this requires prioritization of which supply chains are the most important in terms of competitiveness.

So, what is really the difference between logistics management and SCM? According to CSCMP's definition, logistics management is a 'part of SCM', meaning that SCM has a broader scope. However, the actual difference is vague, and there are alternative interpretations for how to distinguish these terms from each other. A useful distinction between the terms 'logistics' and 'supply chain management' was presented by Larson and Halldorsson (2004), that can also be used for understanding the difference between logistics management and SCM. In short, Larson and Halldorsson (2004) concluded that the difference, if there is any, can be illustrated in the following four views:

- *The Traditionalist* considers SCM as a part of the larger concept of logistics. Here, SCM is associated with logistics outside the company, sometimes referred to as the company's external logistics.
- *The Re-labelling* approach sees no difference between the concepts, and refers to them interchangeably. For instance, one might observe that many logistics managers have had their title changed to 'supply chain manager' without necessarily having their job responsibilities altered.
- *The Unionist* views SCM as a broader concept that encompasses more areas and tasks than logistics. Here, SCM includes a wide range of different company functions where logistics becomes a part of SCM.

- *The Intersectionist* considers the SCM and logistics areas to overlap in content, but SCM tends to contain some strategic tasks that cannot be considered as logistics. Conversely, the concept of logistics contains certain more operational aspects, such as picking and packing in a warehouse, which cannot be included in the SCM concept.

1.4 Logistics strategies

Strategy is certainly not a new term among logistics practitioners and scholars. Indeed, from a logistics management point of view, the planning and organization of material flows has been discussed in numerous different functionally oriented 'logistics strategies' over the years. These strategies have typically been grounded in a 'top-down' reasoning where they have been considered as subordinated to a company's overall corporate and business strategy.

A premise of this book is to go beyond these functional logistics strategies and instead use strategic management theory as a lens to understand how logistics management can be the foundation for a company's sustainable competitive advantage. However, before doing this, it may be insightful to introduce some common (functional) logistics strategies and their fundamentals.

Therefore, in this section the logistics strategy typology that was first presented by the researchers Donald Bowersox and Patricia Daugherty in 1987 (Bowersox and Daugherty, 1987, see also e.g. Autry et al, 2008; McGinnis et al, 2010) and the lean and agile strategies (e.g. Christopher, 2016) are shortly presented. Thereafter follows an explanation of the difference between these functional strategies on the one hand, and business strategy on the other.

1.4.1 The Bowersox-Daugherty strategies

In order to describe and structure the operational patterns of different logistics strategies, a seminal article from the researchers Donald Bowersox and Patricia Daugherty (1987) presented three distinct pathways for how to achieve logistics excellence.

The process strategy primarily aims to coordinate and streamline a range of different company functions internally (e.g. purchasing, manufacturing and distribution) so that the physical flow of goods becomes as cost-efficient and cost-effective as possible. By targeting the underlying processes and outlining included activities and responsibilities of the various involved functions, a better control of the physical flow of goods can be gained. This is expected to result in various cost reductions related to reduction of excess inventories, unnecessary double-work in processes, better use of packaging, better fill-rates in transportations, etc.

The market strategy involves a customer focus where the overarching goal is to align logistics operations with customer demands. For instance, if the company's customer demands revolve around fast deliveries, then its logistics strategy should target mechanisms to ensure fast transportation and minimal lead times. Activities related to customer service are focused on, often in close collaboration with other customer-focused functions, activities such as sales.

The information strategy focuses on the role of information in enhancing logistics operations throughout the supply chain. In particular with respect to recent rapid technology developments and more sophisticated supply chain tools, information has become central to enhance efficient and effective logistics operations. Companies adopting an information strategy prioritize the collection, processing and dissemination of logistics-related information to ensure optimal decision-making.

It is worth noting that while this taxonomy provided a foundational perspective on logistics strategies in the late 1980s, the meaning of the terms logistics as well as SCM has evolved considerably since they were first introduced. Nonetheless, they remain highly valid and offer a good overview of how to organize, plan and execute operational excellence in logistics. In practice, they can be adopted and implemented through a variety of logistics concepts and activities (sometimes also labelled 'strategies') such as vendor managed inventory, collaborative planning, forecasting and replenishment, cross-docking, multimodal transports, etc.

1.4.2 Lean and agile

Two other seminal logistics strategies, also referred to as supply chain strategies, are lean and agile. Both these strategies, discussed as a pair or individually, have had a profound impact on logistics development during the last decades.

The *lean strategy* is based on the fundamental idea of maximizing value for customers while eliminating various kinds of waste. In total, eight types of waste are usually mentioned: transportation, inventory, motion, waiting, overproduction, overprocessing, defects and the unutilized creativity of the workers. In line with these, elimination of non-value-added activities are opted for, which requires a deep knowledge of involved activities and processes, as well as an understanding of customer needs to ensure that products or services are delivered in the most efficient and effective way possible. A lean strategy is best suited when there is a steady flow of materials with little variation and when demand is well known. In such a context, it becomes important to fine-tune logistics operations through continuous small improvements so that the productivity of various resources involved in the flow is maximized, for example, by high-capacity utilization in trucks and storage facilities.

The foundation for *lean* originates from the Japanese automotive industry, especially Toyota, but over time it has evolved to more generally become a viable logistics strategy in other contexts as well, where not only production but also the logistics operations of a company or a supply chain can be included. However, the perception of what the term lean actually covers varies. By some, lean is seen as something much broader and larger than 'only' a strategy – rather, it is considered as a company culture or a change philosophy with a much broader scope than logistics. Conversely, lean can also be seen as a narrower concept than a strategy and instead be framed as a couple of specific tools and working methods used in production or other operations. Some examples of such well-known 'lean tools' are Six Sigma and 5S.

The fundamental idea of the second strategy, *agile*, is about being flexible and adaptable in the logistics operations. In contrast to lean, such a strategy is better suited in a more uncertain environment, where customer demand and needs vary or are uncertain. Under such conditions, the lean strategy's pursuit of being resource-efficient is overshadowed by the ability to deliver at all. To be able to do that, flexibility of various kinds is very important, which, for example, can mean that in an agile strategy, a certain overcapacity in the supply chain is deliberately planned to more easily handle rapid, unpredictable changes in, for example, demand. Since this involves increased costs, an agile strategy fits better in situations where the customers demand high service in the form of high availability and short lead times, rather than low costs.

1.4.3 Logistics strategy vs business strategy

The logistics strategies presented above are all examples of functional strategies, typically designed for managing issues related to the logistics function in isolation. In strategic management theory it is common to allocate strategies to different organizational levels. As well as functional strategies there are, for instance, strategies related to the operating business unit, corporation (company group level) or network (network of independent companies) levels (De Wit and Meyer, 2010). In this book, if not explicitly stated as something else, these higher-level strategies are referred to as 'business strategy'.

Figure 1.3 The relationship between business strategy and logistics strategy

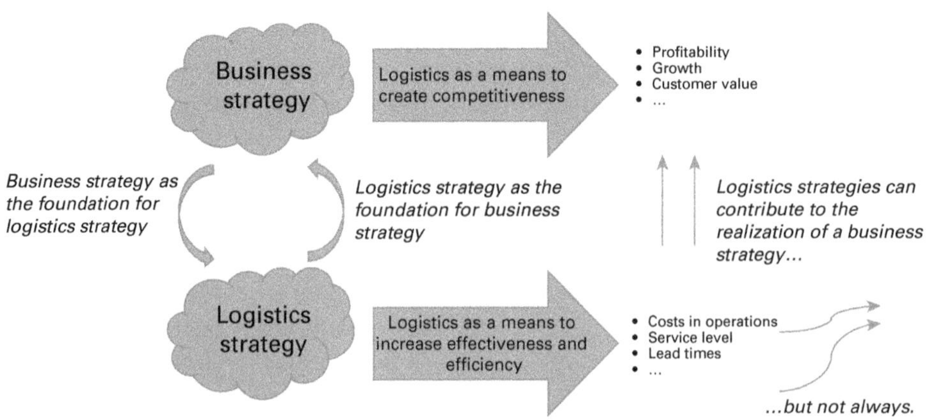

SOURCE Adapted from Sandberg (2015)

As Figure 1.3 illustrates, the business strategy and the logistics strategy are aligned and dependent on each other. However, their overarching objectives when it comes to the role of logistics differ. A business strategy seeks to design and conduct business operations (including logistics practices) in such a way that it can contribute to the company's overall sustainable competitive advantage. A sustainable competitive advantage here refers to a company's overall ability to consistently outperform its competitors and can be measured, for instance, in above-average profitability, company growth and customer value creation. In contrast, a logistics strategy pertains to how logistics as a function can enhance efficiency and effectiveness in physical flows of goods and information. The overall performance of such logistics strategies is often measured with respect to total costs, service and lead times.

A logistics strategy that, for instance, results in reduced costs can also lead to increased overall profitability of a company and hence contribute to a company's business strategy. In fact, superior logistics performance in terms of cost efficiency could be the primary reason why a company can compete based on low prices (an example of this is IKEA – a brief description is provided in Chapter 2). However, the strategic impact from a logistics strategy on the business strategy is not always evident; even if a logistics strategy results in cost-efficient warehousing processes or low transportation costs and may be deemed 'successful' in its own right, such a strategy might have only a negligible impact on the overall business strategy. In fact, it may even negatively affect the overall company performance and subsequently reduce overall profitability. A common illustration of this is when an overly cost-oriented logistics approach undermines an overall business strategy that aims towards unique, differentiated customer offerings. In such a case the low-cost-oriented logistics strategy may be counterproductive, and ultimately jeopardize the entire business strategy. Conversely, from a business strategy viewpoint, logistics can contribute to overall profitability, growth and customer value, even if it is not optimized from a functional perspective. This is often seen when logistics operations are closely tied to overall customer satisfaction. In such scenarios, sometimes expensive and 'inefficient' logistics operations (when evaluated from a strict functional perspective only) can be entirely justified from a business strategy standpoint. One example could be ultra-short delivery lead times that may not be possible to justify from a strict logistics perspective but become a crucial part in a business strategy aiming at creating superior customer satisfaction.

To summarize, a logistics strategy is here considered as a functional strategy and is crucial for our understanding of how to organize, plan and execute logistics. The different logistics strategies demonstrate what pathways and development opportunities there are to follow within the logistics function. As such they are useful for a further examination and elaboration of how different logistics objectives are to be accomplished and how to measure logistics performance. However, in order to fully understand the strategic role of logistics a pure focus on such functional strategies is not enough, as they need to be linked to a company's business strategy. The strategic relevance of logistics – i.e. when logistics contributes to a company's overall sustainable competitive advantage measured by, for instance, profitability, growth and/or customer value – becomes clear first when we can understand how the business strategy utilizes logistics to achieve its objectives.

1.5 Strategic management theory as a lens

As pointed out above, in order to fully understand the strategic relevance of logistics, logistics needs to be put into a larger context where logistics performance not only is measured in terms of costs, service and lead times, but also the company's overall profitability, growth and value creation. Interestingly, this was clarified by the logistics professor Göran Persson already in 1991, who claimed that:

> to understand the important and changing role of logistics in any company, it is insufficient to state that logistics has an important strategic impact. Instead, it is necessary to fully comprehend and reveal the opportunities logistics imply. In order to accomplish this, one has to understand what makes logistics important as well as why, when and how. In other words, one has to consider how the company's logistics activities contribute to creating a competitive advantage. To do this, logistics should be linked to the business strategy – a linkage that is neither evident nor very well explored. (Persson, 1991, p. 1)

In this article, Persson employed the market positioning perspective to move beyond the logistics domain and better elucidate the importance of logistics. This book is based on the same idea as Persson's article – by illuminating the connection between logistics and various perspectives that originate from strategic management theory, we can analyse and understand the strategic relevance of logistics.

Strategic management theory is vast and includes a plethora of dimensions, typologies and concepts. Its objectives are also numerous (see Figure 1.4), including aspects related to markets, competitive priorities and organization. One of the most well-known overviews of the multifaceted concept of strategy was provided by Henry Mintzberg (Mintzberg, 1994) who claimed that strategy can be understood as five different Ps: Plan, Ploy, Pattern, Position and Perspective. A more traditional view of strategy is of a *plan*. For instance, Professor Alfred Chandler defined strategy as: 'the determination of the basic long-term goals of an enterprise and the adoption of courses of actions and the allocation of resources necessary to carry out these goals' (Chandler, 1962, p. 13).

A strategy can, however, also be described as a *ploy*, i.e. a tactical manoeuvre designed to deceive competitors. One can also choose to view strategy as a *pattern* that is derived from activities the company undertakes, or as a certain *position* in the market. Finally, one can also see strategy as a *perspective* where employees and others share a common view of what the company stands for in terms of values, expressions, and more.

Figure 1.4 Objectives of strategic management theory

When it comes to strategic management theory, it is somewhat misleading to address it as strategic management *theory*, as there in fact exist numerous different strategic management *theories*. These have one thing in common: they all aim at explaining the question of *why do some companies outperform others?* (Barney and Clark, 2007), which is indeed a central, but challenging, task for strategic management scholars, characterized as 'the Holy Grail of strategic management' (Helfat and Peteraf, 2009).

There is obviously not one answer to this question, and there are continuously developed new answers to the question, i.e. new theories are presented. The intention in this book is not to provide a complete historical exposé of the development of the strategic management field, nor an exhaustive overview of existing strategic management theories. Rather, the aim here is to present three more aggregated strategic management *perspectives*, each of them representing more specific theories.

Together, these three perspectives provide an overview of the main development paths strategic management theory has taken in the last four decades (see Table 1.1) and will in this book be used to explain the strategic relevance of logistics. In research, it is common for more than one perspective to be used to improve the understanding of a company's strategy. The three perspectives should therefore be seen as complementary rather than competitive. It is also worth noting that the perspectives discussed in this book overlap with each other in many respects and that the 'extremes' and uniqueness of each perspective tend to be emphasized much more

Table 1.1 Main message in the three strategic management perspectives

	Market positioning perspective	Resource-based perspective	Dynamic capabilities perspective
Main question when strategizing	What industry should we operate in and what market position should we take?	Which are our strategically important resources?	How do we change our resources to stay competitive in the future?
Basic unit of competitive advantage	Superior activities and the activity system.	Resources that are valuable, rare and imperfectly imitable.	Superior capacity to renew the resource base.
How customer satisfaction is achieved	A position on the market that creates maximum customer value.	Appropriate resources that create maximum customer value.	Renewal of the resource base to ensure maximum customer value over time.
Emphasis when addressing competitive strength	Competitive market position.	Superior resource(s).	Ability to change resources and practices.

than the similarities and overlaps that exist. There are, for example, similar lines of reasoning about how activities and resources can be seen as important building blocks for the strategy. All three perspectives also emphasize the importance of 'being unique' when competing, and having a fit against environmental elements.

The market positioning perspective revolves around how a company should position itself in the marketplace to gain a sustainable competitive advantage vis-à-vis competitors. Strategizing in market positioning theory consists mainly of answering two questions:

1 In what industry should we as a company operate?

2 What competitive position should we take in that industry?

Tools and theories for how to answer these two questions were first developed by Michael Porter (Porter, 1980; 1985), as well as the five forces model, the value chain concept and the three generic strategies of cost leadership, differentiation and focus. The message of the market positioning perspective forms the basis for a multitude of books, research articles and reports, and has gained significant traction. Its strength lies primarily in the fact that the theories and models presented are relatively simple and robust, and can be used regardless of industry or other environments. Moreover, because they are relatively old and have been used in university and college education for many years, they are also well known to many practitioners in organization, management and strategy. They can still be used as a basis for strategic reviews and form the foundation for strategy development in many companies. Within logistics research, Porter's thoughts are also relatively well-cited – Chapter 2, devoted to market positioning theory, addresses some of these connections.

The resource-based perspective, which primarily includes the resource-based view (RBV) of the firm, was developed largely as a reaction to Porter's approach and came to dominate strategic management research in the 1990s. Inspired by older researchers such as Penrose (1959) and Wernerfelt (1984), proponents of the RBV argued that even if a favourable market position is crucial for a company's competitiveness, it is the company's underlying resources that are decisive. Instead of the market positioning perspective's *outside-in* approach, RBV advocates an *inside-out* approach to strategy. Strategizing therefore becomes about identifying and understanding the company's resource base and how it is linked to the position taken in the marketplace. RBV is relatively commonly used in the domain of logistics and SCM, offering a framework to explore logistics operations, and understand how logistics resources and capabilities can provide the foundation for a sustainable competitive advantage. 'Resources' are here typically understood in a broad sense, including not only physical resources such as a warehouse, but also, for instance, relationships, skills and capabilities. Chapter 3 in this book addresses some of the most prominent works in the field and their connection to logistics.

The dynamic capabilities perspective builds mainly upon the dynamic capabilities theory, sometimes also referred to as the dynamic capabilities view, and was first described in an article written by the researchers David Teece and Gary Pisano in 1994. The main message of this theory takes a stance in the organization's resources and their role in creating competitiveness, and thus has great similarities with RBV. However, in contrast to the resource-based perspective, the dynamic capabilities perspective emphasizes the rapid change in the environment of the organization, for example in terms of market demand and technology developments and the need for renewal of the existing resource base. The very core of strategizing therefore does not become to manage and maintain the *existing* resource base (as in the resource-based perspective) but rather how to embrace and manage an appropriate and timely *change* of the resource base.

An 'evolutionary fitness' (Helfat et al, 2007) should be opted for, where resources are created, extended and modified in such a way so that a competitive advantage can be sustained over time. Since the beginning of the 21st century the dynamic capabilities perspective has received considerable attention in strategic management theory, and the concept has also spread to other research disciplines, such as logistics and SCM. Dynamic capabilities are simply timely when companies are forced to become increasingly agile, flexible and responsive to the megatrends discussed in the beginning of this chapter such as glocalization, increased end consumer demands and technology advancements. The dynamic capabilities perspective is further elaborated and related to a logistics context in Chapter 4.

In this book, the three strategic management perspectives introduced above, together provide an understanding for how logistics management can be relevant from a business strategy point of view.

They also function as a starting point for the second part of this book, in which five contemporary themes of high relevance for strategic logistics management are elaborated on in one chapter each. *Managing logistics development* is addressed in Chapter 5 as a foundational cornerstone to ensure the strategic relevance of logistics in a rapidly changing competitive environment. *Managing paradoxes* is discussed in Chapter 6, highlighting the fact that strategic logistics management must go beyond dealing with trade-offs and instead find out strategies for how to cope with interest conflicts that exist over time in the company and/or supply chain. *Managing supply chain resilience* is thereafter elaborated in Chapter 7 as a major dynamic capability for coping with supply chain disruptions that are increasingly being acknowledged in the business society of today. *Managing logistics-based business models* is targeted in Chapter 8 as a means to provide insights into the role logistics has in the various parts of a company's business model. Finally, *Managing circular supply chains* is addressed in Chapter 9 to highlight the important role of strategic logistics management in society's ongoing transition from a linear to a circular economy.

1.6 Summary

This chapter highlights the existence of logistics-oriented companies, in which the company's sustainable competitive advantage hinges upon logistics management. Due to trends such as glocalization, increased consumer demands and technology advancements, the ability to plan, organize and manage logistics activities of transportation, storing and handling throughout the supply chain has become increasingly strategically relevant for many companies. In these companies, logistics is not only expected to contribute to operational performance in terms of costs, services and lead times, but also company-wide strategic objectives measured in value creation, profitability and growth. In order to provide a ground for the book, this chapter presents and defines key terms used, including logistics, logistics management and the related term supply chain management. Based on a strategic management perspective, it also elaborates the role of logistics management at a business strategy level and a functional level. Finally, it presents the structure and content of the different chapters of the book.

End-of-chapter questions

Discussion questions

1 The book provided some examples of logistics-oriented companies. Provide some more examples and explain in what way logistics is strategically relevant for those companies.

2 How can the definitions of logistics, logistics management and supply chain management be further clarified? When is it especially necessary to clearly distinguish these terms from each other?

3 Provide some more practical, real examples of functional logistics strategies.

Study questions

1 What characterizes a logistics-oriented company?

2 The book presents three contemporary trends that drive the strategic relevance of logistics management. Explain these briefly.

3 Explain how the objectives of logistics management have been developed over the years.

4 What is the difference between a business strategy and a logistics strategy?

References

Autry, C, Zacharia, Z and Lamb, C W (2008) A logistics strategy taxonomy, *Journal of Business Logistics*, 29(2), 27–51

Banker, S (2021) Amazon supply chain innovation continues, *Forbes*, 1 April, www.forbes.com/sites/stevebanker/2021/04/01/amazon-supply-chain-innovation-continues/?sh=444f296277e6 (archived at https://perma.cc/DJ57-89E9)

Barney, J and Clark, D (2007) *Resource-Based Theory: Creating and sustaining competitive advantage*, Oxford University Press, Oxford

Bowersox, D and Daugherty, P (1987) Emerging patterns of logistical organization, *Journal of Business Logistics*, 8(1), 46–60

Chandler, A (1962) *Strategy and Structure: Chapters in the history of the industrial enterprise*, MIT Press, Cambridge

Christopher, M (2016) *Logistics and Supply Chain Management: Creating value-adding networks*, 5th edition, Pearson Education Limited, Harlow

CSCMP (n.d.) Supply chain management definitions and glossary, https://cscmp.org/CSCMP/CSCMP/Educate/SCM_Definitions_and_Glossary_of_Terms.aspx (archived at https://perma.cc/686S-PSGD)

De Wit, B and Meyer R (2010) *Strategy: Process, Content, Context: An international perspective*, 4th edition, Cengage Learning, Andover, Hampshire

Helfat, C, Finkelstein, S, Mitchell, W, Peteraf, M A, Singh, H, Teece, D and Winter, S (2007) *Dynamic capabilities: Understanding strategic change in organizations*, Blackwell Publishing, Oxford

Helfat, C and Peteraf, M (2009) Understanding dynamic capabilities: Progress along a developmental path, *Strategic Organization*, 7(1), 91–102

Larson, P D and Halldorsson, A (2004) Logistics versus supply chain management: An international survey, *International Journal of Logistics: Research and Applications*, 7(1), 17–31

Manners-Bell, J and Lyon, K (2023) *Logistics and Supply Chain Innovation: A practical guide to disruptive technologies and new business models*, 2nd edition, Kogan Page, London

McGinnis, M, Kohn, J and Spillan, J (2010) A longitudinal study of logistics strategy 1990–2008, *Journal of Business Logistics*, 31(1), 217–235

Mintzberg, H (1994) *The Rise and Fall of Strategic Planning*, Prentice Hall Europe, Hertfordshire

Penrose, E G (1959) *The Theory of the Growth of the Firm*, John Wiley & Sons, New York

Persson, G (1991) Achieving competitiveness through logistics, *International Journal of Logistics Management*, 2(1), 1–11

Porter, M (1980) *Competitive Strategy: Techniques for analyzing industries and competitors*, Free Press, New York

Porter, M (1985) *Competitive Advantage: Creating and sustaining superior performance*, Free Press, New York

Sandberg, E (2015) *Logistik och Strategi: För lönsamhet och tillväxt*, Studentlitteratur, Lund

Teece, D and Pisano, G (1994) The dynamic capabilities of firms: An introduction, *Industrial & Corporate Change*, 3(3), 537–556

Wernerfelt, B (1984) A resource-based view of the firm, *Strategic Management Journal*, 5(2), 171–180

The market positioning perspective 02

A major perspective for how to understand a sustainable competitive advantage and why a company outperforms its competitors is to consider the company's position in the market vis-à-vis competitors. A favourable market position is characterized by an ability to provide more value to the customers than competitors, which in turn is expected to translate into higher economic profitability. Profitability above industry average is hence a typical sign of the company having a sustainable competitive advantage.

Centred around the position taken in the market, section 2.1 elaborates the role of activities for achieving a favourable market position. How activities are organized into a value chain, and how they can be arranged to defend a market position, can here be considered as key aspects to consider when strategizing. Thereafter section 2.2 outlines the competitive forces that decide conditions for competition in an industry, and the role logistics plays in these forces. In addition to understanding the competitive forces of an industry, the market positioning perspective also suggests strategies for how to be positioned in the market. From a logistics management perspective, the two strategies of cost leadership and service leadership are here especially relevant, and these are therefore elaborated in sections 2.3 and 2.4. Finally, the application of a combination of these two strategies is discussed in section 2.5. Section 2.6 summarizes the chapter.

2.1 Activities as the basic unit of competitive advantage

In a nutshell, the market positioning perspective is based on an *outside-in* approach to strategizing, by finding out *where* to compete and *how* to compete. This can be further described in two major tasks:

1 Analysing and deciding what industry to operate in. Overall, an industry with relatively weak competitive forces is more favourable to operate in for an individual company than an industry with strong forces. According to Porter

(1980; 1985) there are five competitive forces that are decisive for an industry's overall profitability and hence need to be considered: threat of new entrants, threat of substitutes, bargaining power of customers and suppliers, and rivalry among existing competitors.

2 Ensure a strong position in the market vis-à-vis competitors of that industry. This is made by selecting one of the three generic strategies (Porter, 1980; 1985):

   a Cost leadership, which means that the company offers lower prices than competitors in the industry.

   b Differentiation, which means that the company offers products and/or services that are unique, i.e. not offered by competitors in the industry.

   c Focus, which means that the company offers products and/or services that are targeted to a segment or group of segments of an industry. This enables a more attractive offering for customers in this segment and can be made either by (1) cost leadership in a specific, narrower segment of the market, or (2) differentiation in a specific, narrower segment of the market.

In the targeted industry, the company should position itself in regards to competitors by one of the above-mentioned generic strategies. By doing that, customer value creation (relative to competitors) can be maximized. The three generic strategies are obviously very broad, and for an individual company there are virtually endless opportunities to act in order to position itself advantageously in the market. In a logistics context, it is primarily the strategic advantages in terms of cost leadership and differentiation (in the form of service leadership) that are most important, regardless of whether the entire industry or specific segments are the target group. Therefore, these strategies are addressed in individual sections (see sections 2.3 and 2.4).

Before entering a discussion on the role of logistics on the two above-mentioned tasks for strategizing, this chapter will detail the role of activities in the market positioning perspective. Activities are considered to be 'the basic unit of competitive advantage' (Porter, 1996) that together form various bundled value creation processes, which in turn belongs to an overall activity system. Ultimately, activities must be performed in order to fulfil customer demands and create value. An in-depth understanding of involved activities and the value creation processes and activity system they take part in, is therefore essential for strategizing.

2.1.1 Strategy vs operational effectiveness

A valuable starting point for understanding the importance of activities when strategizing is to consider the uniqueness of the activities that underscore a company's business and intended strategy. In his 1996 article aptly titled 'What is strategy?', Michael Porter argued that to truly have a strategy, it is important to either *perform different activities* compared to competitors or *perform activities differently*. If a company only performs (the same) activities better than competitors, it does not have a strategy but something Porter refers to as operational effectiveness:

> Operational effectiveness (OE) means performing similar activities 'better' than rivals perform them. Operational effectiveness includes but is not limited to efficiency. It refers to any number of practices that allow a company to better utilize its inputs by, for example, reducing defects in products or developing better products faster. In contrast, strategic positioning means performing 'different' activities from rivals' or performing similar activities in 'different ways'. (Porter, 1996, p. 62)

In the article, Porter argued that companies increasingly lack a strategy and instead rely on their operational effectiveness.

By embracing various types of management concepts, such as lean, business process reengineering, and total quality management, their operational effectiveness can be improved, and they all end up close to a so-called 'productivity frontier'. This can be described as the sum of 'best practice' in terms of cost and value creation that can be found in an industry.

The problem with this development, according to Porter, is that it creates a 'hypercompetition' where the entire industry develops into performing the same activities in the same way, and after a while all companies can be found at the productivity frontier. The more similar each company's activities are, the more likely the prices of those activities will be lowered, which in turn results in eroded margins for the entire industry. Although Porter's reasoning about operational effectiveness and hypercompetition was presented as early as 1996, it remains highly relevant, especially in a logistics and SCM setting.

The ongoing rapid development of new technology and various automation solutions is an obvious example of this. This development has caused significant cost savings, and adoption of new technology and automation constitutes a key undertaking for improved operational effectiveness. However, these improvements are often far from unique, and expected competitive advantages based on these technology adoptions are often short-lived, as they tend to diffuse rapidly. Another area that tends to exhibit hypercompetition is that of sustainability practices in logistics. For example, innovative offerings related to fossil-free deliveries tend to spread quickly due to the presence of logistics companies serving competitors with the same type of deliveries. To conclude, a long-term competitive advantage, such as a sustainable competitive advantage, cannot be based purely on imitating competitors but must be grounded on either performing different activities or performing activities differently.

An important insight for how to develop such a uniqueness in the activity system is to acknowledge that activities, whether carried out within the same company or by different companies, are often dependent on each other. Therefore, it is often how the activities are related to each other that forms the basis for how to create a unique value offering towards the customers. As stated by Porter (1996, p. 70), 'While operational effectiveness is about achieving excellence in individual activities, or functions, strategy is about combining activities.' This means that the relationship between activities often constitutes the foundation for a company's market position and thus sustainable competitive advantage; this is very much in line with a logistics and SCM mindset.

The focus on activities in the market positioning perspective underscores the importance of looking deeply into the organization's operations and understanding how activities contribute to broader competitive positioning. By understanding and deliberately choosing which activities to perform and how to connect them, companies can carve out unique positions in the market and achieve a sustainable competitive advantage.

2.1.2 The value chain

To better understand how activities contribute to value for customers, Porter (1985) introduced the concept of the value chain, where a company's activities are schematically presented into various categories of primary and supporting activities. Overall the value chain concept provides an overview and a tool for identification and analysis of how activities (and their interplay) contribute to value creation and, ultimately, the company's profit. Porter's (1985) value chain concept is, however, very generic and can further be contextualized. Figure 2.1 shows such a contextualization from a logistics perspective. With this overview as a starting point it is possible to explicitly clarify the role of different logistics activities further, such as transport, storage and handling (examples of primary activities), as well as planning and controlling the flow of goods (an example of a support activity), in the creation of customer value.

As indicated in the figure, 'the logistics value chain' is here part of the larger generic value chain, which implies that, in addition to understanding the logistics activities' role for value creation, it is also important to consider logistics activities in conjunction with other functional activities. For instance, various technology developments (under 'Technology Development' in support activities) may influence logistics operations in multiple ways by introducing AI-driven supply chain forecasting, block chain solutions, robotics, etc. and the value chain here offers a structured tool for how to identify and reason about these relationships. In a similar vein, based on the value chain logic and an understanding of how different activities may be linked to each other, companies can form strategic partnerships with key suppliers or logistics providers to enhance value creation. In fact, as indicated in Figure 2.1, a company's value chain may be connected to other companies' value chains upstream as well as downstream from the focal company.

Figure 2.1 The logistics value chain

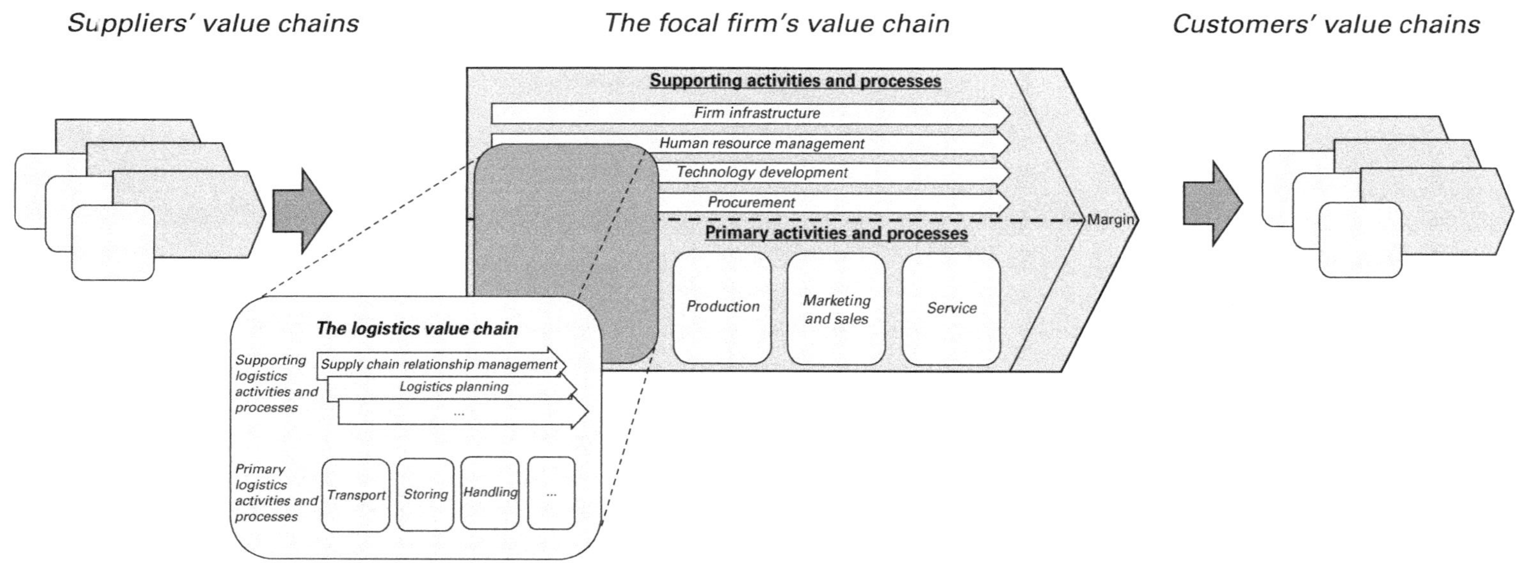

SOURCE Adapted from Porter (1985)

It is interesting to note that Porter's concept of 'value chain' was introduced for the first time in 1985, around the same time when the term 'supply chain' became popular in logistics literature. So, what is really the difference between a value chain and a supply chain? One obvious difference might be that SCM typically has an external focus, beyond the borders of a focal company whereas the value chain mainly revolves around activities and functions internal to a company. (In Figure 2.1 where the value chain concept is expanded upstream and downstream, they can still be understood as individual, company-centred value chains.)

Another way to distinguish the concepts is to consider a supply chain to be focused on the physical structure, i.e. entities/actors that are part of the supply chain, such as companies, organizations or individuals. In contrast, the value chain can be seen as a somewhat broader concept, which primarily focuses on explaining how the included activities and processes together create value for the customer, but also for other stakeholders such as shareholders. To precisely explain how these activities and processes create value, the involved entities/actors are, of course, also essential to describe. In practice, it thus often becomes difficult to entirely separate the two concepts.

Furthermore, to differentiate the concepts could be to focus on what value is created and for whom. In a supply chain, which is the physical structure behind the SCM philosophy, the primary focus is on creating value for the customer through cost efficiency, delivery services and lead times. In Porter's value chain, the goal is also to create customer value that originates not only from the physical flow of goods, but also from other sources such as image and product use.

Finally, it can be stated that while the two concepts may be distinguished from each other, at least for an analytical purpose, they are closely related and very often the two terms are used interchangeably. Indeed, an optimized supply chain can enhance a company's value chain, and vice versa, and hence both perspectives are critical for organizations that seek to maximize value creation and logistics performance.

2.1.3 On the value concept in strategic management theory

When explaining the value chain, it may also be meaningful to elaborate the multifaceted concept of value. In the traditional market positioning perspective presented by Porter (1980; 1985), value was understood based on how the customer perceives the product/service's value and defined as 'the amount buyers are willing to pay for what a firm provides them' (Porter, 1985, p. 38). Although this definition remains valid in many instances, the meaning of value has, in strategic management theory, been expanded over the years, and except for the original understanding of value as defined by Porter, there is not always a clear-cut definition provided. In particular, there are two features of the value concept that complicates its understanding (Sandberg et al, 2018):

1. Value can be considered multidimensional, including economic, monetary value, but also environmental and social aspects, that are not always possible to translate into pure economic ones.
2. In a strategic management context, value is often noted to be subjectively perceived and thus understood differently by different stakeholders.

First, whereas most strategic management literature takes a strict economic, monetary perspective on value and value creation, value can be described as a multidimensional concept. Performance along the triple bottom line, i.e. economic, environmental and social value creation, is often opted for, rather than the narrower scope of economic values. In contemporary logistics, environmental as well as social values are essential ingredients when judging logistics performance, and hence also important to consider when strategizing. That is, today, a position in the market cannot be analysed and understood on the basis of economic considerations alone as it also needs to be considered from an environmental and social point of view. For instance, as will be discussed in Chapter 6, managers are increasingly facing a variety of paradoxes related to requirements on the simultaneous performance along the economic, environmental and social dimensions.

An approach to better understand the second point above may be to distinguish between use value (also referred to as 'value-in-use') and exchange value. *The use value* concerns the customers' perceptions of the product's utility and reflects the specific attributes of the product (or service) with respect to the customers' individual requirements. It is hence a subjective measure determined by each customer at a specific moment in time. In contrast, *the exchange value* equals to Porter's (1980) understanding of value, and refers to the monetary price, and is defined as 'the amount paid by the buyer to the seller for the use value' (Bowman and Ambrosini, 2000, p. 15). In order for a transaction to occur, these definitions mean that the use value, i.e. the customer's perception of the sum of the use value(s), must be higher than the exchange value.

The distinction between use value and exchange value may also be interesting from a triple bottom-line perspective as the use value may not only consist of economic value. In fact, logistics operations may provide the customer with a use value that consists of both environmental and social values as well. However, in order for a transaction to occur, the customer must be willing to pay for these values, i.e. they must be mirrored in the exchange value. This may sometimes be problematic and, when it comes to market positioning, it is therefore fruitful to examine how the use values can be transferred into an exchange value. A typical example of this is the environmental value created through the introduction of fossil-free deliveries which often come with an extra cost for the supply chain members in term of investments. However, this environmental value is seldom not directly related to the specific buyer but is to be found at a higher society level and customers are therefore not always willing to increase the exchange value. As a result, although use value in the form of environmental improvements is created, supply chain members may still be reluctant to make necessary investments, as the exchange value remains the same, i.e. not able to cover the investments.

Another aspect of the value concept that may be fruitful to have in mind with respect to strategizing in the three strategic management perspectives outlined in this book, is to distinguish between the two processes of *value creation* on the one hand, and *value appropriation* on the other. These two processes are both fundamental for shaping a company's sustainable competitive advantage vis-à-vis competitors. Whereas value creation decides the potential magnitude of the value created, value appropriation explains the share of that value that the company is able to acquire (Mizik and Jacobsen, 2003). Both these processes are crucial to have in mind when strategizing.

The value creation process involves efforts made to enhance use value for the customer. In recent years, the idea of 'value co-creation' has gained traction, meaning that the value created may not only be created by the providing company, but should rather be considered as a collaborative, joint process between the provider company and the customer(s). In such a process the use value emerges from the combined efforts of the providing company and customer(s). After all, the use value that is created is by definition a result of the perceptions of the customer (Sandberg et al, 2018).

As the customer, but also many other supply chain members jointly, may be involved in the creation of the use value, the question arises how to appropriate, or capture, the value created. Considering, for instance, members in a supply chain that together create value, it is necessary for long-term stability to get all involved members with a value surplus, but the actual share of the total value could be different. From a strategic management theory point of view, the ability of a company to appropriate value is very much dependent on its strategy, no matter that this strategy is based on a favourable market position, a superior resource base, or an appropriate set of dynamic capabilities (for a further scrutinization of these two latter concepts, see Chapters 3 and 4).

2.1.4 Defence of a market position

A crucial part of having a sustainable competitive advantage based on a favourable market position is the ability of the underlying activity system to defend it from competitors. If the chosen position is not possible to defend over time, a 'first mover advantage' may quickly be eroded. Thus, there must be some entry and mobility barriers established to prevent or discourage new competitors from entering the market or existing competitors from escalating the competitive position. Exactly what these consist of depends on the situation, but some recurring examples in a logistics context of such entry and mobility barriers are the following:

Economies of scale and scope: It is often difficult for smaller companies to compete on price due to the economies of scale and scope that often exist. This perhaps becomes most evident when discussing the purchase price per unit, but also in the use of logistics resources such as central warehouses, transportation, personnel and so on.

Experiences and learning: If the position is built on extensive experiences and learning within the company, it can be difficult for a competitor to quickly assimilate. Often, these experiences and learning are not explicitly explained, making it challenging to pinpoint precisely which experiences and learning are required to be successful in a certain position.

Complexity in the underlying activity system: If the favourable position is based on a variety of complex coordination and integration activities, for instance, in the activity system, it can, just like in the case of experiences and learning, be challenging to explicitly understand what leads to low costs or superior delivery service. In particular, in the case of interorganizational coordination, as in a supply chain, these advantages are often even more complicated to identify, which makes imitation by competitors more difficult.

Switching costs: The higher the costs for changing suppliers, known as switching costs, that a company can create, the more challenging it becomes for competitors to win over the customer. A company that provides good information in conjunction with deliveries, for example, can create switching costs for its customers if they have integrated this information into their existing systems and processes. Similarly, switching costs can also arise due to long and extensive partnership agreements with the customer based on, for instance, securing exclusive transportation routes and use of warehousing facilities.

Network density and geographical coverage: Companies with a dense logistics network can offer faster, more frequent and more reliable service than those without. Building such a network takes time and significant capital investment. Similarly, a wide-reaching logistics network that spans vast geographies can serve as a barrier, especially in industries where quick delivery and service are crucial.

2.2 The role of logistics in competitive forces

From a market positioning perspective, a crucial component in strategizing is to analyse and decide what favourable industry or industries there are to operate in. Everything else being equal, an industry with relatively weak competitive forces is more favourable to operate in, as this implies that it is easier to create customer value and thereby achieve a sustainable competitive advantage in such an industry. An industry refers to a distinct group of companies that are engaged in similar or related activities, or producing similar goods or providing services within a specific category. An industry is typically characterized by common production methods and/or service offerings, market dynamics and regulatory frameworks.

Industries can be discussed and analysed at different levels. For instance, the automotive industry is concerned with the development, manufacturing, repairing and selling of all kinds of motor vehicles. This industry is quite a broad one and can be divided into several others, such as the passenger car, agricultural machineries or bicycle industries. Finding the right level of analysis is crucial from a market positioning perspective, as this may help to identify the sometimes blurred borders between industries where products and services today offered to customers in one industry may also be a valuable offering in other industries. A well-known example of such a development is Apple which has expanded their business from computers to other devices such as mobile phones. Hence, although the market positioning perspective's reasoning of 'selecting' an industry to operate in may seem odd at first glance, an increasing mobility and blurred boundaries between industries paradoxically make it even more important to conduct thorough industry analysis and make good choices around the industry selection (Sandberg, 2015).

A thorough analysis of the competitive forces within an industry can also be valuable in order to change the industry's standard procedures and thus create a superior market position for the individual company. An example of this is the development of e-commerce within the retailing industry, which has, among other things, led to different customer demands and the emergence of services such as last-mile deliveries, from which many entirely new companies have emerged. With the help of new AI-based tools used for route optimizations, new smart ways of delivering to consumers have become increasingly important for achieving customer satisfaction in this industry. Although the market positioning perspective does not delve into it in greater detail, it acknowledges that there is a certain dynamism in industries; their structure and profitability change over time, which, in turn, necessitates that individual companies evaluate their industry choice and adapt their strategy over time.

To evaluate an industry, Porter (1980) introduced a model with the five competitive forces: the threat of new entrants, the threat of substitutes, the bargaining power of customers, the bargaining power of suppliers and the rivalry among existing competitors. Together, these five competitive forces determine how revenues, costs and assets appear for companies in the industry. Revenues, costs and assets, in turn, fundamentally impact a company's profitability (return on investment). The strength, i.e. how strong the competition is in these five forces, determines how easy/hard it is for competitors to reach the same position. In an industry with weak competition, it is therefore easier for a company to achieve higher profitability, and vice versa. All else being equal, a company should thus strive to choose an industry with weak competitive forces, thereby achieving higher profitability.

In line with general megatrends such as those mentioned in Chapter 1 (i.e. glocalization, technology advancements and changed end consumer demands), logistics has come to play an increasingly important role in a company's competitiveness. In this development, the core product often becomes relatively less important, while its surrounding services (including logistics) are becoming increasingly significant. In this context, logistics can be seen as an important tool for creating and sustaining a company's competitiveness. To understand the impact of logistics on a company's competitiveness in more detail, Porter's five competitive forces serve as an excellent framework, which is presented below (see also section 2.1.4 above about entry and mobility barriers).

The *threat of new entrants* poses a risk of new players entering the industry and capturing market share from existing participants. The entry of new players means that more capacity becomes available, which can result in market prices and, consequently, the profitability of existing players being lowered. The industry's requirements for logistics and the general conditions of logistics operations among existing players can be seen as important factors that can hinder new entrants. The higher the demands and expectations among the industry's customers, such as the level of service, the more is simply required from the logistics operations of new companies. The understanding of the logistics requirements in an industry may also not be entirely clear to external players, making it difficult for new companies to establish the right level of service and offer the right type of service. Another important factor that can hinder entry may be the need for significant investments in logistics operations, such as equipment, warehouse facilities and so on. In a similar vein, the need for economies of scale can be another limiting factor in many industries, meaning that new entrants need to quickly capture significant market share to compete with existing players.

A *threat of substitution* to an industry exists when another industry offers different products that have the potential to satisfy the industry's customers as effectively as the industry's 'own' products. The surrounding services to a product, where logistics can play a crucial role, can be decisive in differentiating the industry's products from those of other industries. A clear service offering combined with the product, such as comprehensive service agreements where the customer gains access to spare parts and repair services, can make it challenging for products in other industries because they can no longer be considered equivalent to the industry's own products.

The *bargaining power of customers* can be explained by the level of dependency that customers have on companies in the industry. Typical factors affecting the degree of dependence of individual customers on companies in the industry include how much the customer purchases relative to the industry's total sales, the size of the specific supplier, and how easy or difficult it is for the customer to switch suppliers (e.g. in terms of switching costs). In a logistics context, customers can often be brought closer through investments in various types of logistics solutions. By investing in, for example, a logistics hub or a production facility near the customer's operations, the customer can be offered more frequent and flexible deliveries. This often makes the company's offering unique compared to competitors, and thus, the bargaining power with the customer can become stronger. Of course, the dependency reasoning in this example can also be reversed. The investment made by the supplier increases their dependence on the relationship continuing for a long time, and the customer company may, if it desires (to the disadvantage of the supplier), find itself in a stronger negotiation position. For companies in the industry, investments and long-term relationships with customers can, therefore, be a difficult act of balance.

Suppliers' bargaining power, just like that of customers, can be explained by their dependence on the industry. Decisive factors here are whether suppliers to a certain industry also have customers in other industries (in such a case the suppliers' bargaining powers tend to be stronger) and, in a similar vein, the availability of alternative suppliers to an industry. One way for companies in the industry to increase their bargaining power with suppliers is to integrate vertically, meaning to increase their ownership upstream in the supply chain to gain better control and reduce dependence on suppliers. For example, many companies in the retail industry have established their own purchasing offices and logistics hubs in Asia to get closer to their Asian suppliers. This has allowed them to negotiate better purchase prices and cost control, thereby increasing their bargaining power with suppliers.

Rivalry among current competitors is based on the need to establish a (relatively speaking) more advantageous position in the market. Tactical actions such as pricing, product launches and advertising campaigns are classic examples of this. Rivalry represents an ongoing 'game' among the players in a market, and in this context, logistics can certainly be a tool that can improve a company's position. One way to have a stronger grip on customers is to take over parts of the logistics activities typically performed by the customer. An example of this is the concept of Vendor Managed Inventory (VMI), where the supplier independently plans and takes responsibility for replenishing the customer's inventory without a traditional order being placed (see also Chapter 4 for further explanation of the VMI concept). In many cases, this can be a convenient and cost-effective logistics solution that benefits the customer. This solution also provides the company with an additional advantage over competitors and potential new entrants in the form of better information about the customer and the customer's customer; it is common for the company in a VMI solution, in order to plan and control replenishment, to have access to the customer's sales information, Point of Sales (POS). Another important competitive tool has been the ability to assist and provide services in conjunction with customers' internationalization. In order to retain fast-growing customers expanding into new markets and thus exclude competitors (and potential new entrants), suppliers may also need to internationalize their businesses. From a logistics perspective, this may involve the establishment of new transportation networks, either in-house or through agents, or new warehouse solutions.

2.3 Logistics in a cost leadership position

In addition to industry analysis and selection, the market positioning perspective also encompasses the critical question of which generic strategy to be deployed in the market. Given the historical development and managerial focus of logistics, the most traditional and obvious way for logistics to contribute to a favourable market position is based on cost leadership. If a company can reduce its logistics costs more than its competitors, everything else being equal, there is an opportunity to achieve cost leadership based on logistics superiority. This becomes particularly relevant in industries where logistics accounts for a significant portion of the total cost structure.

In order for the company to keep its logistics costs lower than its competitors and thus contribute to cost leadership, there is a need to identify and understand (Sandberg, 2015):

- the key types of logistics cost to focus on
- the structural factors that impact the size of logistics costs

A good starting point for identifying and understanding the key logistics cost types of a company can be to use a standardized total logistics cost model. A total logistics cost model refers to the comprehensive calculation and analysis of all costs associated with the logistics activities of a company. This includes all expenses incurred in the planning, execution and management of material flows throughout the supply chain. A generic total logistics cost model may cover, for instance, the following cost categories:

- *Transportation costs*: Expenses related to the movement of goods, such as shipping, freight, fuel, carrier services and transportation infrastructure costs.
- *Inventory carrying costs*: Inventory carrying costs encompass expenses associated with the inventory held, including the cost of capital tied up, insurance, risk of obsolescence, etc. This cost usually depends on the volume stored.
- *Administrative costs*: Costs that originate from activities related to order management and processing, including, for instance, order entry, documentation, information sharing, forecasting, etc.
- *Warehousing costs*: Expenses include the operation, maintenance and rental of warehouse facilities, as well as material handling costs within the warehouse.

- *Information technology*: These costs pertain to logistics software, technology infrastructure, data management, and any investments in technology to support logistics operations.
- *Packaging costs*: Expenses associated with packaging materials and the packaging process.

Based on these generic cost types, more specific models can be generated, suitable for a company's specific context. For instance, more specific transportation costs may be preferable for a haulier company, whereas inventory carrying costs or warehousing costs may be relevant to specify further in a manufacturing company. The total logistics cost model approach provides a structured method for comprehending the potential for cost reductions in various cost categories. This potential can be understood partly by considering the cost type's relative share of the total logistics costs and partly by comparing the company's cost position in a specific cost category with that of its competitors.

In addition to understanding a company's costs based on different cost types, many companies may also benefit from selecting a specific part of the supply chain, such as material procurement or distribution, and focusing on implementing cost rationalizations in that area. Ideally, the focus should be on the part of the supply chain with the greatest potential for improvement, meaning it represents a relatively significant portion of the company's total logistics costs. Besides the size of the costs chosen to focus on, another crucial factor is how controllable these costs are for the company. Does the company have control over the activities involved, and can they realistically be changed?

It is also important to emphasize that since it is the company's total costs that need to be kept low, changes leading to a more cost-effective logistics should not jeopardize the company's overall costs. Changes in various cost items in the total cost model should, therefore, not only be compared with each other but also with other cost items within the company. When changing, for example, a company's distribution structure, a wide range of other functions and activities in the company can be affected, such as:

- production capacity and utilization
- procurement processes and routines
- the need for skills development
- involvement and new requirements for the marketing function
- relationships and agreements with other companies
- various types of financial costs

As such, these considerations require systems thinking, which is further presented in Chapter 5.

In addition to understanding the logistics cost structure, another important prerequisite for cost leadership is a good understanding of the structural factors that impact the size of logistics costs.

Perhaps the single most important factor to understand and consider is how *economies of scale and scope* affect logistics operations and associated costs. Economies of scale and scope often play a crucial role for cost efficiencies, and the need to create these economies is and remains one of the main tasks of logistics. A more detailed description of economies of scale and scope follows in Chapter 5 in conjunction with managing logistics development (where economies of scale and scope obviously have a central role). Another related crucial factor, which will also be discussed in Chapter 5, is *economies of integration*. Economies of integration, both internally within the company and between companies in a supply chain, can enable various types of cost efficiencies when organizational barriers are broken down. Coordination among activities, functions and companies is here expected to eliminate various forms of waste, such as duplicate work, unnecessary handling and packaging, etc.

Another important logic that impacts logistics costs is different types of *experience and learning*. By performing an activity over time, one can learn how to perform it in a better and more efficient way, which can lead to lower costs. For example, through their own experiences, individuals can reorganize their work to complete it more quickly, perhaps by performing activities in a different order or in a different way. Through better planning, waste can also be more effectively avoided.

There are also factors related to *geographical location* that need to be taken into consideration. One example is the company's warehouse location, which is often explained by the company's historical background. In many cases, the reason for the warehouse location is not the most cost-effective one, but is due to the fact that the company was originally established in that location, and that it is expensive to carry out a major relocation. Some strategic warehouse locations, such as in free trade zones around the world, can also have a significant impact on the company's logistics costs. Another structurally significant factor in this context is *agreements and collaborations* with customers and suppliers. For example, outsourcing various logistics services is an important factor here.

REAL-WORLD EXAMPLE Logistics as a part of Lidl's cost leadership strategy

Lidl is a German discount grocery chain that operates more than 12,000 stores and some 200 logistics centres in 31 countries around the world, mainly Europe and the US. Since the first store was opened in Germany in 1973 the company has had cost leadership as its main competitive strategy in the market. In combination with high purchasing volumes that ensure low prices, a restricted product range, and vertical integration in the form of a high share of private labels (around 80 per cent), the latter, for example enhanced by an individual coffee roastery, efficient logistics operations throughout the entire supply chain play a decisive role for the cost leadership strategy.

In the very heart of Lidl's logistics philosophy is standardization that enables streamlined supply chain operations. Standardization at Lidl encompasses operational working processes (such as picking and packing) in the various supply chain nodes, but also product range and use of technology. In addition, standardization is also a key theme in Lidl's store concepts with regards to, for example, layout and planograms.

The outspoken focus on standardization is crucial in order to identify and understand the structural factors that explain the strategic role of logistics in Lidl's cost leadership. For instance, standardization in the working processes allows for *economies of scale and scope*, for example in conjunction with use of picking equipment, optimization of labour capacity, etc. In addition, standardized store layouts and planograms enable fewer types of packaging, which in turn simplify the storing and handling at the logistics centres as well as the replenishment process to the store shelves. Standardization of working processes as well as technology is also vital for *economies of integration* as this ensures predictability and a joint understanding among the various involved logistics functions in the supply chain.

Apart from these 'economies of', standardization at Lidl is also considered to be a key element for *experience and learning* that further drives cost rationalizations of various kinds. In line with a lean philosophy (see Chapter 1) standardized working processes at Lidl constitute an important ground for efficient and effective development and innovation, as well as training of staff. The *geographical location* of Lidl's logistics centres is another crucial element for cost-efficient logistics operations, in particular full truck loads in the transportation networks are here in focus. The size of the standardized logistics centres is carefully designed to optimize the total logistics costs of transportation, handling and storing. In Germany, around 80 stores are served from each logistics centre – for that country deemed to be a suitable number. Finally, *supplier agreements and collaborations* are central in Lidl's strategy of providing a high share of private labels. Long-term relationships in combination with large product volumes here ensure cost-efficient, stable logistics operations.

SOURCES www.lidl.de, Beer (2024)

2.4 Logistics in a service leadership position

Apart from cost leadership, logistics can also play a crucial role in creating a sustainable competitive advantage based on a differentiation strategy (see section 2.1). In such a strategy, logistics can form the basis for some kind of unique offering, which distinguishes the company from competitors and thus gives the company an opportunity to charge higher prices. A prerequisite for this is, of course, that the offering not only differs from other companies but also that it provides a use value for the customers that is higher than the exchange value (see section 2.1.3).

In particular, a unique offering based on logistics can enable an extraordinary customer service. In a broad sense, customer service is understood as: 'Activities between the buyer and seller that enhance or facilitate the sale or use of the seller's products or services' (CSCMP definition, see CSCMP, n.d.).

From a focal company perspective this means to assist and meet the various needs and demands of customers to ensure satisfaction, by means of both the internal activities as well as collaboration and coordination with other involved players in the supply chain, such as suppliers and third-party logistics providers.

Of particular importance from a logistics point of view is the role physical delivery plays to achieve customer service. This part of the customer service concept is sometimes called delivery service and revolves around the physical transfer of the product or service to the customer, be it a manufacturer that receives supply of raw materials to its factory or a consumer receiving a home delivery in an e-commerce purchasing process.

Although often understood as a narrower concept than customer service, delivery service is still a vast concept and includes customer interactions with customers before, during as well as after the transaction (see Figure 2.2 for some examples of aspects to consider).

In order for the company to compete based on superior logistics in a service leadership strategy, it is especially important to identify and understand:

- what type of delivery service is valuable to the customer
- how to enhance and improve the delivery service

Ultimately, it is the customers who determine if they are receiving good service, and that is why it is important to fundamentally understand what type of service is valuable to the customers. A good starting point to analyse and delve into this is to divide delivery service into various delivery service elements. Figure 2.3 shows some of the most common elements, but these can be further defined depending on the specific context of a company.

Figure 2.2 Logistics aspects in the delivery service before, during and after the transaction

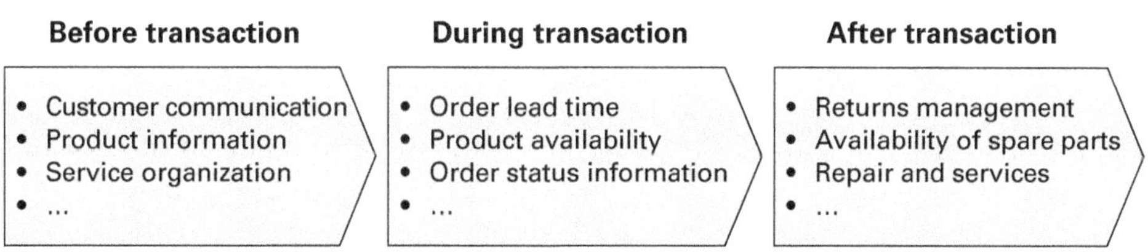

SOURCE Adapted from Sandberg (2015); Christopher (2016)

Figure 2.3 Commonly discussed delivery service elements

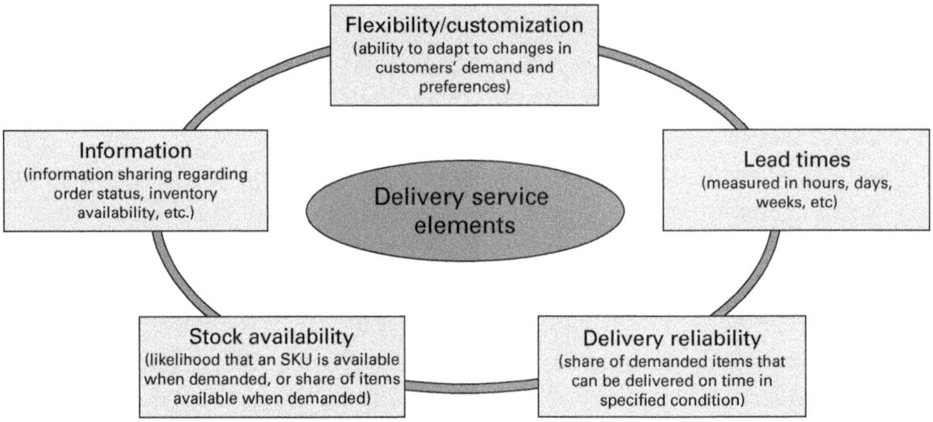

SOURCE Adapted from Sandberg (2015) and Sandberg and Abrahamsson (2019)

Just like in a total logistics cost model approach, it is these elements that together determine the total delivery service offered and performed towards the customers. Different customers or customer groups may have completely different preferences regarding the various elements, and therefore it is very important to understand the real needs of the customers. A relatively common misjudgement, for example, concerns the customer's wishes regarding lead time and delivery reliability. Several customer surveys in different industries have shown that customers generally do not need as short lead times as suppliers believe – instead, it is delivery reliability that is important (Sandberg and Abrahamsson, 2019).

Companies can both underperform and overperform in terms of the different delivery service elements, given their importance to the customer. A crucial aspect of a service leadership strategy based on logistics is hence to perform the right level of delivery service, rather than always perform the best. When overperforming, such as very short lead times that do not provide any added value to the customers, many unnecessary costs may arise, for example high transportation costs due to poor planning, fill rate or expensive modes of transport.

Given the different delivery service elements, there are essentially two main approaches for how to enhance and improve the delivery service. Fundamentally, these are based on the company's value chain and its underlying activity system; and aim to strengthen and/or change this in such a way that the chosen, unique position in the market is supported.

The first approach is about coordinating and integrating the supply chain so that people, functions, and activities work in the same direction, both within and between involved companies. If, for example, delivery reliability is an important service element for the customer, all parts of the supply chain that influence this need to be synchronized. Perhaps information about the location of goods in the central warehouse needs to be complemented with product training for the picking staff, in order to increase recognition and judgement ability among the staff? Another example is to work more closely with suppliers to get better support from them, such as regarding sustainability of packaging. It might be worth looking at what type of resources are already available and/or used by other parts of the company to explore coordination opportunities.

A second main approach to improving delivery service is to add new services to the existing offering, thereby enhancing customers' overall perception of the value of the delivery service. If customers have varying needs for appropriate lead times (which can be influenced by, for example, the customer's own clients), it might be suitable to bolster the offering with some form of express delivery that occurs outside of regular deliveries. Another type of enhancement to the offering is to add various information services to the physical delivery, such as the ability to track goods in transit, and environmentally related reports (e.g. emissions reports). Furthermore, in an era of increased circular efforts, e-commerce last-mile deliveries could be complemented by, for instance, various pick-up services at consumers' homes for returns and donations of second-hand goods. Consumer convenience is at the heart of a service leadership position, and hence last-mile deliveries should be complemented by first-mile services (see also Chapter 9).

REAL-WORLD EXAMPLE HAVI Group's service leadership strategy

HAVI Group was founded in 1974 based on a 'handshake agreement' with McDonald's to serve their restaurants in Chicago, USA. HAVI Group is today a global player in the logistics and supply chain sector that operates in more than 45 countries in North America, Europe and Asia. The very core of the company is a vast network of logistics centres, warehouses and a transportation fleet, that offers the customers customized and localized logistics solutions, while global expertise can be ensured to fulfil the various, often extensive and demanding, customer requirements.

The company's customers are mainly to be found in the foodservice and retail industry including gas stations, convenience stores, catering firms, cafés, restaurants, etc. Although operating very differently, these customers are typically in need of high-level logistics services including, for instance, the storing, handling and delivery of temperature-sensitive products.

HAVI's offering towards its customers is comprehensive, in which HAVI Group typically functions as an integral part of the customer company, for instance taking care of procurement and supplier contacts, storing as well as transportation and deliveries. In order to excel in these advanced, often long-term undertakings and fulfil the high service levels offered to the customers, HAVI relies upon advanced technology services. For instance, this includes the use of big data and tools for predictive analytics to forecast demand, optimize delivery routes and manage inventory in real-time.

A profound customer to HAVI has, since the handshake agreement in 1974, been McDonald's.

Today in many countries HAVI collaborates extensively with McDonald's and acts as McDonald's' extended logistics function. For McDonald's, HAVI's in-depth knowledge and capabilities in logistics and SCM is pivotal for a well-functioning supply chain, from suppliers to the restaurants, for example with respect to:

- Inventory availability at suppliers and warehouses – the restaurants themselves have typically very small storage facilities, and hence the availability of 'raw materials' upstreams in the supply chain is decisive.
- Delivery reliability – deliveries to the stores need to arrive within certain time windows so that staff efforts can be optimized.
- Product quality – the raw materials delivered have very strict quality requirements, including, for example, demands on temperatures.

An integral part of the service leadership strategy is HAVI's extensive commitment towards sustainability. This includes investments in technology to utilize used cooking oil from McDonald's restaurants as fuel, and utilizing more eco-friendly and reusable packaging solutions. The latter was acknowledged in 2023 when HAVI Germany won the German Award for Sustainability Projects in the Package Solution category. This was for its development of a reusable packaging system for McDonald's Germany, which had been implemented at 1,450 McDonald's restaurants across Germany during 2022.

SOURCES www.havi.com; www.tmsv.com

2.5 A combination of cost and service leadership

A very important and widely discussed message from Porter (1985) is his view that companies should choose only one of the three generic strategies. If a company tries to implement more than one, there is a risk of failing to achieve a clear, profitable position in the market, and become what Porter labels 'stuck in the middle'. In order to avoid this, a key managerial task when strategizing becomes choosing *what to do*, and *what not to do*.

In practice, this means that a critical part of strategizing is to refrain from various initiatives and activities based on the chosen position on the market. A cost leadership position may result in limited possibilities to offer extensive, costly services in conjunction with deliveries. Of course, however, as also clearly pointed out by Porter

(1996), an operational effectiveness (see section 2.1.1 above) is still desirable in activities that are not prioritized in the strategic position. Significant improvements in terms of efficiency and effectiveness can, according to Porter, be made simultaneously in different areas, without it necessarily being a strategy.

While most academics agree with Porter that strategy indeed involves making choices and thus actively opting out of certain things, the question of whether only one generic strategy at a time can be applied has been debated. For instance, logistics professor Martin Christopher (2016) highlighted that there are three major approaches for how to gain a competitive advantage in the market (see Figure 2.4):

1. by offering a product or service at a lower price than competitors (a cost leadership strategy)
2. by offering a product or service that brings more customer value through superior customer service (a service leadership strategy)
3. by offering a product or service that can render both lower price and higher customer value than competitors (a combined cost and service leadership)

In fact, the third alternative, which brings superior customer value to lower cost, is the most favourable position Christopher points out, and achieving that position is thus an important strategic task for logistics management. This also goes well in line with the overarching objective of SCM which is to establish processes and practices for achieving low costs and good service simultaneously, in order to enhance superior customer value.

Figure 2.4 Strategic approaches for gaining competitive advantage in the market

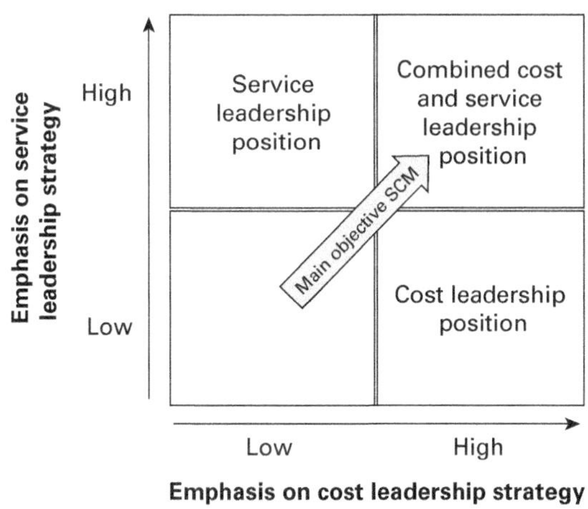

SOURCE Adapted from Christopher (2016)

A common example of how to achieve cost leadership and service leadership simultaneously is to reduce tied-up capital that is held in inventory. From a theoretical point of view, in a completely optimized logistics system, the relationship between inventory costs and service level can be expressed as the dotted line in Figure 2.5, in which a close to 100 per cent product availability service becomes immensely expensive. On this line, a change in inventory costs would always result in a direct result on the service level, i.e. a reduction of the inventory levels and hence inventory costs would result in a reduction of the service level and vice versa.

In practice, however, the actual existing cost and service performance of the inventory can always be placed to the left of the dotted curved line. Many times, in fact, it is possible to reduce the inventory level and related inventory costs without lowering the service level in terms of product availability. This can for instance be achieved by scrapping and removing obsolete products, i.e. products that are no longer demanded by, and thus have no value for, the customers. Likewise, it is often possible to improve product availability without increasing the total inventory value. This can be done, for example, through product segmentation, which means assigning different products with different availability levels where typically high-value products are given lower availability while low-value products are given higher.

Another example of how to achieve a combined cost and service leadership position is to target time reductions of various types in the supply chain. For instance, by reducing the order and delivery lead times, or the throughput time internally within the company, both reduced costs and improved service can be achieved simultaneously. Overall, reduction of lead times is hence often a universal approach for cost as well as service leadership.

Figure 2.5 The relationship between inventory costs and service level in the form of product availability

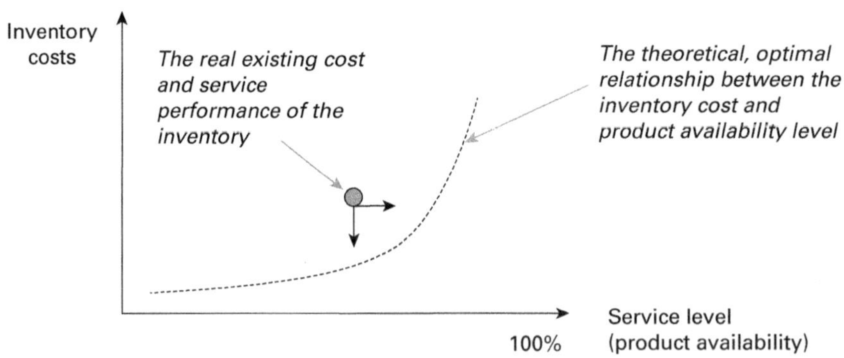

One might wonder how the examples above and the reasoning around whether cost and service leadership can be achieved simultaneously aligns with Porter's call for selecting only one of the generic strategies. The ambition to position oneself in the upper right quadrant of Figure 2.4 might seem close to what Porter calls being 'stuck in the middle'? It is also tempting to describe the aforementioned examples of inventory management and time reductions in terms of operational effectiveness, rather than strategy? There is, of course, no clear answer to these questions; we can only note that there is some disagreement between Porter's view and logistics and SCM scholars. One way to reconcile the different perspectives is to consider the boundary as fluid between what forms the basis of a competitive advantage, in terms of, for instance, superior cost reductions, and what is 'only' general cost improvements (i.e. operational effectiveness). The larger the cost savings and service improvements that are made, and the more they help to strengthen the company's position for customer value creation, the more plausible it is to argue that a competitive advantage has been achieved.

Moreover, if one looks at the competitive situation over time, meaning adopting a more dynamic perspective as will be discussed in Chapter 4, it often becomes easier to justify a market position built on combined cost and service leadership position. In such cases, it could be argued that in a situation where the company is always ahead of its competitors, by constantly cost-optimizing its logistics operations, a competitive advantage can be created that largely relies on always having a slight edge, a so-called 'first mover advantage', against the competitors.

2.6 Summary

This chapter has presented the market positioning perspective, in which strategizing revolves around (1) analysing and deciding what industry to operate in, and (2) ensuring a strong position in the market vis-à-vis competitors of that industry by selecting one of the three generic strategies: cost leadership, differentiation or focus. Overall, the market positioning perspective is based on an *outside-in* approach to strategizing by finding out *where* to compete and *how* to compete.

Activities in the market positioning perspective are considered to be 'the basic unit of competitive advantage', and it is thus crucial to understand how activities and the entire activity system create value. For that, the value chain concept provides an overview and a tool for identification and analysis of how activities (and their interplay) contribute to value creation and, ultimately, the company's profit.

In this chapter 'the logistics value chain' was presented as a part of the larger, generic value chain. It was also highlighted that value can be considered multidimensional, including economic, but also environmental and social values, and that value can be understood as (1) use value, i.e. a customer's subjective perception of the product's value at a specific moment in time, and (2) the exchange value, i.e. the monetary price actually paid by a customer for a product. Furthermore, it was emphasized that activities play a role in defending a market position from competitors. If the chosen position is not possible to defend over time by the underlying activity system, a 'first mover advantage' may quickly be eroded. In a logistics context, examples of such entry and mobility barriers (anchored in the activity system) are economies of scale and scope, experiences and learning, complexity in the underlying activity system, switching costs, network density and geographical coverage.

The market positioning perspective suggests that industry analysis is a vital part of strategizing.

An industry with relatively weak competitive forces is more favourable to operate in than an industry with strong forces, as this implies that it is easier to create customer value and thereby achieve a sustainable competitive advantage in such an industry. To evaluate an industry, Porter (1980) introduced a model with the five competitive forces: the threat of new entrants, the threat of substitutes, the bargaining power of customers and suppliers, and the rivalry among existing competitors. Together, these five competitive forces determine how revenues, costs and assets appear for companies in the industry. This chapter further outlined these five forces and discussed how they relate to logistics activities.

In addition to industry analysis and selection, the market positioning perspective also encompasses the critical question of which generic strategy to be deployed in the market. From a logistics management perspective, the two strategies of cost leadership and service leadership are here especially relevant and these were therefore further elaborated in individual sections. Finally, the application of more than one generic strategy was brought forward. According to the market position perspective, a company may be 'stuck in the middle' if it tries to implement more than one generic strategy. In order to avoid this, a key managerial task when strategizing becomes choosing *what to do*, and *what not to do*. Although the need for making choices is not questioned in general, logistics and SCM scholars, supported by the general SCM literature, have another view when they emphasize a combined cost and service leadership strategy as the most preferable strategy. This also goes well in line with the overarching objective of SCM which is to establish processes and practices for achieving low costs and good service simultaneously, in order to enhance superior customer value.

End-of-chapter questions

Discussion questions

1 The chapter brought up some examples of possible differences between a value chain and a supply chain. How do you understand the difference between these two terms?

2 The chapter brought up a number of ways in which a market position can be defended. Provide some real-world examples on how logistics can contribute to such a defence.

3 Provide examples of companies that compete based on cost leadership and service leadership. What role does logistics have in these companies?

Study questions

1 What are the two fundamental tasks when strategizing according to the market positioning perspective?

2 What is the difference between a strategy and operational effectiveness?

3 What does hypercompetition mean?

4 The value concept is a multifaceted concept which may be difficult to grasp. Explain two factors that complicate its understanding.

5 What are the key managerial concerns in cases when logistics contributes to a cost leadership position?

6 What are the key managerial concerns in cases when logistics contributes to a service leadership position?

References

Beer (2024) Decoding Aldi and Lidl's success: A logistics perspective, blog post Beer-Management.de, www.beer-management.de/decoding-aldi-and-lidls-success-a-logistics-perspective/ (archived at https://perma.cc/G7JE-6H6K)

Bowman, C and Ambrosini, V (2000) Value creation versus value capture: Towards a coherent definition of value in strategy, *British Journal of Management*, 11(1), 1–15

Christopher, M (2016) *Logistics and Supply Chain Management: Creating value-adding networks*, 5th edition, Pearson Education Limited, Harlow

CSCMP (n.d.) Supply chain management definitions and glossary, https://cscmp.org/CSCMP/CSCMP/Educate/SCM_Definitions_and_Glossary_of_Terms.aspx (archived at https://perma.cc/686S-PSGD)

Mizik, N and Jacobsen, R (2003) Trading off between value creation and value appropriation: The financial implications of shifts in strategic emphasis, *Journal of Marketing*, 67(1), 63–76

Porter, M (1980) *Competitive Strategy: Techniques for analyzing industries and competitors*, Free Press, New York

Porter, M (1985) *Competitive Advantage: Creating and sustaining superior performance*, Free Press, New York

Porter, M (1996) What is strategy? *Harvard Business Review*, 74(6), 61–78

Sandberg, E (2015) *Logistik och Strategi: För lönsamhet och tillväxt*, Studentlitteratur, Lund

Sandberg, E and Abrahamsson, M (2019) *Logistikdriven Affärsutveckling*, Studentlitteratur, Lund

Sandberg, E, Pal, R and Hemilä, J (2018) Exploring value creation and appropriation in the reverse clothing supply chain, *International Journal of Logistics Management*, 29(1), 90–109

The resource-based perspective 03

Whereas market positioning adopts a strategy based on the relative position in the market, an alternative approach for understanding the origin of a sustainable competitive advantage begins internally with a company's resources. This approach, particularly represented by the resource-based view (RBV) of the firm, means that the market position is viewed as an *outcome*, rather than a starting point when strategizing. Thus, the position in the market is primarily not a matter of *selection*; rather, it is the company's resource base that *enables* a market position. In line with this, the main message in the resource-based perspective is that the position in the market is still important for understanding how value is created for customers, but it is the company's resource base that should be in focus when strategizing. Sometimes it may be a *single resource*, such as a patent, that forms the basis for a sustainable competitive advantage. However, as will be discussed later in this chapter, a *combination of resources* is often more likely to be the foundation for a sustainable competitive advantage.

This chapter aims to introduce the fundamentals of a resource-based perspective and explicate the role of logistics management in this perspective. Section 3.1 provides an understanding of how resources are understood in this context, and how various resources can be categorized. Section 3.2 thereafter outlines the concepts of economic and monopolistic rents that can be considered as the ultimate goal and main indicators for a sustainable competitive advantage according to the resource-based perspective. The chapter thereafter elaborates on how to identify and understand the resources that are strategically relevant. For this, section 3.3 presents the four resources attributes of valuable, rare, imperfectly imitable and organization. Finally, section 3.4 presents a model for analysing logistics resources at four different organizational levels, ranging from a subset of resources within an organization's logistics function, to a set of resources across company borders.

3.1 Organizations as bundles of resources

In general, when examining the difference between a market positioning perspective and the resource-based perspective, there are primarily two fundamental assumptions on how to consider resources that distinguish the perspectives:

- The market positioning perspective tends to assume that all companies possess or have access to the resources needed to achieve a certain market position, while the resource-based perspective contends that this is not the case. On the contrary, advocators of a resource-based perspective suggest that there is a *firm resource heterogeneity*, i.e. companies do not normally have the same access to resources. In addition, resources are also often asymmetric, meaning they perform differently across different companies.
- The market positioning perspective also tends to assume that resources are mobile and easily transferable, meaning that companies can quickly acquire them if needed. According to the resource-based perspective this may not always be the case, i.e. there is a *firm resource immobility*.

In line with these two assumptions advocators of the resource-based perspective acknowledge that market characteristics tend to be more volatile, resources can be perceived to be more stable in the long term, and thus a more reliable foundation of the company's strategy. In the literature, this resource base is often described as something internal, which is why the resource-based perspective is often referred to as an 'inside-out' perspective on strategizing (while the market positioning perspective is considered to be an 'outside-in' approach). According to both viewpoints, the position in the market, the company's activities, and the company's resources are important, and it is of course impossible to treat these parts independently of each other. However, as Figure 3.1 shows, the starting point for strategizing is different in the two perspectives.

Figure 3.1 The starting points for strategizing in the market positioning and resource-based perspectives

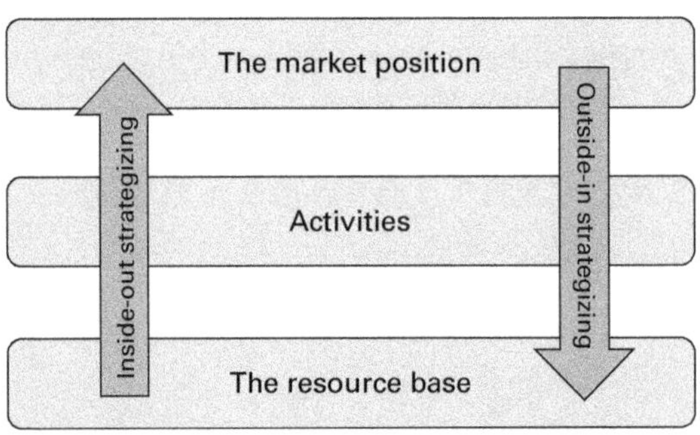

SOURCE Adapted from de Wit and Meyer (2010); Sandberg (2015) and Sandberg and Abrahamsson (2019)

According to a resource-based perspective, a company consists of a network of intertwined resources, often discussed as 'bundles of resources'. This view, originating from older seminal work by, among others, Edith Penrose (1959) and Birger Wernerfelt (1984), highlights the importance of resources in a similar way to how the market positioning perspective recognizes activities as the basic unit of analysis in strategizing. The term 'resources' is often given a very broad meaning here. An example of such an all-embracing definition of resources is that of Jay Barney (1991): 'all assets, capabilities, organizational processes, firm attributes, information, knowledge, etc. controlled by a firm that enable the firm to conceive of and implement strategies that improve its efficiency and effectiveness' (Barney, 1991, p. 101).

According to this definition by Barney (1991), resources may include tangible as well as intangible ones. Examples of more tangible resources are:

- financial resources (capital, cash reserves, securities, etc.)
- physical resources (buildings, machines, production facilities, etc.)
- organizational resources (corporate structure, planning processes, etc.)
- technological resources (patents, proprietary technology, etc.)

Examples of more intangible resources, that are often more difficult to measure and observe, include:

- human resources (skills, expertise, knowledge of employees, organizational culture and beliefs, etc.)
- innovation resources (R&D capabilities, learning abilities and related processes, etc.)
- reputational resources (image and business reputation, relationships with stakeholders, etc.)

Compiling an exhaustive list of all the various resources a company actually possesses is difficult, if not impossible. However, business systems, budgets and balance sheets can provide an indication. Further assistance for resource identification can be obtained by using some form of structured classification of different resources, for example based on tangible and intangible ones as presented above. In a logistics context, a rough categorization of relevant resources can, for example, be:

- physical items – warehouse facilities, forklifts, trucks, and access to land
- organization – reporting structures and planning systems
- information – information systems and information sharing
- relationships – formal as well as informal collaborations with other actors in the supply chain
- individuals – knowledge, experiences, and social contacts of the employed staff (Sandberg, 2015)

The term 'capability' also plays a major role in the resource-based perspective, and it may therefore be worth explicating the difference between these terms and how they are viewed in this book.

Resources, as was described above, can be physical things as well as intangible assets and can in themselves serve as the basis for a sustainable competitive advantage. However, it is often capabilities that are considered to have the greatest significance for creating competitive advantages. Capabilities are here seen as a specific type of resource whose main task is to combine and coordinate different resources. Thus, while a resource is something an organization *has*, a capability is something an organization *does*. Following the same line of thought, logistics researchers Olavarrieta and Ellinger define capabilities as: 'complex bundles of individual skills, assets and accumulated knowledge exercised through organizational processes, that enable firms to co-ordinate activities and make use of their resources' (Olavarrieta and Ellinger, 1997, p. 563).

As we proceed in this book, the term 'resource' will be used for simplicity, unless otherwise stated, where capabilities, as described above, can be considered a specific type of resource.

3.2 Resources are fundamental for the creation of rents

For all strategic management theories, understanding how companies generate superior profitability is a pivotal issue. The resource-based perspective draws on the notion of rents when doing this. Rents is a term rooted in economics and represents the surplus, extraordinary return a resource can generate that is *above the average profitability* level in an industry and is the ultimate goal when strategizing from a resource-based perspective. Rents are not just regular profits, but are the *additional earnings* that arise when a firm has resources that are superior to the competitors'. Having such superior resources, sometimes labelled *distinctive* resources (or capabilities), indicates that the company has a sustainable competitive advantage against competitors (Olavarrieta and Ellinger, 1997). In accordance with this, companies in the resource-based perspective are sometimes labelled 'rent-seekers' (Olavarrieta and Ellinger, 1997).

Of particular relevance for understanding how a company can gain a sustainable competitive advantage based on the resources, are the two fundamental types of rents, economic and monopolistic.

Economic rents originate from the fact that some resources are more efficient than others. This allows the company in possession of those resources to operate more efficiently than competitors and hence achieve a sustainable competitive advantage.

Historically, the economic rent concept was primarily associated with land. The English economist David Ricardo observed that a more fertile piece of land, due to its inherent higher productivity, could result in a higher price than less fertile counterparts. In contemporary strategic management theory, this idea has been broadened to encompass any resource or capability that allows a company to earn returns above the industry average.

Logistics resources of various kinds could definitely be the grounds for the generation of economic rents. For instance, a packaging function in the outbound area of a warehouse may consist of a successful combination of people, processes and technologies that result in a more productive packaging performance than competitors, which results in packaging at a lower cost than competitors, which, everything else being equal, results in higher profit margins. In a similar vein, an optimized route planning may render better fill-rates in trucks compared to competitors. The extra profit made due to a better packaging performance or route planning, beyond what is typically expected in that industry, is the economic rent derived from resources involved.

Monopolistic rents stems from resources with some form of monopolistic position on the market. This type of rent is based on a company having a resource which, regardless of the efficiency of this resource, other companies are prevented from having. A monopolistic rent typically emerges when a firm achieves a degree of market power, allowing it to price its offerings above what would be the case in a perfectly competitive scenario. This market power often arises from differentiation – a unique selling proposition that resonates with customers and is not easily replicable by competitors. In a logistics context, monopolistic rents may originate for instance from a shipper's long-term collaboration and agreement with a very dominant third-party logistics provider in a certain market. A perfectly competitive situation may be obstructed as the agreement may hinder competitors from entering agreements with the third-party logistics provider and thereby operating under the same conditions in the market.

It may be worth noting that a competitive advantage that stems from having resources that generate a monopolistic rent does not imply that the company operates on a market with restricted legal opportunities for a free market competition. Instead, a monopolistic rent refers to the company's ability to differentiate its offerings in a manner that grants pricing power and shields it from a relentless price competition at a perfect competitive market.

To summarize, economic rent originates from the existence of resources which allow a company to operate more efficiently or effectively than its rivals. In contrast, monopolistic rent stems from a situation where a company has, often by means of a powerful market position, managed to differentiate its resource base and in some way exclude competitors. This in turn allows a pricing power and rents beyond the industry average. While both forms of rent can lead to superior returns, they also present distinct challenges. Typically, economic rents erode if competitors successfully replicate or substitute the distinctive resource, while monopolistic rents can diminish if differentiation wanes or if customer preferences shift (thus making the resource less relevant).

3.3 Logistics resources as a basis for competitive advantage

When considering a company to consist of bundles of resources, it becomes evident that not all of these resources are strategically important. In fact, most of them are to be considered as 'commodities', available on the open market and to competitors and are hence not useful for the creation of rents and a sustainable competitive advantage. When strategizing it therefore becomes important to identify and understand more precisely which resources – or combinations of resources – are strategically important, i.e. the distinctive resources.

In line with this, one of the most significant theoretical contributions within the resource-based perspective was made by Barney (1991), when he developed the attributes for such distinctive resources. In a 2007 book co-authored with Delwyn Clark, Barney expanded on this reasoning, arguing that the resource in question must possess the following four attributes, collectively known as the VRIO model:

1. It must be *Valuable*. The resource should contribute to creating value for the company by exploiting business opportunities and/or neutralizing threats.
2. It must be *Rare*. Not many of the company's current and future competitors should possess this resource.
3. It must be *Imperfectly Imitable*. The resource must be difficult or very costly for competitors to replicate.
4. The company must also have an *Organization* that can fully exploit the resource in question.

Figure 3.2 illustrates how these attributes are aligned to a sustainable competitive advantage.

3.3.1 Valuable

According to the VRIO model, a resource is valuable if it enables the company to implement strategies that either captures (business) opportunities or neutralizes (business) threats thus improving efficiency and/or effectiveness in the company's operations. From an economic perspective, the improved efficiency and/or

Figure 3.2 The VRIO attributes and how they align to sustainable competitive advantage

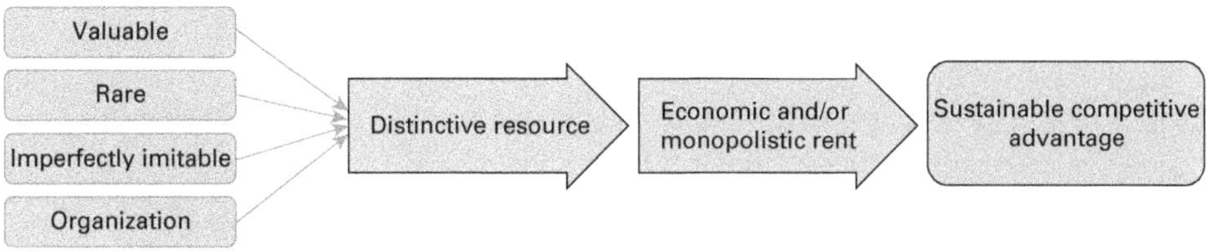

effectiveness enables either cost savings for the company and/or allows for higher prices towards customers. The way logistics can create value is often discussed in a similar manner, where, just as described in Chapter 2, value can be created by contributing to lower prices for the customer, and/or contributing to better service. Service here is implicitly expected to enable prices to be raised towards the customer, or maintained at the same level if the current market is under price pressure. By that above-average profitability can be created and hence rent.

Some typically common areas where logistics resources may contribute to the criterion valuable are:

- *Cost efficiency*: Efficient logistics operations and their underlying resources can significantly reduce a company's operational costs. This includes, for instance, costs associated with transportation, warehousing, inventory management, and order fulfilment.
- *Customer service and satisfaction*: Quick and reliable delivery services, accurate order fulfilment, and responsive customer service are all aspects of logistics that directly contribute to customer service and, by extension, satisfaction. As was also highlighted in Chapter 2, a company that is able to consistently meet or exceed customer expectations creates value and can differentiate itself from competitors.
- *Flexibility and responsiveness*: In today's rapidly changing business environments, the ability to quickly respond to changes in market demand is crucial. Effective and efficient logistics resources here provide companies with the agility needed to adapt to changes, manage disruptions, and capitalize on new opportunities.
- *Inventory management*: Effective and efficient logistics resources, including for instance planning processes and logistics-related technology applications, helps in maintaining optimal inventory levels, ensuring that products are

available when customers need them, without incurring the high costs associated with excess inventory. Indeed, this balance is valuable as it contributes to customer satisfaction while minimizing holding costs.

- *Visibility*: Advanced logistics operations often involve the use of technology to track and manage the movement of goods. This visibility enables, for instance, better decision-making, risk management, and performance analysis, all of which contribute to creating value.
- *Strategic partnerships and relationships*: Logistics often involve working with a network of suppliers, distributors, and other partners, combining and pooling resources. The ability to manage these relationships (and involved resources) effectively is valuable as it, for instance, contributes to unique service offerings towards customers, cost-efficient flows of products and related information throughout the supply chain.

Note that in the VRIO model, the primary focus is on the creation of economic values in the long term. This means that values related to environmental or social aspects are not directly considered in this model as it was originally conceived. However, it should be noted that indirectly these values may play a role. For instance, increasing efficiency or effectiveness in operations may lead to environmental value creation, which in turn may be, at least partly, translated into economic gains.

3.3.2 Rare

In order to form the basis of a company's competitive advantage, a resource must be able to generate value. However, if the resource in question is commonly found, it means that several companies will be able to create the same value, and thus the resource cannot be the source for an above-average profit, i.e. the creation of rent. This means that the attribute of being *rare* is just as important as the attribute of being valuable.

What is actually meant by rare? Where to draw the line for when a resource can be deemed rare is, in practice, not always clear. A general rule of thumb that is commonly referred to is that as long as the number of companies, possessing a valuable resource, is less than the number that would be required for a perfect competition, the resource in question has the potential to generate a competitive advantage (Barney and Clark, 2007; Barney, 1991).

At first glance, meeting the rarity attribute within logistics may seem challenging. The inclusion of logistics resources in a company's operations is hardly rare. Likewise, more specific logistics resources such as physical logistics assets, warehousing systems or logistics-trained personnel are not uncommon. However, the more precisely the resources are described, the more their rarity can emerge. For instance, zooming in on a distribution system, not all companies operate a (valuable) cross-docking system with a specific, superior type of information system. Thus, it is the details in the description of the logistics resources that are important for understanding and determining what is truly a rare resource.

Furthermore, another aspect that may improve the rareness of logistics resources is their combination with other resources, one example being that individual resources may not be rare, but in combination they are. For instance, accurate forecasts of future customer behaviours, coupled with the ability to provide cost-effective deliveries with long lead times from a supplier, may have the potential to be rare, although these resources individually may not fulfil the criteria of being rare (or even valuable).

3.3.3 Imperfectly imitable

According to the VRIO framework, the criteria 'valuable' and 'rare' can together mean that a company obtains an initial first mover advantage. However, as long as the resource in question can easily be acquired by competitors it will only be a matter of time before this advantage disappears. Therefore, a third attribute is needed, which means that the resource in question must be imperfectly imitable (i.e. difficult and/or costly to imitate). It is only then the resource can form the basis for a long-term competitive advantage. As mentioned at the beginning of the chapter, the difficulty of imitation is based on the fact that, according to the resource-based perspective, there is a resource heterogeneity and resource immobility.

There are a wide variety of reasons as to why a resource can be difficult to imitate. These reasons strongly overlap with the market positioning perspective, where, in a similar way, it is argued that there is a need for an ability to defend a market position, for instance against the establishment of new companies and substitute products. A few common examples in a logistics context are (these may also be relevant from a market positioning perspective):

- *Complex networks*: If the logistics operations at hand involve an intricate network of suppliers, distributors and customers that has been built for a long time, it would probably be challenging for competitors to imitate this network quickly.
- *Unique relationships*: In a similar vein, firms may have unique relationships with suppliers, logistics partners or distributors within these networks, leading to

preferential treatment, better terms or exclusive access to resources. These relationships, built over time, are hard for competitors to replicate.

- *Proprietary technology*: Some firms may develop their own unique logistics software or technologies that optimize their supply chain, reduce costs and improve efficiency.
- *Culture:* A company's culture that emphasizes, for instance, efficiency, continuous improvement and excellence in logistics operations can be a significant asset. This culture, coupled with a highly skilled and experienced logistics team, often creates a capability that is not easily replicated by competitors.
- *Location*: Being strategically located close to key suppliers, distribution hubs or customers can provide logistics-related advantages that are not easily imitable. For instance, one such advantage can be grounded in short delivery lead times or quick repair services.
- *Economies of scale and scope*: Companies with large-scale logistics operations can achieve economies of scale or scope, that result in lower transportation, handling and/or storage costs. Smaller competitors may find it difficult to match these cost efficiencies.
- *Learning curve*: Companies with long-standing logistics operations have often been able to advance on the learning curve, understanding the nuances and complexities of efficient and effective logistics operations. For new entrants or competitors, it can be argued, it would take time and investment to reach a similar level of proficiency.

On a more general level, three different general reasons why a resource – or a combination of resources – is difficult to imitate can be identified (Barney, 1991):

- The involved resources are historically conditioned, i.e. there is a *path dependency* to acknowledge. This means that the resource has been created and built up over a long time internally in the company, often based on experiences, lessons learned and knowledge related to the company's historical development. This does not necessarily have to be the consequence of a diligent, conscious effort by the company. It could also be coincidences in the past such as the purchase of land for a warehouse, transitioning to a new IT system, or initiating a new collaboration with a new supplier, which in the future can prove to be of great strategic importance. Another example is a good, strong reputation among both customers and suppliers.

- The involved resources are *causally ambiguous*. Often, it can be difficult to distinguish the exact composition of involved resources and what really is the source of the competitive advantage. However, this ambiguity can paradoxically be seen as something positive from a competitive standpoint. If any company, including the company holding the competitive advantage, were to have complete insight into exactly how the resources are interconnected, and exactly how they contribute to a competitive advantage, it would be considerably easier to imitate the resources in question. The fact that the competitive advantage is somewhat 'shrouded in mystery' can therefore be an advantage.
- The involved resources are *socially complex*. Resources that lead to a long-term competitive advantage often include people and their knowledge and experiences, as well as their personal connections. These relationships are often an important part of the corporate culture, which is difficult to imitate. For example, information transfer can take place through such informal contacts, which often makes them difficult to imitate.

The reasons mentioned above can be seen as the main explanation for why capabilities or the combination of resources are more likely to be the foundation for a sustainable competitive advantage compared to individual resources. Individual resources might be seen as valuable, and sometimes even rare, but they are often easier to imitate, or copy, compared to a capability or a combination of several resources.

The above points can also be seen as an explanation why in logistics there has been a strong emphasis on pointing out that IT systems in themselves, or various logistics-related management concepts such as ECR (Efficient Consumer Response), VMI (Vendor Managed Inventory) or CPFR (Collaborative Planning, Forecasting, and Replenishment) are not in themselves the foundation for a company's competitive advantage.

In their generic form they are neither rare nor historically conditioned, causally ambiguous, or particularly socially complex phenomena. In order to play a role from a strategic point of view and be a source for a sustainable competitive advantage, these systems and concepts need to be further developed internally and adapted to the situation. Only then can they become strategically relevant. This line of reasoning is in many ways similar to Michael Porter's distinction between operational effectiveness on the one hand, and strategy on the other, as was presented in Chapter 2.

3.3.4 Organization

In addition to one or more resources that are valuable, rare and imperfectly imitable, the company also needs to have an organization that can exploit the full potential of the resources. Here, 'organization' mainly refers to its formal aspects, such as reporting structure, control systems and compensation strategies for employees.

A functioning organizational 'infrastructure' like this does not necessarily need to be particularly valuable, rare or difficult to imitate, but it is still required in order for the strategic resources to be utilized effectively.

It is well known that the company's overall organization plays a significant role in how well logistics resources can be utilized in the company. Historically, logistics has often been organized under either a production or a marketing function, which has made it difficult for many companies to clearly see and understand the full significance and potential of logistics resources. Since strategically important logistics resources typically cross boundaries, they have often been difficult to see and oversee in such an organization. It is often only when logistics is elevated to a more strategic level that it can be fully used to create profitability and growth. When logistics as a business function gets more room to operate, and is positioned higher up in the corporate hierarchy, the proximity to the company's management becomes clearer. This, in turn, increases the opportunities to fully exploit valuable, rare and difficult-to-imitate logistics-related resources.

3.4 Analysing logistics resources at different organizational levels

As previously pointed out in this chapter, a single, individual resource may fulfil the VRIO criteria and hence be considered as a distinctive resource, for instance, a patent or a completely unique, advantageous location of a warehouse. However, in a logistics context, with the VRIO attributes in mind, it is far more likely that a *combination of resources* provides the foundation for a sustainable competitive advantage. When it comes to the value criteria, value is often co-created among resources, functions or even organizations. Regarding the rareness criteria, a combination of several resources, often including a capability to coordinate them, makes it more unusual compared to a single resource. Finally, the imitation of the resource (or combination of resources) is likely to be more difficult in the case of several resources combined.

It is therefore relevant to consider combinations of resources as a source of a competitive advantage when strategizing. These combinations can be found at four different organizational levels (see Figure 3.3):

Level 1: Within an organization's logistics function

Level 2: At the organization's logistics function as a whole

Level 3: Across functions in an organization

Level 4: Across organizational borders

Figure 3.3 Strategically relevant combinations of logistics resources at four different organizational levels

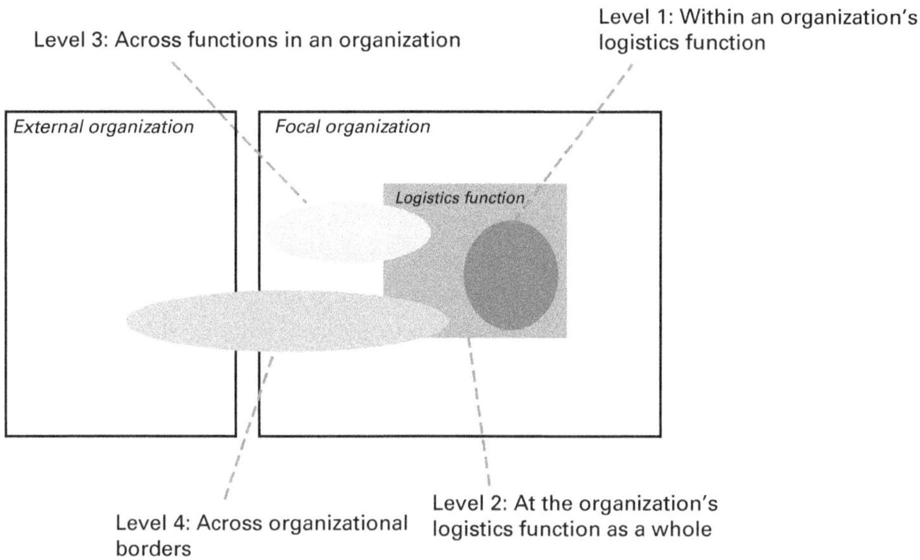

3.4.1 Level 1: Within an organization's logistics function

A first possible category of distinctive logistics resources may be found in a subset of the logistics function. Internally to the logistics function, it is possible to distinguish at least four typical combinations of logistics resources that hold the potential for a sustainable competitive advantage: customer-oriented resources, supplier-oriented resources, information-oriented resources and coordination-related resources (Mentzer et al, 2004).

Customer-oriented resources broadly aim to ensure that customers are satisfied in the best possible way. The goal can be said to be the traditional logistical service requirements of delivering the right goods at the right time, in the right quality and quantity, while transporting and storing products as cost efficiently as possible. To achieve this, a customer-centric distribution network is often a pivotal overall logistics resource. In addition, flexibility and tailored logistics solutions towards different customer requirements are other important aspects for customer-oriented resources. Examples of involved individual resources include, in addition to physical resources such as warehouse buildings and picking equipment, personnel, demand forecasting and the design of operational processes in the flow, such as picking and packing.

An important common denominator for *supplier-oriented resources* is their focus on ensuring a smooth, efficient and reliable supply chain upstream in the supply chain where total costs should be balanced against service-related aspects. Often supplier-oriented resources also have the task of ensuring that innovative logistics solutions are created for better customer orientation downstream in the supply chain. Examples include standardized work methods, risk management and contingency planning, and performance measurement systems that enable control and understanding of sourcing practices.

Information-oriented resources are based on the understanding that logistics is a process-oriented function, where the collection and analysis, as well as the storage and distribution of information across the company's functional boundaries, play a crucial role. Typical resources included are information technology (hardware and software, as well as networks and their design) and the sharing of useful information itself (exchange of technical as well as strategic and operational data). Alongside these aspects related to the information infrastructure itself, there are also more informal capabilities for effective information and knowledge exchange, between functions as well as individual people. For instance, cultural aspects such as willingness to share information, team spirit and systems thinking here come into play.

Closely related to information-oriented resources, *coordination-related resources* can also be a source of competitive advantage. Broadly, these contribute to efficiency as well as effectiveness in the flows of products and materials by linking downstream service and product needs with upstream availability. These types of resources include, for example, cross-functional and cross-border teams within the organization, as well as other organizational solutions that promote a high degree of integration internally within the company.

3.4.2 Level 2: The organization's logistics function as a whole

In some contexts, instead of focusing on subsets or parts of the company's logistics function, it may be more meaningful to consider the entire company's logistics function as a strategic resource that provides the company with a sustainable competitive advantage. At this functional level, it is often difficult to designate certain parts (resources) as more important than others – here, it is rather the logistics function as a whole, and how the various logistics resources interact, that contributes to the competitive advantage. One way to describe the strategic significance of the logistics function was presented by Abrahamsson, Aldin and Stahre (2003), who argued that in cases where logistics plays a role in the company's overall strategy, the company has a well-functioning *logistics platform*. The logistics platform can be defined as follows:

> We define a logistics platform as a homogenous part of the logistics system, which a logistics organization centrally manages and controls, and has the power to design in a

> way that it is a resource base for new market positions. The logistics platform includes concepts for logistics operations, a physical structure, processes and its activities as well as the information systems needed for design, operations and reporting (Abrahamsson et al, 2003, p. 104).

In line with this definition, the logistics platform can be described as a uniform function with a clear direction and a clear goal. It can then be seen as a means for supporting and enabling the company's strategies regarding, for example, expanding the product range, implementation and utilization of new market channels, expanding the company's operations into new markets, extracting synergy effects in acquisitions and/or scalability, etc. Another feature is its ability to efficiently and effectively link operational activities with strategic decisions in both directions, that is, both top-down and bottom-up.

Given these features, not all companies' logistics functions can be described as a logistics platform. In fact, very few companies have a logistics function that can be considered to be a logistics platform and hence fulfil the VRIO attributes.

REAL-WORLD EXAMPLE The valuable, rare and imperfectly imitable logistics platform of Apple Inc.

Apple Inc. is a US-based technology company with logistics and SCM operations that fit well into the description of a logistics platform. Founded in 1976 with the business idea of designing and selling personal computers, Apple has today developed into a global giant that designs and sells not only computers, but also other well-known hardware such as iPod, iPhone, Apple TV, Apple Smartwatch, etc. Apple also provides its own operating systems, macOS and iOS, for its devices as well as a variety of online services such as iTunes, App Store and iCloud.

With headquarters and a design-organization mainly based in California, USA, the various Apple products are produced, stored and transported across the world based on a massive logistics platform that stretches from a global sourcing of components to retail stores, via production and distribution networks. In line with Abrahamsson et al's (2003) definition of a logistics platform, Apple's logistics system is characterized by a high level of control, centralized decision-making, as well as systems thinking, in which logistics and supply chain operations constitute an integral part of Apple's business strategy.

In accordance with the VRIO framework, Apple's logistics platform can be considered *valuable* mainly due to its focus on control and lean approach in the global logistics operations that stretches from suppliers of raw materials to retail stores and end consumers. A lean inventory management approach is here especially emphasized, as components in the tech industry may rapidly become obsolete. From an organizational point of view, Apple's physical supply chain operations are to a high extent outsourced to manufacturers and third-party logistics providers, often based on close, long-term collaboration.

Around 200 suppliers, mainly concentrated in China but also other parts of the world, represent some 98 per cent of Apple's total procurement. The close collaboration with these suppliers allows the company to launch products simultaneously in multiple countries with high availability even during massive demand peaks, such as those for new iPhone models. As such, thanks to control and close collaboration in the supply chain, Apple manages to provide products when and where the customers want them.

Apple's logistics platform may also be considered as *rare*. Many other players in the industry Apple rely upon external manufacturing resources as well as logistics services, but in contrast to many other players Apple has been able to keep an extensive control of the flows of materials and products. This level of integration and overview is rare and enables Apple to ensure high supply chain performance throughout the supply chain and at the same time innovate and continuously develop its practices in line with new technology and customer demands.

The logistics platform can also be deemed as *difficult to imitate* by competitors due to a number of reasons. An obvious first aspect has to do with the economies of scale and scope – Apple is today able to exploit its size in terms of sales volumes when negotiating contracts with manufacturers as well as logistics service providers. As indicated above, another crucial factor that hinders imitation is Apple's long-term, close collaboration with suppliers. As a result of these close relationships there is often a path dependency to consider, as well as the existence of socially complex, sometimes personal, boundaries between Apple and their suppliers. In a similar vein, the close collaboration with suppliers, as well as the extensive supply chain control by Apple, may also be considered to be somewhat causally ambiguous. At least as an outsider, it may be difficult to fully grasp how these features are being turned into a superior logistics performance. Indeed, control here implies more than just hard figures and facts of supply chain conditions – it also needs to be translated into activities and performance.

Finally, Apple also has an *organization* that is able to exploit its logistics platform for strategic purposes. In particular, the organization in conjunction with logistics and supply chain matters is characterized by centralized decision-making. This is, for instance, an important ingredient when it comes to necessary investment decisions in new technology, supplier collaborations or new logistics facilities.

SOURCES Fámúwàgún (2021); www.apple.com; DFreight (2023); Kaponda (2020); Ross and de Naoum (2023)

3.4.3 Level 3: Across functions in an organization

The entire logistics function, or parts of it, can also be a subset of a resource that fulfils the VRIO attributes. In these cases, logistics becomes strategically interesting only if it interacts and coordinates with other parts of the company. Some typical constellations with other internal functions can be logistics resources combined with resources in the IT function, the marketing function or the company's production. It may also be the entire logistics function, often in cases when this function can be described as a logistics platform, as presented above, that is combined with other functions.

A well-functioning logistics platform is expected to be able to interact with other units and, together with them, be the foundation for a strategic resource. It is primarily the interaction of the logistics platform with the marketing function that has been most acknowledged. This combination can play a crucial role in linking the operations in the supply chain with customer demands. Typical areas that require a well-functioning collaboration between logistics and marketing functions are assortment issues, distribution structures and e-commerce. The logistics platform can often also be seen as an important 'engine' and prerequisite for being able to realize the marketing strategy in the company. Typical examples here are growth through geographic expansion, effective launch of new products, and acquisitions and integration of companies into one's own operations.

3.4.4 Level 4: Across organizational borders

Finally, a combination of resources that fulfils the VRIO attributes can also be found across organizational borders. In fact, considering real existing contemporary companies and their business environment, the resource base is often not limited to the company's internal resources, which one might get the impression of in early literature that refers to the resource-based perspective such as RBV.

Within the field of logistics, there is a natural understanding that it is the collective resources in the entire supply chain that must be considered, and it is therefore logical that a competitive advantage which is valuable, rare and difficult to imitate increasingly depends on external relationships with various types of customers and suppliers. In the literature, this is described in the relational view, a framework which was coined by the researchers Jeffrey Dyer and Harbir Singh in 1998 (Dyer and Singh, 1998). Given that logistics and supply chain operations generally encompass a range of interorganizational relationships and extend across numerous stages of supply, production, distribution and sales, the principles of the relational view become especially pertinent.

In essence, drawing from RBV which posits that superior resources can lead to rents and sustainable competitive advantage, the relational view examines interorganizational resource combinations. When these are effectively integrated, often within the framework of long-term collaborative alliances, they are believed to have the potential to generate relational rents. These are defined as:

> 'We define a relational rent as a supernormal profit jointly generated in an exchange relationship that cannot be generated by either firm in isolation and can only be created through the joint idiosyncratic contributions of the specific alliance partners' (Dyer and Singh, 1998, p. 662).

According to Dyer and Singh (1998), there are four different sources of competitive advantages, all of which are based on a company's alliances, and all are highly relevant from a logistics perspective:

- relation-specific investments
- knowledge-sharing routines
- complementary resources and capabilities
- effective governance (of the alliance)

Relation-specific investments

Regarding *relation-specific investments* for the alliance, it is often by adapting its own operations, for example through investments or changed working methods and routines, that a company can fully take advantage of a partner's resources and competencies. Specific investments also contribute to making the relationship itself unique and difficult to imitate, which is an important prerequisite for a sustainable competitive advantage. A general rule of thumb is that the potential for the relationship in question to be the basis for a competitive advantage increases with the size of the investments, which for example can be measured in both the time the alliance has lasted as well as money invested in the relationship. Within the field of logistics, relation-specific investments are a relatively often recognized source of sustainable competitive advantage.

Knowledge-sharing routines

Another important part is *knowledge-sharing routines* and the diffusion of 'know-how' between the partners, which can contribute to learning and development. A common example within logistics is the collaboration that can exist between a shipper company and its logistics provider. Through continuous dialogue and exchange with each other, there are great opportunities for the shipper to better take advantage of the logistics provider's knowledge about, for example, a new market, while the provider can learn about the customer's products, needs and conditions.

Complementary resources and capabilities

In addition to the exchange of knowledge, the exploitation of *complementary resources and capabilities* that 'match' each other can also be an important foundation for a competitive advantage. By combining resources, synergies can be created, which in turn can result in more valuable, rare and difficult-to-imitate resources. Examples of such combinations of resources can for instance be found between a manufacturer and its supplier, where pre-assembly operations and related resources can be located to the supplier in order to facilitate smoother operations at the manufacturer.

Effective governance

Finally, the fourth source of a competitive advantage is the *effective governance* of the alliance, i.e. how well one manages to keep down the costs associated with the alliance, for example in terms of involved personnel. In cases where one manages to have a more effective governance of one's alliance, there is potential for a competitive advantage. In addition to cost-effectiveness, the ability to initiate value-creating initiatives is important – the better conditions one can create in the relationship for new initiatives and development, the better governance the alliance can be considered to have.

REAL-WORLD EXAMPLE The collaboration between Telia and PostNord

The collaboration between the Swedish telecom company Telia and PostNord, one of the dominating logistics service providers in the Nordic region, represents an example where logistics-related resources across company borders are combined in order to fulfil the VRIO attributes. Telia offers a large selection of telecom services related to mobile, broadband and TV services to businesses as well as private consumers. It has a long record of exploiting its own expertise in telecom and logistics to develop and improve customer-centric and technology-oriented supply chain solutions. Telia's supply chain operations are to a great extent outsourced to PostNord, which spans a broad range of supply chain-related services, including logistics planning, warehousing and distribution.

Telia and PostNord have had a collaboration for more than 10 years, with close relationships and interactions at strategic, tactical as well as operational levels. Over the past decade, the two companies have jointly undertaken several logistics development projects in order to improve the overall supply chain performance. In accordance with Dyer and Singh's (1998) relational view, the collaboration has generated relational rent. In particular, the collaboration especially hinges upon *knowledge-sharing routines* and *complementary resources and capabilities.*

An example of *knowledge-sharing routines* between the companies is the formalized, recurrent joint meetings about Telia's end consumer experiences in conjunction with the PostNord-operated delivery of a Telia-product. At these meetings, some 10–20 employees from both companies participate and discuss statistics in the form of delivery service rate and the results from follow-up interviews with individual end consumers about their experiences. Based on the statistics and end consumer responses, the companies can jointly identify shortcomings in the delivery system and discuss improvements. The actual, hands-on examples of the supply chain performance here constitute a valuable ground for a mutual learning about the companies' knowledge, processes and resources.

In a number of joint logistics development projects, the companies have also taken advantage of the fact that they have *complementary resources and capabilities*. For instance, Telia's knowledge and development resources in the area of telecom has been combined with PostNord's physical operations to develop a tracking device to be used in PostNord's distribution system. As such, this device has enabled an estimated 65 per cent reduction of thefts and losses of Telia's products on the Swedish market. Other examples of how the companies' resources have successfully been combined includes a new automated packaging machine to be used in PostNord's warehouse and new routines in conjunction with an express delivery service.

SOURCE Based on the author's interviews with the two companies.

3.5 Summary

This chapter has presented the main principles of strategizing from a resource-based perspective. The resource-based perspective acknowledges that a favourable market position is not a matter of selection. Rather, it is the company's resource base that *enables* a market position. The company's resource base is therefore what should be in focus when strategizing.

According to a resource-based perspective, a company consists of a network of intertwined resources, often discussed as 'bundles of resources'. The term 'resources' is given a broad meaning, encompassing tangible resources such as physical assets and organizational structures as well as intangible ones such as skills and learning abilities, etc. One type of resource of particular importance is capabilities. Capabilities are typically occupied with combining and coordinating other resources. Categories of logistics-related resources include physical items (e.g. warehouse facilities), organization (e.g. planning systems), information (e.g. information systems), relationships (e.g. collaborations) and individuals (e.g. their knowledge and experiences).

The resource-based perspective draws on the notion of rents when explaining what constitutes a sustainable competitive advantage. Rents are understood as the surplus, extraordinary returns a resource can generate that are above the average profitability level in an industry. Having resources that are able to generate such rents becomes the ultimate goal when strategizing according to a resource-based perspective. Two types of rents exist, economic and monopolistic rents. Logistics resources can in various ways contribute to both of these types of rents.

When strategizing it becomes important to identify and understand more precisely which resources – or combinations of resources –have the potential to generate rents. The VRIO model, including the four attributes of valuable, rare, imperfectly imitable and organization, were in this chapter presented as a means to identify strategically relevant resources. This chapter discussed how logistics resources may contribute to the fulfilment of these criteria.

Finally, this chapter highlighted that combinations of logistics resources that are valuable, rare and difficult to imitate can be found at four different organizational levels: within an organization's logistics function, at the organization's logistics function as a whole, across functions in an organization, and across organizational borders.

End-of-chapter questions

Discussion questions

1 Consider the logistics-related resources of a company you know well. How would you like to categorize those resources?

2 From a managerial viewpoint, which one of the criteria in the VRIO model may be most difficult to judge and manage?

3 Distinctive resources can be identified at different organizational levels. Discuss and provide examples of distinctive resources at various organizational levels.

Study questions

1 Explain the fundamental assumptions that distinguish the resource-based perspective from the market positioning perspective.

2 How can a resource respectively a capability be understood? How are these two terms related to each other?

3 Explain the concept of rent.

4 What is the VRIO model?

5 Under what circumstances can a resource (or a combination of resources) be considered as imperfectly imitable?

6 What is the main message of the relational view of the firm?

References

Abrahamsson, M, Aldin, N and Stahre, F (2003) Logistics platforms for improved strategic flexibility, *International Journal of Logistics: Research and Applications*, 6(3), 85–106

Barney, J (1991) Firm resources and sustained competitive advantage, *Journal of Management*, 17(1), 99–120

De Wit, B and Meyer R (2010) *Strategy: Process, Content, Context: An international perspective*, 4th edition, Cengage Learning, Andover, Hampshire

DFreight (2023) Blogpost, dfreight.org/blog/an-insight-into-apples-supply-chain-strategy/ (archived at https://perma.cc/F8K9-YYSB)

Dyer, J H and Singh, H (1998) The relational view: Cooperative strategy and sources of interorganizational competitive advantage, *Academy of Management Review*, 23(4), 660–679

Fámúwàgún, O (2021) The role of global operations management in Apple and its role in the company's competitiveness in the marketplace, dx.doi.org/10.13140/RG.2.2.29078.88644 (archived at https://perma.cc/ERX2-Y8PJ)

Kaponda, K (2020) Optimization of profits by benchmarking supply chain costs: A case for Apple Computers Incorporated, dx.doi.org/10.2139/ssrn.3609113 (archived at https://perma.cc/V2C5-XGAX)

Mentzer, J T, Min, S and Bobbitt, L (2004) Toward a unified theory of logistics, *International Journal of Physical Distribution & Logistics Management*, 34(8), 606–627

Olavarrieta, S and Ellinger, A (1997) Resource-based theory and strategic logistics research, *International Journal of Physical Distribution & Logistics Management*, 27(9/10), 559–587

Penrose, E G (1959) *The Theory of the Growth of the Firm*, John Wiley & Sons, New York

Ross, L and de Naoum, K (2023) How the Apple supply chain stays top ranked in the world, www.thomasnet.com/insights/apple-supply-chain/ (archived at https://perma.cc/P3UG-6V9B)

Sandberg, E (2015) *Logistik och Strategi: För lönsamhet och tillväxt*, Studentlitteratur, Lund

Sandberg, E and Abrahamsson, M (2019) *Logistikdriven Affärsutveckling*, Studentlitteratur, Lund

Wernerfelt, B (1984) A resource-based view of the firm, *Strategic Management Journal*, 5(2), 171–180

The dynamic capabilities perspective

04

In line with an increasingly volatile and fast-moving business landscape, strategic management theory has increasingly emphasized the ability to cope with changes in the environment as the overarching task for strategizing. The dynamic capabilities perspective has its roots primarily in RBV, and can be considered as a natural extension of this theory. As RBV, the dynamic capabilities perspective considers the resource base to be the prime tool for strategizing. However, instead of planning and managing distinctive resources that are valuable, rare and difficult to imitate, strategizing according to the dynamic capabilities perspective concerns the *capacity to change* the resource base. The principal argument is that in a volatile and unpredictable environment with rapidly changing customer requirements and technology advancements, the existing resource base may explain how we 'earn a living now' (Winter, 2003) at 'a given point in time' (Teece, 2007), but becomes less relevant for sustaining a competitive advantage over time. If not coupled with dynamic capabilities, what is today a superior resource base will quickly become outdated. Dynamic capabilities (DC), i.e. the key concept of this line of thinking, can accordingly be defined as: 'the capacity of an organization to purposefully create, extend, or modify its resource base' (Helfat et al, 2007, p. 4).

This chapter outlines the meaning of having a dynamic mindset when strategizing (as opposed to a static one) (section 4.1) and highlights the capacity to change as the basic unit of competitive advantage (section 4.2). It thereafter further explains the content of the dynamic capabilities perspective by means of dynamic capabilities in a hierarchical and horizontal categorization (section 4.3). Finally in section 4.4 the nature of interorganizational dynamic capabilities is further explained.

4.1 A dynamic mindset for strategizing

Understanding how changes in external factors such as consumer trends and technology advancements may influence the strategy of a company has always been an important factor in strategic management theory. For instance, with respect to the marketing positioning perspective and RBV that have been described in this book, Porter (1985) pointed out that if a company's competitive advantage is to last over time, the company's market position also needs to be favourable in the future, meaning it needs to be defensible against competitors and the overall industry development. Similarly, within RBV it is suggested that an important component for a competitive advantage to be sustainable is that the resource underlying the competitive advantage *over time* is valuable, rare and difficult to imitate.

However, a fundamental premise to the dynamic capabilities perspective is that although previous strategic management theories acknowledge the need for change, they do not offer a satisfactory answer to the critical question of *how* a (new) position or resource base is *created*. To offer a more dynamic mindset for strategizing, opposed to the more 'static' perspectives of, for example, market positioning and RBV, the dynamic capabilities perspective advocates that there is a need to establish an *evolutionary fitness* between the organization and its continuously changing environment. For this to continuously stay tuned with environmental developments and changes, and have a suitable, superior resource base in place that is able to capture and shape business opportunities, dynamic capabilities are required. In accordance with this, Helfat et al (2007) defined evolutionary fitness as: 'Evolutionary fitness refers to how well a dynamic capability enables an organization to make a living by creating, extending, or modifying its resource base' (Helfat et al, 2007, p. 7).

Although the concept of evolutionary fitness may be relatively straightforward and easy to understand, the step from a static to a dynamic mindset when strategizing can be difficult in practice. In many cases there is a considerable risk to embrace a dynamic mindset at an overarching level; meanwhile a static thinking still prevails in the more actual strategizing processes of the organization. In Table 4.1, some common differences between a static and dynamic mindset when strategizing are presented.

Table 4.1 Examples of the differences between a static and dynamic mindset when strategizing

Example area	A static mindset	A dynamic mindset
The balance between low price and high service in logistics performance	***Predetermined plan:*** Prioritization of stability and predictability in the balance, often based on long - term planning of, e.g. product range.	***Explorative strategic orientation:*** Flexibility and market responsiveness is sought for, with high internal expectations on continuous improvements in operations and customer-centric-related decisions.

(continued)

Table 4.1 (Continued)

Example area	A static mindset	A dynamic mindset
Omnichannel design	***Efficient utilization:*** A combination of e-commerce and physical stores that are built on long-term agreements and operational effectiveness in terms of, e.g. economies of scale and scope.	***Innovation:*** Flexible design of involved market channels, embracing the customer journey to optimize customer convenience and experience.
Acquisition of new knowledge	***Close knowledge gaps:*** Utilization and trust in fixed channels of knowledge supply, often with an emphasis on newly recruited staff and in conjunction to specific operations with a clear 'end' of the learning phase (such as implementation of a new packaging machine).	***Continuous learning:*** A wide range of knowledge sources, both internally and externally, are utilized. Acquisition of new knowledge is seen as a source for innovation and continuous development, sometimes with less-defined objectives.
Supplier base	***Optimizing existing performance:*** Long-term agreements with minimal governance, opting for predictability in terms of supplier performance.	***Development of new performance:*** Continuous work with a supplier portfolio that matches the company's current and future objectives, and sometimes facing challenges in collaboration with suppliers.

The essence of evolutionary fitness and a dynamic mindset can also be related to a discussion on how to understand the productivity frontier, as was discussed in Chapter 2. Whereas Porter acknowledges that the productivity frontier of an industry can be moved and transformed, he does not recognize how an individual company's performance relates to the productivity frontier. A common view supported by a dynamic capabilities perspective is that a sustainable competitive advantage is created through a series of short, temporary competitive advantages that are constantly being replaced with new ones (Eisenhardt and Martin, 2000). Related to Porter's productivity frontier the task of the company's dynamic capabilities is to continually – and ahead of competitors – push the frontier outward (see Figure 4.1).

Figure 4.1 Dynamic capabilities can push the productivity frontier

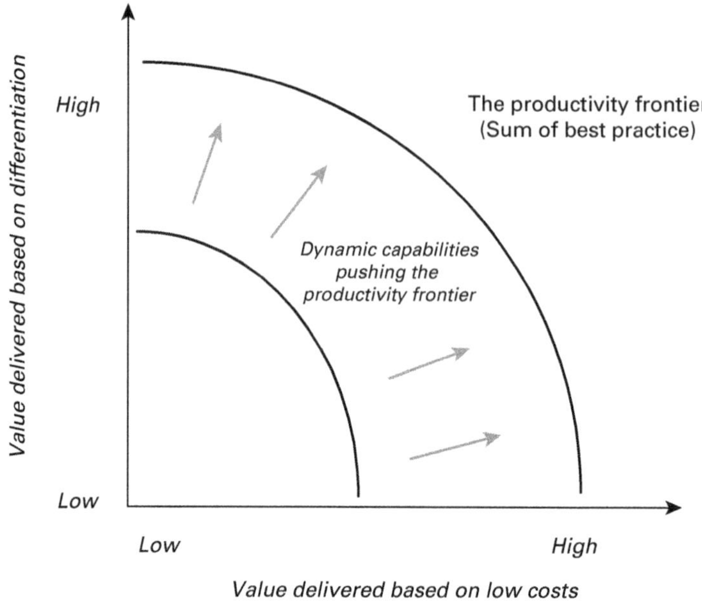

SOURCE Adapted from Sandberg and Abrahamsson (2011) and Porter (1996)

The approach of constantly moving the productivity frontier also means that operational effectiveness, as was also outlined by Porter (1996) and in Chapter 2 in this book, despite Porter's argumentation, can be considered a ground for a sustainable competitive advantage. Rapid improvements of the operational effectiveness become in this context essential for moving the productivity frontier *before* the competitors. By doing this, the hypercompetition that Porter warns of can also be avoided. Companies with superior operational effectiveness do not place themselves together at the productivity frontier – they are pushing it outwards ahead of competitors. This argumentation goes well in line with arguments raised by logistics scholars for many years (e.g. Sandberg and Abrahamsson, 2011), in which the general sequential top-down strategic thinking has been questioned in favour of a focus on operational performance, such as logistics and supply chain management performance.

In the long run, this means that successful companies with strong dynamic capabilities do not have to worry about competitors imitating their resource base, working processes or customer offerings – they can trust that their operations will look different tomorrow. In line with a dynamic mindset these companies know that their success does not lie in their current resource configuration, but in their ability to change it.

4.2 Capacity to change: the basic unit of competitive advantage

At the beginning of this chapter, perhaps the most common definition of dynamic capabilities was presented, in which the company should have the 'capacity' to create, extend and modify its resource base. If activities and resources were considered the basic units of competitive advantage in the market positioning and resource-based perspectives, then the 'capacity to change' may be considered as the basic unit of competitive advantage in a dynamic capabilities perspective.

In traditional DC literature, it is argued that this capacity consists of repeatable organizational routines or processes. Teece et al (1997) described these processes as: 'the way things are done in the firm, or what might be referred to as its routines, or patterns of current practice and learning' (Teece et al, 1997, p. 518).

For the organizational routines, their fundamental task is to contribute to the integration and coordination of the company's resources and activities. New, changed and improved linkages between the company's activities, processes and functions are the core of the company's ability to update its resource base.

An alternative (and to a large extent overlapping) view on what underscores dynamic capabilities was presented by David Teece in his seminal article from 2007 (Teece, 2007). Based on earlier work on organizational routines, this article developed the capacity concept further and argued that there are a number of organizational 'microfoundations' that collectively build up a company's dynamic capabilities. In this context, microfoundations were defined as: 'distinct skills, processes, procedures, organizational structures, decision rules and disciplines' (Teece, 2007, p. 1319).

In recent years, partly as a result of the paper from Teece (2007), the understanding of the capacity to change as the basic unit for competitive advantage, has expanded to include not only routines but also other types of managerial tasks which are less repeatable. For instance DCs may also be considered to contain entrepreneurial abilities, aiming to find completely new ways to operate. This aspect is less routinized and repeatable than the original understanding of DCs as presented in, for example, Teece et al's (1997) original description of DCs. Therefore, apart from managerial and organizational routines characterized by repeatability, dynamic capabilities can also be interpreted as a capacity or ability to change in a broader sense. An important component of such a capacity is, for instance, the sensing of business opportunities and threats (Teece, 2007), and timely and market-oriented decision-making (Barreto, 2010).

4.3 Categorizing dynamic capabilities

As outlined above, the foundation for dynamic capabilities lies in adequate organizational routines and other managerial tasks that collectively provide the company with a capacity to change the resource base. However, despite considerable research interest, knowledge on dynamic capabilities remains relatively fragmented. Consequently, recent years of research on dynamic capabilities have been characterized by efforts to clarify and operationalize the concept of dynamic capabilities, primarily by making various classifications. Such classifications can be made both from a hierarchical and a horizontal point of view.

4.3.1 Dynamic capabilities in a capability hierarchy

As a natural evolution of RBV, a company's resources and capabilities can be classified into different hierarchical levels. Together, they constitute the logic in how static 'here-and-now'-resources are combined with dynamic capabilities to provide a sustainable competitive advantage.

As indicated in Figure 4.2, the actual, 'vertical' scope of dynamic capabilities may be discussed as it is interpreted differently among research scholars. A distinction can be made between (1) resource change-oriented dynamic capabilities that focus on the ability to change the resource base, and (2) learning-oriented capabilities that may be

Figure 4.2 Hierarchies of capabilities

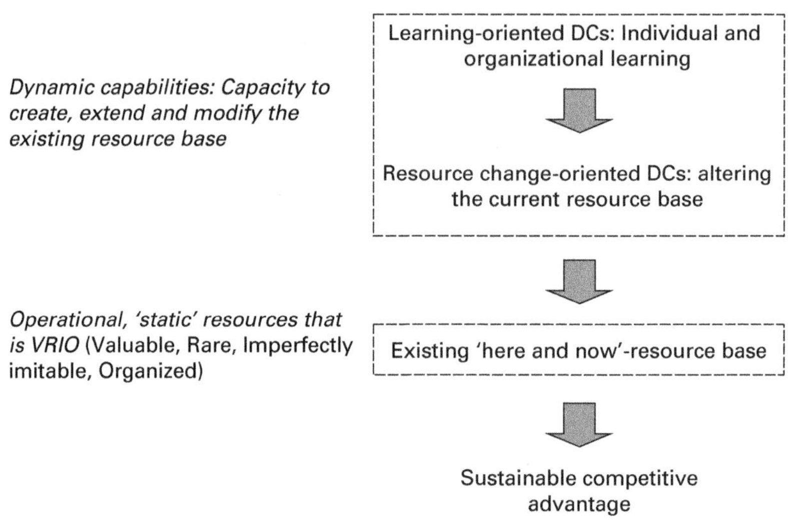

SOURCE Adapted from Sandberg and Åman (2010), a similar figure also appears in Sandberg and Abrahamsson (2011)

seen as antecedent to resource change-oriented dynamic capabilities, sometimes addressed as the 'competence to build new competences' (Danneels, 2008).

Thus, the actual scope of dynamic capabilities may differ depending on whether learning is considered as a dynamic capability or a 'higher-order' capability that is placed 'above' the dynamic capabilities. However, the distinction between these two types of dynamic capabilities is often difficult to make in practice, as the meaning of 'capacity' as referred to in Helfat et al's (2007) definition may incorporate dynamic capabilities related to resource change as well as learning. Therefore, in this book, dynamic capabilities refer to learning-oriented as well as resource change-oriented capabilities. Organizational learning, as a dynamic capability in itself, is further discussed in Chapter 5.

Another confusing concern about terminology that becomes clear when considering hierarchies of capabilities is the matter of how to distinguish between the static, 'here-and-now', focus in the market positioning and resource perspectives on the one hand, and the focus on development over time in the dynamic capabilities perspective on the other. Reason for this concern is that the criteria of 'imperfectly imitable' as put forward in RBV implies that the resource in question should resist imitation over a period of time and hence exceeds the indicated 'here-and-now' focus. Thus, the VRIO framework could, just as the dynamic capabilities perspective, claim that a sustainable competitive advantage over time is targeted.

However, the argument of being imperfectly imitable in a resource-based perspective remains static in the sense that it refers mainly to the defence of *one, particular market position*, based on *one specific resource base*. In contrast, the dynamic capabilities perspective considers a competitive advantage over time based on *different positions and resource bases*. Thus, dynamic capabilities are concerned with the ability to transform from one preferable, competitive position and resource base to another. A metaphor here could be a favourable position at the top of a mountain that provides the company with an above-average profitability and growth based on a certain market position. In the static resource-based perspective, the position on the mountain should be 'defended' over time by a resource base that is imperfectly imitable. As long as no other competitor is able to gain the same position at the mountain, the sustainable competitive advantage remains. In contrast, a sustainable competitive advantage based on dynamic capabilities refers to a situation where a company is able to swiftly move from the top of one mountain to another, more preferable one. This new, more favourable position at the new mountain top may be based on another market position than the former mountain, and may require another resource base.

4.3.2 Horizontal classes of dynamic capabilities

In addition to placing different types of capabilities in a hierarchy, strategy research has increasingly come to identify different types of dynamic capabilities in terms of content, i.e. a horizontal classification. Based on such a classification, a better understanding of the significance of dynamic capabilities can be obtained, while conscious and long-term development work can be systematized and implemented. One of the most recognized categorizations, which has gained relatively wide acceptance, was presented by the researcher David Teece (2007). He identified three different general classes of dynamic capabilities that have come to be used and developed in a variety of contexts (Teece, 2007; Sandberg, 2021).

Sensing (and shaping) business opportunities and threats

The dynamic capability class sensing consists of a variety of processes aimed at 'discovering' business opportunities and/or threats, and the subsequent analyses and sensemaking processes regarding the potential and magnitude of these. When considered as a framework, it could be argued that sensing precedes the other two dynamic capability classes of seizing and reconfiguring, as are outlined below. In relation to these, the value of sensing lies in its potential to offer a first mover advantage that enables the company to acknowledge opportunities and allows the company to allocate resources and adjust strategies more swiftly and effectively than their competitors, i.e. effect processes related to seizing and/or reconfiguring.

Sensing includes environmental scanning processes to detect shifts in consumer preferences, emerging technological trends, regulatory changes and new competitive threats such as new business models and disruptive products. This typically involves continuously gathering intelligence and applying analytical processes to discern patterns and possibilities that others may overlook. In practice, sensing capabilities are often found in activities related to the market and customer partnering and information exchange inside as well as outside the industry, and investments in various technologies to gather information. In recent years, in line with digitalization, big data and technology advancements, it has been noted that data may often be available, but instead the main challenge for sensing is to have the right tools and abilities for the identification of meaningful patterns in the data. Currently, not least in a logistics and SCM context, when making sense of 'big data' there is a need for appropriate business analytics, artificial intelligence and machine learning tools.

In addition to a scanning of business opportunities external to the company, internal scanning of trends and available capabilities and resources is also required. Sensing hence includes an organizational structure that allows for an internal vertical as well as horizontal flow of information to ensure that valuable insights reach the right decision-makers in the organization. Organizations often benefit from developing cross-functional teams that bring together diverse perspectives, which is critical for discovering business opportunities and threats. From a cultural point of view, there must be a propensity in the organization towards knowledge sharing, and an openness for changes and a willingness and preparedness to share relevant insights with the rest of the organization.

Once business opportunities have been identified, they must also be shaped, i.e. further defined and contextualized. This may involve analysis concerning the choice of technologies to leverage, market strategies as well as logistics and supply chain operations. It also includes an evaluation of potential moves by other stakeholders in the company's environment such as competitors, suppliers and customers. In these analyses and shaping processes, when relevant from a logistics and supply chain point of view, it is pivotal for the logistics function to play a role. As an example, even though the sensed business opportunity may have little to do with logistics in the first place, such as customer requirements on a new product, logistics function may play a crucial role for the shaping of the sensed business opportunity. For successful launch of a new product, indeed, logistics is fundamental for its success. This example implies that sensing processes, to make them effective, typically stretch over functional boundaries.

Seizing business opportunities

The capability class of seizing revolves around the development and commercialization processes for sensed business opportunities, i.e. seizing is about translating the business potential recognized in a sensed business opportunity into concrete, specific outcomes such as new processes, products or services. Hence seizing processes stretch from the management of initial, competing potential offerings and solutions, via analysis and decision-making where development paths are narrowed down, to the final launch of a new specific process, product or service.

At a general level, seizing business opportunities often means some kind of change of the current business model, for instance in conjunction with crafting new value propositions, entering new markets or enhancing the firm's position in an existing market. These opportunities could originate from customer needs but could also be grounded in internal effectiveness and efficiency improvements through the use of new technologies. Overall, Teece (2007) identified changes and developments in customer markets and technologies as the two main sources for business opportunities to be sensed. As a result, seizing capabilities revolve around better value creation and capture related to these two factors.

In a logistics context, seizing processes mainly result in new processes or services such as a third-party logistics provider's launch of a new last-mile delivery option in e-commerce, a supplier's establishment of a new regional warehouse that enables shorter delivery lead times towards customers, or new packaging working processes that enable cost efficiency improvements internally at the company. The outcomes of a seizing capability are typically relatively easily identified and address a specific business opportunity sensed.

Decision-making, including an appropriate, supporting organizational infrastructure, is a vital component along the seizing processes. This also calls for a commitment among management and the internal organization as well as external relationships when appropriate. Furthermore, new products, processes and services that are to be launched to capture the sensed business opportunity need to be underpinned by an appropriate basis for decision and resources that ensure that the perceived business opportunity is indeed realized. Just as is the case with sensing, new technology here plays an important role in understanding and evaluating the most appropriate path towards implementation and follow-up.

Reconfiguring

The capability class of reconfiguring, sometimes also referred to as transforming, includes the long-term orchestration of tangible as well as intangible resources, internally as well as externally to the company. The objective of reconfiguring processes is to *adapt* the resource base to changing customer and technology developments, but also to *shape* the market and the industry where the company operates. In contrast to seizing capabilities they do not aim to fulfil a specific business opportunity sensed, but could rather be considered as a means to be better positioned to sense and seize in the future (e.g. Sandberg, 2021).

The outcome of a reconfiguring capability typically results in a new resource base that is better positioned for long-term evolutionary fitness. As outlined by Teece (2007), this may require radical innovation, beyond more comfortable, incremental development paths of the company. Reconfiguring processes may, for instance, include larger changes in the organization such as mergers, joint ventures or liquidations, entrance or exits from markets, or investments in new knowledge and technology. Again, these changes in the resource base are not primarily focused on the capture of one specific business opportunity, but rather changes that are sensed to be important for the company's future evolutionary fitness. In the field of logistics, a contemporary example is the increased interest for investing in AI competence related to logistics operations; although the exact benefits of using AI may still be somewhat vague and unpredictable in a logistics and SCM setting, AI is coupled with vast expectations related to improved customer service performance as well as cost reductions of various kinds. Hence, when adding AI competence to the existing resource base a 'preparedness' for future sensing and seizing is the primary objective.

Making these changes, as the competitive landscape evolves, requires a number of more 'soft' managerial skills. For instance, the organization must be innovative in problem-solving and have a willingness and openness to challenge and look beyond the current resource base. There must be a proactive mindset that is guided by clear vision and company goals. In this context, as outlined by Teece (2007), learning and knowledge management is a key ingredient.

REAL-WORLD EXAMPLE Example: H&M's dynamic capabilities for the creation of logistics flexibility

The Swedish fashion retailer H&M Group (H&M) operates in more than 75 countries, with total sales of more than US$20 billion mainly through 5,000 retail stores accompanied by a growing share of online sales (in 2023 30 per cent). As well as the H&M brand, the group also includes several other fashion brands with different profiles, including COS, & Other Stories, Sellpy, Monki, Weekday, Afound and ARKET. In the very heart of H&M's supply chain operations are some 80 warehouses located around the world. While design and retailing operations such as logistics, marketing and sales are conducted in-house, production is provided by around 700 independent manufacturers located in Asia, Europe and Africa, that together contract in total more than 1,600 first-tier factories. The production is supervised from 20 local production offices.

In order to navigate the rapidly changing competitive landscape of retail fashion, swift and continuous change and development in H&M's very large, global and complex supply chain network is pivotal. New business opportunities related to technology advancements, customer requirements and new business models emerge on a continuous basis, but these must also be captured.

In order to do so, logistics flexibility throughout the supply chain network is a key ingredient. From an academic point of view, the concept of logistics flexibility can be understood in many ways, but is often acknowledged to encompass the two dimensions of *logistics range flexibility* respectively *logistics response flexibility* (Sandberg, 2021, p. 704):

- *Logistics range flexibility* is defined as the number of potential states it is possible to achieve in the physical supply and distribution and related purchasing and demand functions.
- *Logistics response flexibility* is defined as the ease (measured in logistics performance indicators such as costs, speed, service, environmental impact etc.) with which changes can be made within the logistics flexibility range.

In H&M's supply chain network the need for logistics flexibility becomes especially pertinent in conjunction with the industry's ongoing omnichannel development. Flexibility here becomes a key component in order to synchronize sales via physical stores and online, and create a seamless end consumer experience. There is also a need to create economies of scale and scope in production as well as distribution on a global basis, while simultaneously being able to meet demands for local adaptations and governance. At H&M, this 'glocal' challenge requires transparency across the production facilities and the extensive distribution network. Another feature that calls for increased flexibility in H&M's supply chain network is the need to coordinate and manage the many different brands, whose profiles and market positions often require different logistics solutions; meanwhile synergies should be found when combining operations related to different brands.

From a dynamic capabilities perspective, it can be argued that in order to create a logistics response and range flexibility in H&M's supply chain network, dynamic capabilities with respect to seizing and reconfiguring, respectively, are required. Moreover, sensing capabilities to discover and analyse various opportunities for logistics flexibility is a prerequisite for seizing and reconfiguring capabilities (see diagram below).

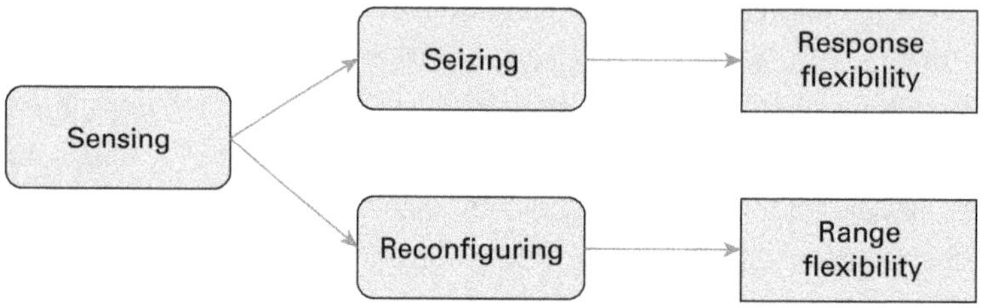

Sensing capabilities at H&M is an important prerequisite for reconfiguring as well as seizing capabilities, and therefore, ultimately, a ground for logistics range as well as response flexibility. Examples of sensing capabilities include:

- Formal as well as informal sharing of information among logistics development projects internally at the company to disseminate insights on, e.g. new technology and markets.
- Qualitative and quantitative methods to detect the latest demand and trends of customers, e.g. boosted by technologies related to AI and machine learning.
- Close formal as well as informal collaboration and boundaries with universities and the academic community as a means to update the knowledge base regarding, e.g. new technology, circularity and consumer behaviour.

Seizing capabilities for the enhancement of response flexibility in H&M's supply chain network are mainly related to the organizational structure and decision-making. Examples include:

- Differentiation of the physical flow of goods, e.g. based on sales volumes and dependence on season, enabling the right product availability at various markets.
- Alignment and in-depth communication between the global logistics and design functions to achieve a harmonized and uniform product range, which improves, e.g. capacity planning and forecasting.

Finally, *reconfiguring capabilities* at H&M are mainly characterized by coordination and resource sharing across functional borders in the company as a means to enhance range flexibility, i.e. a preparedness for the capture of a broad palette of future business opportunities. More specific examples in the H&M supply chain network encompasses:

- The use of product labels that are independent of sales channel and market.
- Combined transportation services between different brands and types of goods.
- Coordinated procurement of logistics services among company brands.
- A conscious, planned and systematic sharing of human resources and competencies between H&M's functions and development projects in order to boost overall knowledge sharing and pace of innovation.

SOURCE Sandberg et al (2022); www.hm.com; author's research notes

4.4 Interorganizational dynamic capabilities

From primarily focusing on a focal company's internal resource base, the dynamic capabilities perspective has increasingly taken into account the company's environmental context. In line with the fundamentals of SCM and the relational view presented in previous chapters of the book, it is recognized that a company can achieve new, competitive combinations of resources through the integration of external resources, which would not be possible to achieve solely through its internal resource base. In fact, maintaining all relevant resources internally in a fast-paced volatile competitive landscape may simply not be possible and/or be extremely costly, and it is therefore necessary to rely upon external resource integration. A capacity to create, extend and modify such an interorganizational resource base, i.e. a combination of internal and external resources, is therefore increasingly identified as a critical source for a sustainable competitive advantage.

Figure 4.3 Interorganizational dynamic capabilities and their origins

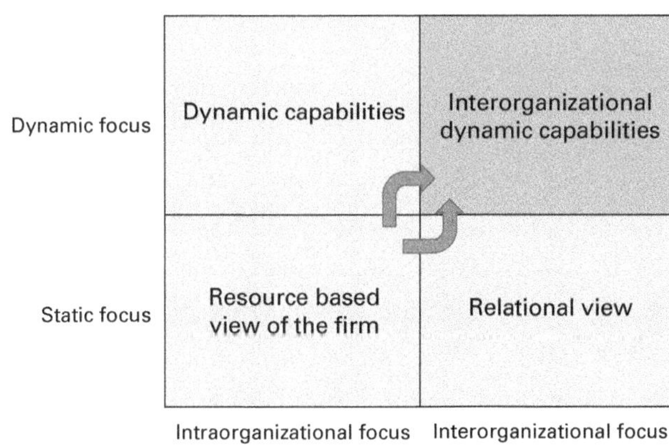

Interorganizational dynamic capabilities, IDCs, is here considered as an umbrella term for such a capacity. As indicated in Figure 4.3, originally grounded in RBV, the foundations for IDCs can be traced back to the traditional intraorganizational dynamic capabilities perspective as well as the relational view (described in Chapter 3). As an umbrella term, a considerable number of terms and concepts for what constitutes IDCs have been brought forward in various research disciplines. For instance, in a marketing research context terms such as 'dynamic networking capabilities' (e.g. Mitrega et al, 2012), 'supplier relationship capabilities' (Forkmann et al, 2016), or 'network management capabilities' (Möller and Svahn, 2003) have been used to capture the essence of IDCs. In strategic management research, 'ecosystem capabilities' (Kay et al, 2018), and 'alliance management capabilities' (Schilke and Goerzen, 2010) have been addressed in a similar manner. Finally, in a logistics and SCM context, which will be further developed later in this chapter, 'dynamic supply chain capabilities' (Beske, 2012; Defee and Fugate, 2010) have been elaborated.

The creation, extension and modification of a resource base across company borders imply some form of interaction between the involved companies, often described in terms of collaboration, partnership or alliance. However, such an interaction can be challenging and difficult to navigate, and what it really means for the underlying resource base and its development is not always clear.

In their research on business networks, Håkansson and Ford (2002) proposed the existence of three paradoxes that need to be navigated for a company when building external networks and partnerships. Together, these three paradoxes highlight the many challenges related to IDCs and their management:

1. *Opportunities and limitations*: A network relationship comes with some kind of joint investments in time and efforts, creating bonds and a mutual dependence. On the one hand, the stronger the bonds the more opportunities are given to the participating partner companies. For instance, a long-term supply chain collaboration where both parties are deeply involved may provide excellent knowledge exchange and planning opportunities. However, on the other hand, such a partnership also comes with limitations and a 'lock-in effect', as innovation as well as change of partners and hence more radical changes, may be hindered.
2. *Influencing and being influenced*: From a focal company perspective it can be argued that the company can influence the network and its other members. However, the network (and its other members) may also be able to influence the focal company. Hence, the focal company's own strategies and goals may be influenced by the goal and strategies of the network. That is, in a supply chain that is characterized by collaboration and joint efforts to enhance end customer satisfaction, an individual company is partly dependent on the other supply chain members when strategizing.
3. *Controlling and being out of control*: Similar to the second paradox, a tension

also arises from a control perspective. If a focal company attempts to take full control and utilize the network in a too self-centred manner, there is a risk that the network overlooks different perspectives, innovation abilities and other opportunities that may be more beneficial long term. Hence a focal company should to some extent accept that it cannot have full control of the network and its objectives and leave some degree of control to the network level.

As such, these paradoxes illustrate that a mutual interaction needs to be taken into consideration when organizations develop a joint resource base. As suggested by Qiu et al (2022), in an interorganizational setting, the frequently applied framework of sensing, seizing and reconfiguring capabilities at a focal company should be accompanied by appropriate 'being sensed', 'being seized' and 'being reconfigured' capabilities at the partner company for an appropriate two-way interaction. In a similar vein, as will be further elaborated in Chapter 5, an *absorptive* capacity (an organization's ability to capture and exploit external knowledge) focused on a focal company's learning and utilization of external knowledge should be complemented with a *desorptive* capacity at the knowledge-transmitting company.

4.4.1 Orchestration capabilities

The interorganizational dynamic capability that has perhaps gained the most recognition, and is thus the most theoretically substantiated, is the orchestration capability. This is, for instance, defined as 'the dynamic capability of a central actor to efficiently and effectively integrate and coordinate resources and relationships within an ecosystem to adapt to the continuously changing dynamic environment' (Shi and Shen, 2021, p. 15). The concept of an orchestration capability has been developed through the unification of several different literature streams, as illustrated in Figure 4.4.

In the very centre of an orchestration capability is the ability to coordinate *resources* and *relationships* effectively, as shown in Figure 4.4. Resource coordination stems from previous strategic management theories, especially RBV, and includes a number of subprocesses, for instance the processes of structuring, bundling and leveraging resources (Sirmon et al, 2007). The coordination of relationships, sometimes labelled network orchestration, is instead geared towards the coordination of the network members themselves (rather than the network members' resources). Examples of relationship coordination capabilities are goal alignment, knowledge sharing and relationship governance.

Orchestration capabilities are often considered to be controlled and employed by powerful, strong leader companies, in a logistics context for instance referred to as a 'channel captain', or 'ecosystem captain', the latter defined as a 'lead enterprise that provides coordinating mechanisms, rules, key products, intellectual property, and financial capital to create structure and momentum for the market it seeks to create' (Kay et al, 2018, p. 633). The following example indicates some questions relevant to consider for an ecosystem captain in conjunction with its orchestration capabilities.

Figure 4.4 Orchestration capabilities and their theoretical origins

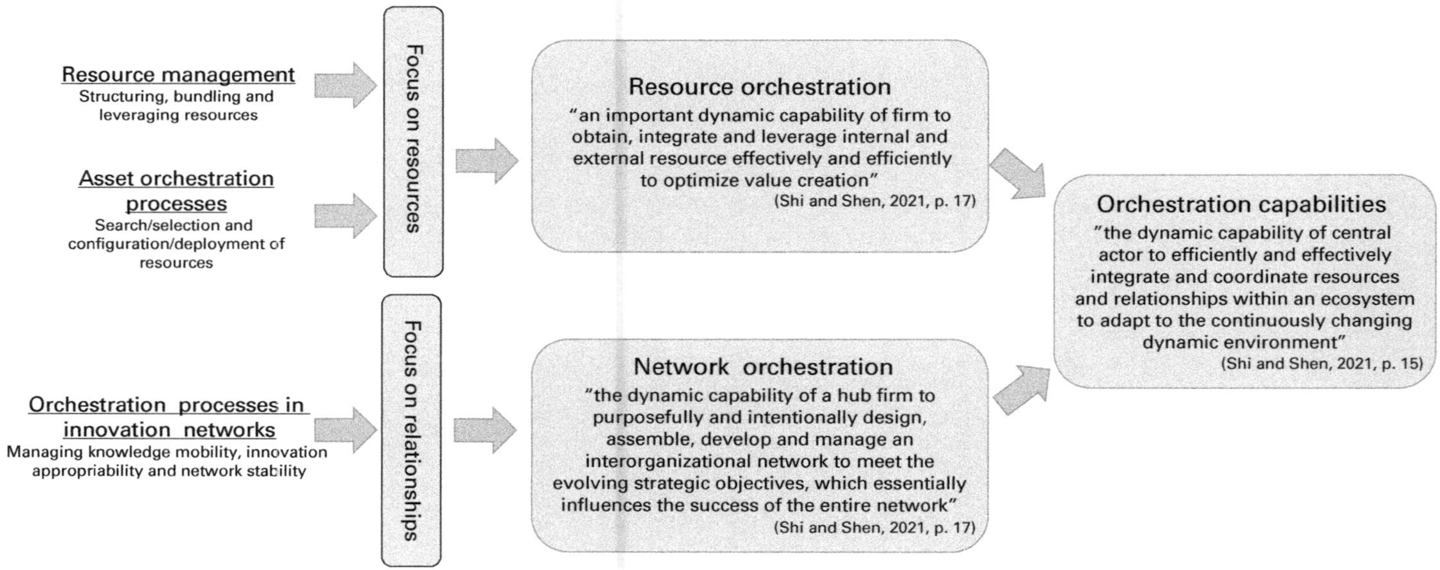

SOURCE Author's own figure, adapted from Sandberg (2023) and Shi and Shen (2021)

EXAMPLE: QUESTIONS RELEVANT FOR AN ECOSYSTEM CAPTAIN'S ORCHESTRATION CAPABILITIES

Resource coordination	Relationship coordination
- What are the main resources relevant for the supply chain's long-term success, and where are they located? - How can resources be maintained within the supply chain? - How can new resource combinations be probed and tested? - What values (economic, social and environmental) should be targeted when resources are combined? - Who should be in charge of the various resources? - How is the existing resource base influenced when new resources are added?	- How can the various supply chain members benefit from pooling and coordinating their resources? - How can a balance be achieved between benefits and sacrifices among the supply chain members with respect to the joint resource base? - What are the main joint goals and visions that should guide the overall supply chain performance? - Are there any risks and conflicts in conjunction with the merge of resources from different supply chain members? - How should information exchange and transparency among supply chain members be enhanced? - What new supply chain members could be included to further enhance and strengthen the resource base?

4.4.2 Dynamic supply chain capabilities

In logistics and supply chain management (SCM) research, the importance of IDCs has been recognized primarily through a focal company's supply chain collaboration with suppliers and customers in a supply chain context. An example of this is Defee and Fugate's (2010) dynamic supply chain capabilities of *knowledge accessing* and *co-evolving*.

Knowledge related to logistics and supply chain management plays a fundamental role in building efficient and effective resource bases, no matter whether an intraorganizational or interorganizational resource base is opted for. Given the vast amount of various knowledge required for building a strong resource base, and the uncertainty about which knowledge will be needed in the future, means that it is usually not possible to always have and maintain all knowledge internal in the company. In such a situation, *knowledge accessing* becomes important, i.e. the ability to know where (that is, with whom) different types of knowledge and competencies are available in the supply chain. By having such an overview, one can quickly and efficiently build new resource configurations that can meet new customer needs when needed. For example, a company's geographical expansion can be drastically facilitated if it hires and collaborates with the 'right' third-party logistics provider who has knowledge about, for example, customs regulations and logistics conditions at the new market.

Some examples of indicators that are often found in companies with a good knowledge accessing capability include:

- Differentiation of various types of knowledge and competencies available in the supply chain, in order to more effectively create an overview.
- Proactive collaboration in cross-functional teams to improve understanding of what type of knowledge is available in the company's environment.
- Clear roles between different functions and companies involved in the supply chain that facilitate an overview of the resource base and related knowledge.

In addition to an overview of knowledge and competencies in the supply chain, its members also need to continuously combine their resources so that a new, competitive resource base can be built. Joint development of the resource base, i.e. *co-evolving*, is therefore an important capability. Similar to what has been described above, the fundamental point is to be able to see and utilize the entire supply chain's resources and from that create new synergies and opportunities. Another critical aspect in co-evolving is the ability to align the full range of various hierarchical levels in both organizations. Otherwise, there is a risk that one party lacks authority, insight and/or understanding of details that the other party has.

Co-evolving often occurs in conjunction with logistics-related business concepts, in which resources within logistics, marketing and IT are combined across company borders. Based on various technology developments that support integration of a company's own operations with other companies in the supply chain, a holistic overview and end customer orientation can be gained. Common examples include ECR (Efficient Consumer Response), VMI (Vendor Managed Inventory) and CPFR (Collaborative Planning, Forecasting, and Replenishment). These concepts cannot in themselves be seen as a source of sustainable competitive advantage, but may serve as a good platform for more effective collaboration and information exchange, which can be seen as a prerequisite for building a common resource base.

Some examples of indicators that are often found in companies with a good co-evolving capability include:

- Clear mandates at different hierarchical levels in the company to drive effective collaboration and development of a common resource base with external partners.
- Access to a well-functioning information system that is adapted to the activities and processes important for both the company itself and the supply chain as a whole.
- The capacity to quickly reallocate resources, for example, between different projects, in order to rapidly support the development of the 'new' resource base.

BUSINESS CONCEPTS IN LOGISTICS AND SCM

As referenced in Chapter 2, some of the most prominent business concepts in logistics and SCM are ECR (Efficient Consumer Response), VMI (Vendor Managed Inventory) and CPFR (Collaborative Planning, Forecasting, and Replenishment). By means of technology and related logistics processes such as replenishment and storing, these concepts aim to improve supply chain performance within and across companies in the supply chain.

Originally launched in the grocery industry during the 1990s, ECR aims to strengthen collaboration between retailers and their suppliers with the overall objective of more efficient response towards changes in end consumer demands, increase on-shelf availability, improve product range and reduce costs. Efficient campaigns and product introductions are also essential parts of the ECR concept. Optimization of the entire distribution system is here included to achieve these objectives.

Established in the grocery industry as well as other industries such as automotive, VMI is a concept where the supplier (vendor) controls and replenishes the customer's inventory based on agreed service and inventory levels. The traditional order is in this system removed and instead it is the responsibility of the supplier to maintain satisfactory inventory levels at the customer. The concept requires intense sharing of data with respect to, for example, sales volumes, forecasts and inventory levels, mainly through a shared data system. Expected advantages of VMI include possibilities for a more efficient replenishment system, in which the supplier has better ability to plan deliveries in advance.

Also grounded in the grocery industry, but today present in other industries, CPFR can be described as a concept that embraces collaboration among supply chain members regarding the supply chain processes of forecasting and replenishment. The concept has many similarities with ECR, but is more focused on these two processes. It typically requires extensive information sharing and joint planning with respect to sales forecasts and inventory levels and has the overall objective to better align supply and demand throughout the supply chain.

4.4.3 A generic framework of interorganizational dynamic capabilities

Another, more generic way to categorize IDCs originates from the fact that the *locus of control* as well as the *beneficiary* of an IDC may differ (Sandberg et al, 2021). The locus of control here refers to who controls the IDC in question.

In an interorganizational setting, such as a supply chain or network, it cannot always be assumed that this control falls to a focal company in the network, as some

IDCs may also be found at a higher entity level, such as the network itself. In other words, the network as an entity could be the owner and control an IDC. Similarly, it cannot always be assumed that the beneficiary of an IDC is the individual company that controls it, as is the traditional view in an intraorganizational context. In an interorganizational setting, it is relevant to extend the nature and location of beneficiaries to also include other companies or even the entire network.

To further scrutinize the existence of different types of IDC and based on these two dimensions, Sandberg et al (2021) delineated four categories of IDCs (see Figure 4.5). Although it is in practice difficult to draw a distinct line between these four categories, they demonstrate the multidimensional aspects and complex challenges related to IDCs and how to understand them when strategizing.

Exploitative IDCs is the most commonly discussed type of IDCs and has long since been acknowledged, although seldom discussed in any great detail. For instance, Teece et al (1997) argued in their seminal paper that (dynamic) competencies 'may extend outside the firm to embrace alliance partners' (Teece et al, 1997, p. 516). Exploitative IDCs are governed by an individual company, and enable the company to use external resources in a way that complements its existing resources to form a sustainable competitive advantage for the company. A key aspect of this IDC is for the company to mobilize and attract valuable resources residing with other members of the network. In line with this, some examples of exploitative IDCs are resource identification (in the network) and the subsequent utilization of these, as well as the ability to construct and manage a network of (for the focal company's point of view)

Figure 4.5 A generic framework to classify IDCs based on their beneficiary and locus of control

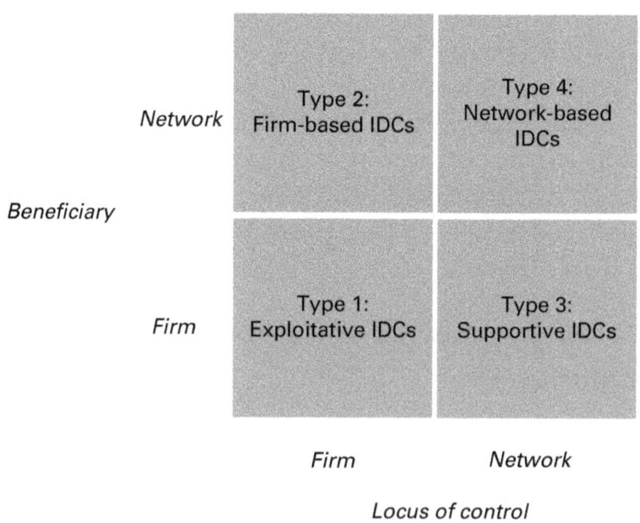

SOURCE Sandberg et al (2021), p. 8

relevant partner companies. In real existing supply chains, these IDCs can, for instance, be found among powerful companies with a purchasing strategy based on price pressure and arms-length agreements.

Firm-based IDCs are controlled by an individual company in a network, but render benefits also to other companies in the network. This type of IDC is often controlled by powerful companies that share and provide leadership for the entire network. In a logistics and SCM context, such companies have been referred to as 'channel captains'. Firm-based IDCs are close to the orchestration capability described above, as this is often presented as fundamental for the creation of new organizations, markets as well as ecosystems, which is deemed beneficial not only for the individual company in control of the IDC, but for the entire network. Another example is a 'timing capability', i.e. the ability to change resource base at a favourable *pace* (not too fast, not too slow) and identify *when* in time changes are appropriate. As a channel captain it could be argued that the Swedish furniture retailer IKEA possesses firm-based IDCs, in particular in conjunction with sourcing and in-depth knowledge of the wood and forest industry around the world. In Chapter 8 the Swedish furniture retailer IKEA as a channel captain is further explained.

Supportive IDCs are controlled at a network level, but render benefits primarily at an individual company level (among network members). Each individual company in the network leverages through their participation various benefits. Often, the supportive IDCs are characterized by underlying larger investments or knowledge accumulations that may be difficult for an individual company to maintain and control on their own. Instead, a higher-order entity, controlled at a network level, such as a venture association, controls these joint capabilities. Supportive IDCs typically include sharing of knowledge and experiences, as well as identification and utilization of complementarities among network members' individual resource bases. An example is the Swedish agricultural cooperative Lantmännen, owned by some 18,000 Swedish farmers. Supportive IDCs at Lantmännen include the continuous supervision and sharing of knowledge among the farmers with respect to, for example, new products and farming processes. It also has a responsibility to develop an improved supply chain resilience and availability of products such as grain, spare parts and fuel.

Network-based IDCs are controlled at a network level, and benefit the entire network. With some kind of interorganizational agreement in place, whether more or less formalized, the main idea of these IDCs is that the network members should be able to jointly achieve benefits that were not possible to achieve at an individual company level. The network level could be considered as an extended enterprise level in which resources are created, extended and modified to be beneficial for the entire network.

Hence, network-based IDCs provide a network with a sustainable competitive advantage vis-à-vis other networks, and are close to Martin Christopher's argument that nowadays it is not companies that compete with other companies, but supply chains that compete with other supply chains (see Chapter 1). Examples of network-based IDCs include interorganizational pooling of resources from which innovation and new resource configurations can be attained. The resource identification and monitoring in such complex, boundary-spanning resource bases is also a vital network-based IDC. Finally, in conjunction with this, visioning and goal alignment for the network are also crucial network-based IDCs. Examples of organizations with network-based IDCs are different business and employer organizations, and purchasing cooperatives.

4.5 Summary

This chapter outlined the basics of the dynamic capabilities perspective, one of the dominant streams in strategic management theory during the 2000s. In the very centre of this perspective are dynamic capabilities that create, extend and/or modify an existing resource base. The importance of having capacity to change, and a dynamic mindset when strategizing, is fundamental for an organization's ability to cope with a continuously changing environment.

Grounded in previous, more static theories such as RBV, it is argued that if not coupled with dynamic capabilities, a company's resource base that 'here and now' fulfils criteria of being valuable, rare and difficult to imitate, may quickly become outdated. In essence, a dynamic capabilities perspective considers this capacity to change as the basic unit of competitive advantage. The capacity may be described as organizational routines or microfoundations present in the organization.

To further structure dynamic capabilities, they can be placed into a capability hierarchy, where they are placed above the operational, static resources. They can also be further (vertically) separated into learning-oriented and resource-oriented dynamic capabilities. From a horizontal perspective, dynamic capabilities can be classified depending on their content. This chapter presented the three dynamic capability classes of sensing, seizing and reconfiguring as an example of such a horizontal, content-based dynamic capabilities framework.

Apart from intraorganizational dynamic capabilities, IDCs may also play a crucial role in the creation of a sustainable competitive advantage, not least in the context of logistics management. Mainly originating from an intraorganizational perspective on dynamic capabilities and the relational view of the firm, IDCs can be considered as an umbrella term that has been explored and scrutinized in various research disciplines, including logistics and supply chain management. The two dynamic supply chain capabilities of knowledge accessing and co-evolving are here explicated as examples of logistics-related IDCs. Finally, this chapter presents a more generic framework of four fundamental types of IDCs depending on whether they are firm- or network-oriented when it comes to beneficiary (i.e. does the individual firm or the entire supply chain/network benefit from the IDC?) and locus of control (i.e. does the individual firm or the supply chain/network control the IDC?).

End-of-chapter questions

Discussion questions

1 Consider a company or organization you are familiar with. Provide examples of strategizing with a static and dynamic mindset in that company.

2 In what way do the fundamentals of a supply chain orientation and supply chain management practices support the role of interorganizational dynamic capabilities? What do they have in common?

3 As a powerful 'channel captain' or 'ecosystem captain', why is it important to coordinate both resources and relationships in the supply chain(s)?

4 Consider Figure 4.5. Provide examples of different types of interorganizational dynamic capabilities based on their beneficiary and locus of control.

Study questions

1 Explain the concept of evolutionary fitness.

2 Explain the role of dynamic capabilities in a capability hierarchy.

3 Explain the essence of the three general dynamic capability classes of sensing, seizing and reconfiguring.

4 Describe briefly the meaning of orchestration capabilities.

5 Explain the dynamic supply chain capabilities of knowledge accessing and co-evolving.

References

Barreto, I (2010) Dynamic capabilities: A review of past research and an agenda for the future, *Journal of Management*, 36(1), 256–280

Beske, P (2012) Dynamic capabilities and sustainable supply chain management, *International Journal of Physical Distribution & Logistics Management*, 42(4), 372–387

Danneels, E (2008) Organizational antecedents of second-order competences, *Strategic Management Journal*, 29(5), 519–543

Defee, C and Fugate, B (2010) Changing perspective of capabilities in the dynamic supply chain era, *International Journal of Logistics Management*, 21(2), 180–206

Eisenhardt, K and Martin, J (2000) Dynamic capabilities: What are they? *Strategic Management Journal*, 21(10–11), 1105–1121

Forkmann, S, Henneberg, S, Naude, P and Mitrega, M (2016) Supplier relationship management capability: A qualification and extension, *Industrial Marketing Management*, 57, 185–200

Håkansson, H and Ford, D (2002) How should companies interact in business networks?, *Journal of Business Research* 55(2), 133–139

Kay, N, Leih, S and Teece, D (2018) The role of emergence in dynamic capabilities: A restatement of the framework and some possibilities for future research, *Long Range Planning*, 27(4), 623–638

Mitrega, M, Forkmann, S, Ramos, C and Henneberg, S (2012) Networking capability in business relationships: Concept and scale development, *Industrial Marketing Management*, 41(5), 739–751

Möller, K and Svahn, S (2003) Managing strategic nets: A capability perspective, *Marketing Theory*, 3(2), 209–234

Porter, M (1985) *Competitive Advantage: Creating and sustaining superior performance*, Free Press, New York

Porter, M (1996) What is strategy? *Harvard Business Review*, 74(6), 61–78

Qiu, X, Holmen, E, Havenvid, M, De Boer, L and Hermundsdottir, F (2022) Open for business: Towards an interactive view on dynamic capabilities, *Industrial Marketing Management*, 107, 148–160

Sandberg, E (2021) Dynamic capabilities for the creation of logistics flexibility: A conceptual framework, *International Journal of Logistics Management*, 32(2), 696–714

Sandberg, E (2023) Orchestration capabilities in circular supply chains of post-consumer used clothes: A case study of a Swedish fashion retailer, *Journal of Cleaner Production*, 387, 135935

Sandberg, E and Åman, P (2010) Logistics learning mechanisms and capabilities: Towards an understanding of sustainable competitive advantage, *Logistics Research*, 2(2), 97–108

Sandberg, E and Abrahamsson M (2011) Logistics capabilities for a sustainable competitive advantage, *International Journal of Logistics: Research and Applications*, 14(1), 61–75

Sandberg, E, Kindström, D and Haag, L (2021) Delineating interorganizational dynamic capabilities: A literature review and a conceptual framework, *Journal of Inter-Organizational Relationships*, 27(3–4), 98–113

Sandberg, E, Abrahamsson, M, Björkman, M and Sondell, M (2022) *Dynamiska förmågor i handelns logistiksystem: För ökad grad av innovation och flexibilitet*, Forskningsrapport, 8, Handelsrådet, handelsradet.se/app/uploads/2019/11/Rapport-2022_82.pdf (archived at https://perma.cc/8LVK-MEF7)
Schilke, O and Goerzen, A (2010) Alliance management capability: An investigation of the construct and its measurement, *Journal of Management*, 36(5), 1192–1219
Shi, Q and Shen, L (2021) Orchestration capability: A bibliometric analysis, *Kybernetes*, 51(10), 3073–3094
Sirmon, D G, Hitt, M A and Ireland, R D (2007) Managing firm resources in dynamic environments to create value: Looking inside the black box, *Academy of Management Review*, 32(1), 273–292
Teece, D (2007) Explicating dynamic capabilities: The nature and microfoundations of (sustainable) enterprise performance, *Strategic Management Journal*, 28(13), 1319–1350
Teece, D J, Pisano, G and Shuen, A (1997) Dynamic capabilities and strategic management, *Strategic Management Journal*, 18(7), 509–533
Winter, S (2003) Understanding dynamic capabilities, *Strategic Management Journal*, 24(10), 991–995

PART TWO
Managing Strategic Logistics

Managing logistics development 05

In cases when logistics plays a decisive role for the company's business strategy and the ability to achieve a sustainable competitive advantage, managing logistics development becomes pivotal. Not the least recognized in the dynamic capabilities perspective, in which the capacity to create, extend and modify the resource base is targeted, logistics development becomes essential. Whereas the strategic management perspectives presented in previous chapters together provide an overview of how to understand the strategic role of logistics management, logistics development is required to put this understanding into practice. The theme managing logistics development therefore initiates the second part of this book, in which a number of contemporary themes relevant for strategic logistics management are presented. An aligned logistics development could here be considered as a prerequisite for these themes and hence a suitable starting point.

This chapter begins with a presentation of some of the fundamental premises of logistics development (section 5.1), including systems thinking, economies of scale, scope and integration, and the design and use of key performance indicators, KPIs. Section 5.2 thereafter introduces organizational learning, which is a crucial prerequisite for all kinds of development, including logistics development. Finally, in section 5.3, organizational learning in a logistics context is presented and outlined as a logistics learning capability.

5.1 Fundamentals of logistics development

At the very heart of logistics management are some fundamental logics that provide a sound guidance for logistics development practices. This chapter elaborates three of the most significant ones: systems thinking, ensuring economies of scale, scope and integration, and the design and use of KPIs.

5.1.1 Systems thinking

Strategic logistics management is typically grounded in the ability to design, manage and leverage on various 'systems' that consist of various organizational 'building blocks' such as resources, competencies, relationships, strategies, values, beliefs and personnel. Systems thinking acknowledges that for an optimal functionality of such a system (e.g. an organization, a process, a warehouse, supply chain or something else) it is important to have the ability to zoom in and improve specific details and parts of the system, as well as to zoom out in order to 'get the full picture' of the entire system. A swift and smooth change between different system levels is key for successful logistics development practices.

Systems thinking is thus based on the idea of the existence of a system-of-systems (e.g. Maier, 1998), in which resources and objectives in a number of more narrow systems are combined and understood to be subsystems of a more holistic, larger system. This larger system is typically more complex, with other objectives and functionalities than the sum of the constituent subsystems. Due to interconnectivity between the different subsystems, the sum of the subsystems may not be the same as the larger system, i.e. synergistic effects can make two subsystems together contribute more than the two subsystems individually. For instance, if considering a company's two warehouses as two separate systems, analysing them one by one, a manual picking and packing processes may be viewed as the most cost-efficient solution. However, when considering the system-of-systems, i.e. both the warehouses as one larger system, a centralization and an investment in an automated picking and packing process may be identified as a better, more cost-efficient solution due to the creation of economies of scale and scope (see section 5.1.2 below).

Systems thinking is an important starting point for analysing and understanding logistics systems. It allows for a structured reasoning on the objectives of different parts of the system, i.e. subsystems, and what is possible to influence by different subsystems. It is also a valuable approach for the understanding, and elimination, of various interest conflicts and other obstacles that exist in a system. Furthermore, in case of several stakeholders in the system, a systems thinking may provide insights for different incitements among these, and how areas of responsibilities are to be designed in the system. In terms of logistics development, a systems thinking hence allows for:

- Understanding and defining goals for the system as a whole as well as the subsystems that are better aligned with the overall business strategy.
- Identification of the need for new roles, responsibilities and stakeholders in the system.
- Defining new and more efficient interfaces and joint planning among different subsystems as well as among different stakeholders.

A common managerial approach for how to deal with complex systems is to analytically break down a system to more manageable pieces, without taking into account how the different pieces influence each other. This was described by organizational researcher and author Peter Senge in the following way:

> From a very early age, we are taught to break apart problems, to fragment the world. This apparently makes complex tasks and subjects more manageable, but we pay a hidden, enormous price. We can no longer see the consequences of our actions; we lose our intrinsic sense of connection to a larger whole. (Senge, 2006, p. 3)

In contrast, systems thinking instead embraces the need for learning and controlling the entire system as a whole; although zooming in on details is important, the recognition of the interconnectivity and dependency among the subsystems means that the entire system always needs to be considered. This allows for an ability to understand the entire system and see the opportunities given by the entire system, and at the same time be able to go into details and improve the various subsystems.

EXAMPLE 5.1

Important questions for an organization with systems thinking

At the very heart of systems thinking is to acknowledge that a system can be divided into subsystems, and that these may interact and influence each other. This approach is valuable to recognize patterns and relationships among various building blocks in the system such as activities, people and processes, and anticipate how a change in one subsystem influences the other subsystems as well as the system as a whole. Characteristic questions in conjunction with a systems thinking for a logistics organization are for instance:

1 How can our logistics organization be described as a system, and what subsystems exists?
   - Aim to describe in a holistic way the scope of the logistics organization, its operations and responsibilities.

2 How do the different organizational units interact with each other? What communication and feedback loops exist?
   - Aim to understand interdependencies among the different building blocks, for instance different departments, processes and activities in the organization.

3 What will the consequences be of a change in one part of the organization on the other parts and on the organization as a whole? How can these changes be measured?
   - Aim to identify causal relationships and ripple effects among, e.g. functions and processes and organizational units, and how these can be either reinforced or mitigated.

4 How does our organization and inherent operations impact its surroundings and vice versa? What is possible for the organization to influence and what is not?
   - Aim to understand the exchange the organization has with the external environment with respect to, e.g. customer demands, regulations, suppliers, new technology, etc.

5 How can different organizational functions, both internal and externally to the organization, be better aligned with each other in order to break down functional silos?
   - Aim to foster a process orientation and an understanding for what is required to improve process performance.

A systems thinking can be considered as inherent in the DNA of logisticians and is a fundamental, although seldom explicitly stated, starting point for logistics development. As a further operationalization and contextualization of systems thinking the concept of supply chain orientation (SCO) has been forwarded. This concept was coined by Mentzer et al (2001) and defined as: 'the recognition by an organization of the systemic, strategic implications of the tactical activities involved in managing the various flows in a supply chain' (Mentzer et al, 2001, p. 11).

An SCO represents the more philosophical, underlying message of SCM, and can be seen as a prerequisite for SCM activities such as collaboration and information sharing to be 'implemented' in real existing supply chains. It can be described as a mindset that emphasizes the need for a holistic thinking of the supply chain, beyond an individual company's borders, with the overall objective of designing efficient and effective supply chains. Without an SCO in place among the supply chain members, there is an obvious risk that all the positive benefits expected from SCM will never be realized. In particular, an SCO can be summarized into the following three basic principles:

- A focal company that is situated in the larger context of a supply chain, and is dependent on other supply chain members for its performance and, in the extension, its competitiveness. When strategizing, a holistic view that extends beyond the particular company's borders is therefore necessary.
- A focal company and the other supply chain members must synchronize and coordinate their activities and processes in order to achieve an efficient and

effective supply chain. By doing this, various suboptimizations can be discovered and eliminated.

- The focal company, as well as the other supply chain members, are all dependent on the end customers. Therefore, the overarching objective when synchronizing and coordinating the supply chain should be to enhance end customer satisfaction.

5.1.2 Ensuring economies of scale, scope and integration

Another fundamental starting point for logistics development is to anchor development efforts around the three financial logics of economies of scale, scope and integration. Together, these can be seen as three guiding principles for how to understand what constitutes efficient and effective logistics practices.

Economies of scale are achieved by concentrating volumes of products or services to fewer resources, and thereby increasing resource utilization. By doing this, the unit cost of a product or service can be reduced as more units will share the fixed, overhead costs of involved resources. Economies of scale thus arise when the average cost per unit produced (a product or service) decreases as volumes increase. One way to achieve economies of scale, for example, is to concentrate logistics operations to fewer warehouses, administrative units or transports. In this way, the unit cost can decrease as various fixed costs, such as warehouse buildings, IT systems or fuel costs, can be distributed over more units.

Economies of scope are created when the same resources can be used for several different products, services, sales activities, customer groups, etc. Economies of scope are, for instance, created when several different products are stored and distributed by the same resources (mainly resources such a warehouse and trucks), or when the same resources are utilized when expanding operations into a new market or use of a new sales channel. In general terms, in a manufacturing context, Panzar and Willig (1981, p. 268) argued that economies of scope occur 'where it is less costly to combine two or more product lines in one firm than to produce them separately'. Compared to economies of scale that aim to reduce the cost of a product, economies of scope instead aim to lower costs for the entire company (regardless of how many units are involved). Furthermore, from a strategic perspective the main motivation for economies of scale is often to achieve lowest possible total costs (per unit), whereas the primary driving force for economies of scope is to achieve flexibility (e.g. for the company).

Finally, *economies of integration* revolve around economic advantages that can be achieved through collaboration and coordination of resources. Such integration can improve information sharing and eliminate various types of waste, such as duplicative work. The ultimate goal is to create high value for customers in the form of unique goods and services by combining internal resources as well as with those of suppliers or those of the customers themselves. The focus here is to remove functional silos by improving the boundaries and interfaces internally between departments and functions, as well as externally with customers and suppliers. A simple example of this is the concept of vendor managed inventory, VMI (see also Chapter 4 for a further description), when a supplier, through information sharing, can gain access to customers' sales of a product, i.e. point-of-sales data, and thereby automatically (without the need for a purchase order from the customer) replenish the customer's inventory or store with an appropriate quantity. Other typical examples include the synchronization of quality control in outbound flows of a supplier and inbound flow of a customer (to avoid double work), and the use of packaging that facilitates operations across the entire supply chain.

5.1.3 Design and use of key performance indicators (KPIs)

Another fundamental requirement for logistics development, also anchored in systems thinking, is the design and use of key performance indicators, KPIs. Appropriate and purposeful KPIs enable organizations to identify areas for improvement, make informed decisions, and track progress throughout development and implementation processes of various kinds. KPIs are also needed for the alignment between operational logistics practices on the one hand, and the overall business strategy on the other.

This becomes especially clear in more complex logistics systems such as a supply chain network, where an overview of, for example, logistics costs, CO_2 emissions or service performance becomes very difficult to achieve. As a result, with limited overview and understanding of the performance of different parts of the system, an effective and efficient comprehensive logistics development becomes challenging.

When considering the definitions of logistics, logistics management and SCM, and provided that strategic logistics management includes a triple bottom-line perspective, the number of potential KPIs to be used is indeed vast. Although far from exhaustive, an indication and overview of potential areas to measure are provided by the SCOR model, i.e. the supply chain operations reference model. This model is provided by the cross-industry association of ASCM (Association for Supply Chain Management) and offers a structured set of KPIs which can be used for evaluation and improvement of logistics and supply chain operations. Suggested KPIs are placed into different hierarchical levels and as such the standardized framework enables advanced benchmarking opportunities against other users of the SCOR model. At an overall level, the SCOR model includes the following six main processes:

1 Plan: Activities that aggregate and combine the overall supply and demand of the company in order to manage and allocate involved resources and functions effectively. This typically includes forecasting, resource planning, production scheduling, etc. Some examples of KPIs include *forecast accuracy* (percentage of

accuracy between forecasted and actual demand during a time period) and *inventory days of supply* (number of days the current inventory will last under average daily demand).

2 Source: Activities that involve the procurement of products and services to meet actual and planned customer demand, including activities such as ordering, receipt of goods and payment processing. Examples include *supplier on time delivery* (percentage of orders delivered on time by a supplier), and *payment accuracy* (percentage of payments made in time).

3 Make: Activities that are occupied with the actual conversion of raw material into finished products, or the actual work done in conjunction with a service execution. This includes for instance various production activities and quality testing. Examples include *cost of goods sold* (the actual costs for production of a unit produced) and *production cycle time* (total time from beginning to end of the production process of a unit).

4 Deliver: Activities covered in the order and delivery process, for example including order management, transportation, warehousing and distribution. Examples include *order fulfilment cycle time* (average time taken from order receipt to order delivery) and *perfect order rate* (percentage of orders meeting promised delivery performance).

5 Return: Activities that are concerned with bringing back products in the supply chain (both from customers and to suppliers), including post-delivery customer support and the management of returned products due to, for example, defects or obsolescence. Examples include *return rate* (percentage of products returned relative to products sold) and *cost of returns* (the total costs of all activities related to the returns process).

6 Enable: Activities that are associated with the support of the other processes. This includes for instance various activities related to IT management and performance measurement. Examples include *total logistics development costs* (total costs of development activities), and *IT costs* (the total costs of the IT system).

Although the SCOR model may provide an idea of potential KPIs to be used, the choice and design of actual KPIs depends on a number of factors such as the characteristics of the industry and products, the organization and related business strategy and supply chain, etc. It is therefore, at the end of the day, a vital task for logistics management to develop and decide upon a number of more specific KPIs that together capture the logistics performance of the particular business and indicate development opportunities. Such a performance measurement system, PMS, is close to a balance scorecard (Kaplan and Norton, 1996). A balance scorecard is based on the idea that a more efficient and effective management of a company, in which the company's business strategy is aligned with its operations, can be achieved by the continuous monitoring of a number of critical KPIs. These KPIs, in combination, should cover the essential dimensions of the business to monitor, and hence provide an overview of the company's performance. In order to be relevant, KPIs included in a balance scorecard typically stretch beyond the traditional, financial measures such as sales, but include also non-financial indicators that better capture and provide an understanding of the company's performance in relation to its business strategy.

The availability and collection of KPIs in most organizations today is not a problem. In fact, since long before the era of digitalization that has further overloaded the availability of KPIs, the major challenge of performance measurement has not been to *get access* to KPIs, but to find out *the right* KPIs, and subsequently, the *right combination* of KPIs (i.e. a PMS). What constitutes then a 'good' KPI, and what characterizes a good combination of KPIs, i.e. a PMS? Some years ago, the researchers Chris Caplice and Yossi Sheffi delved into these questions in the beginning of the 1990s, and presented two excellent scientific articles on these matters. Table 5.1 and Table 5.2 summarize the main quality criteria of an individual KPI (metric) and a PMS that still holds today.

Of particular importance when designing a PMS in a logistics context is to take notion of the fact that a logistics system needs to be efficient and effective in its inherent functions as well as processes. When designing a PMS it is therefore necessary to

Table 5.1 Summary of evaluation criteria for an individual KPI

Criterion	Description
Validity	It measures what is really desired, i.e. the KPI accurately captures what is intended to be measured.
Robustness	It provides an outcome that all parties have agreed upon how it should be interpreted, and it is repeatable
Usefulness	It is understandable for users, and provides guidance for actions to be taken
Integration	It captures performance across individual activities and functions, hence promoting process performance
Economy	The benefits of using the KPI exceeds the costs for extraction and use of it
Compatibility	It is aligned with, and possible to extract from existing data sources
Level of detail	It is provided at a relevant level for users, i.e. it is not too aggregated nor too detailed.
Behavioural soundness	It minimizes the risk and incentives for counter-productive actions to be taken by stakeholders in the organization or supply chain

SOURCE Adapted from Caplice and Sheffi (1994)

Table 5.2 Summary of evaluation criteria for a performance measurement system

Criterion	Description
Comprehensive	Included KPIs together capture all relevant aspects for the user(s)
Causally oriented	Included KPIs create an understanding of current practices, but provide also guidance about the future
Vertically integrated	Included KPIs together align overall business strategy with the various operational activities and processes conducted
Horizontally integrated	Included KPIs together cover all relevant functions, processes and organizations along the supply chain
Internally comparable	Included KPIs should be possible to illuminate the existence of trade-offs among different performance dimensions such as cost vs service.
Useful	The PMS should be easy to understand by its users and provide support for actions to be taken

SOURCE Adapted from Caplice and Sheffi (1995)

ensure that there is a balance between KPIs that bring productivity and performance in individual functions on the one hand, and KPIs that emphasize the performance of processes that stretch across the functions on the other.

Given higher complexity and fragmented managerial attention, process-oriented KPIs are often underrepresented in PMS, and individual functional organizational units, such as a warehouse or a purchasing department, therefore tend to be developed independently from each other, hence with risk for various suboptimizations. In many companies there is therefore a need for increased managerial attention for including process-oriented KPIs in the PMS, which in turn often means a need for an understanding of logistics management among top management. Some examples of process-oriented KPIs that may be included in a PMS are the following:

- *Lead time from order to delivery* with the goal of reducing all included lead times (e.g. measured in days or hours).
- *Delivery service*, which assesses performance against the customer internally between different functions and units and externally towards customers and from suppliers (e.g. measured in percentage of delivered products in time).
- *Total costs*, which are the sum of all costs included in the system being measured, whether it is a production system, a logistics system for distribution to customers, or the entire supply chain.
- *Throughput times*, which show the total time for several interconnected systems, such as manufacturing, warehousing and distribution, across internal as well as external units (e.g. measured in days).
- *Total CO_2 emissions*, which show the system's environmental impact, should be measured for individual processes and for the system as a whole.

Especially relevant to note in conjunction with the process-oriented KPIs above is the importance of being able to align these to customer satisfaction, i.e. an improved KPI must correspond to increased customer satisfaction. In reality, this is often challenging. For instance, it is common to mistakenly translate the internal KPI of product on-shelf-availability when a customer orders, into a measure on customer value and, in the extension, customer satisfaction; the on-shelf-availability is just one out of many aspects that may influence customer value and customer satisfaction. In a similar vein, a delivery service, or for instance the lead time, is often measured in relation to what has been promised by the delivering company – not necessarily what the customer has really asked for or demanded.

Finally, it is again worth highlighting that except for more process-oriented KPIs, there is a need to embrace a triple bottom-line perspective when designing PMS. In functional as well as process-oriented KPIs there is a tendency to neglect the environmental and social dimensions. In particular from a strategic logistics management perspective, aiming at developing a logistics system that contributes to a sustainable competitive advantage, the economic-oriented KPIs of, for example, costs, services and lead times become too narrow and are not enough. These must be complemented with KPIs related to, for instance, corporate social responsibility (CSR) and environmental ones such as CO_2 emissions.

5.2 Organizational learning

'Behind the scenes' of the above described fundamentals of logistics development stands organizational learning. It is therefore relevant here to highlight some of the key aspects of this vast topic. As indicated in Chapter 4, from a hierarchical capabilities perspective, organizational learning can be seen as a dynamic capability, but also an antecedent to resource change-oriented dynamic capabilities. In line with this, research often brings forward organizational learning as the principal means of achieving strategic renewal of a company (e.g. Crossan et al, 1999), hence a vital prerequisite to logistics development.

Organizational learning theory is a multidisciplinary research area that has been addressed in a wide range of research disciplines such as marketing, sociology and psychology, and it thus extends far beyond strategic management theory as emphasized here. In essence, it revolves around a number of coupled processes that include how knowledge is discovered, interpreted, expressed, formalized and transformed and thus serves as an essential ingredient for logistics development as well as strategizing in general. A clear-cut definition of organizational learning is difficult to provide, but an important ground for learning in general was provided by Huber (1991), who argued that: 'An entity learns if, through its processing of information, the range of its potential behaviors is changed' (Huber, 1991, p. 89) and that 'an organization learns if any of its units acquires knowledge that it recognizes as potentially useful to the organization' (Huber, 1991, p. 89).

The use of 'entity' and 'unit' in Huber's reasoning above indicates that organizational learning is relevant at several organizational levels. A common division of levels is the individual, group and organizational levels (Crossan et al, 1999). These levels each have a specific role and significance for well-functioning organizational learning, although the main focus in this book is on the latter level, i.e. the organizational level. The *individual level* emphasizes that for organizational learning to take place, the cognition and memory of individuals is required for initiating learning processes. The learning of individuals is seen as an important prerequisite for organizational learning, but not sufficient, as important knowledge can 'get stuck' with individuals and is thus not spread in the organization. At the *group level*, for instance a function or a department, learning occurs as a collective process among the individuals. A dialogue between individuals leads to a mutual understanding and joint actions to be taken by the group of individuals.

Finally, at an *organizational level*, when the shared understanding about something has been achieved in the group of individuals, this understanding can be codified and transformed into explicit rules and standards that define how the organization works. This institutionalizing 'is the process of embedding learning that has occurred by individuals and groups into the organization, and it includes systems, structures, procedures, and strategy' (Crossan et al, 1999, p. 526). The organization is typically treated metaphorically as an individual, with the ability to, for example, have its own memory and cognitive properties (Hedberg, 1981).

This level also stretches beyond the individual organization, emphasizing the fact that learning may also occur *between* organizations. A well-known concept at this level is absorptive capacity, which revolves around an organization's ability to capture and exploit external knowledge. Absorptive capacity has been defined by Zahra and George (2002, p. 186) as 'a set of organizational routines and processes by which firms acquire, assimilate, transform, and exploit knowledge to produce a dynamic organizational capability'.

In line with this definition, four sequential subprocesses that together enable firms to identify, understand and use knowledge can be described as:

1 Acquisition: a firm's ability to identify and acquire external knowledge.

2 Assimilation: a firm's routines and processes for analysing, processing, interpreting and understanding external knowledge.

3 Transformation: a firm's ability to develop and refine routines that facilitate the combining of existing knowledge with acquired and assimilated knowledge.

4 Exploitation: a firm's ability to refine, implement and leverage existing and new competencies based on acquired and transformed knowledge (Zahra and George, 2002).

Figure 5.1 A framework of absorptive and desorptive capacities

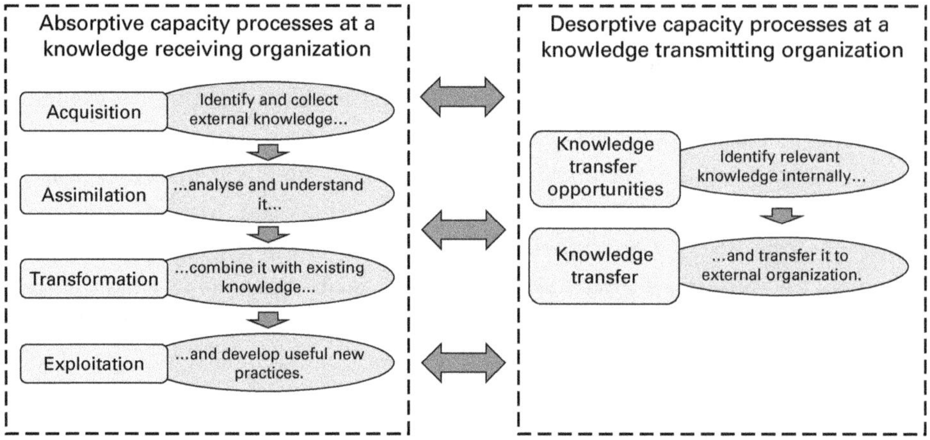

Finally, when discussed from an interorganizational lens, an absorptive capacity at a knowledge-receiving organization could be considered as dependent upon, and coupled with, a desorptive capacity at a knowledge-transmitting organization (see Figure 5.1). Overall, it can be assumed that the better desorptive capacity there is at a knowledge-transmitting organization, the better absorptive capacity there is at the knowledge-receiving organization, and vice versa. The desorptive capacity that matches, strengthens and facilitates the absorptive capacity processes can be divided into two sequential subprocesses (Lichtenthaler and Lichtenthaler, 2009):

1 Identify knowledge-transfer opportunities: the ability to identify knowledge-transfer opportunities.

2 Transfer knowledge and facilitate application: the ability to transfer knowledge to the recipient.

5.3 A logistics learning capability

Organizational learning in a logistics and SCM context has been further elaborated and contextualized through the concept of a 'logistics learning capability' defined as 'the ability of a logistics organization to 1) effectively maintain and manage learning organization characteristics and 2) convert learning outcomes to new logistics management strategies, tactics, and operations in support of future development of other logistics capabilities' (Esper et al, 2007, p. 63).

Grounded in the absorptive capacity concept as outlined above, the scope of a logistics learning capability hence covers both the conditions, or antecedents, to

Figure 5.2 The logistics learning components

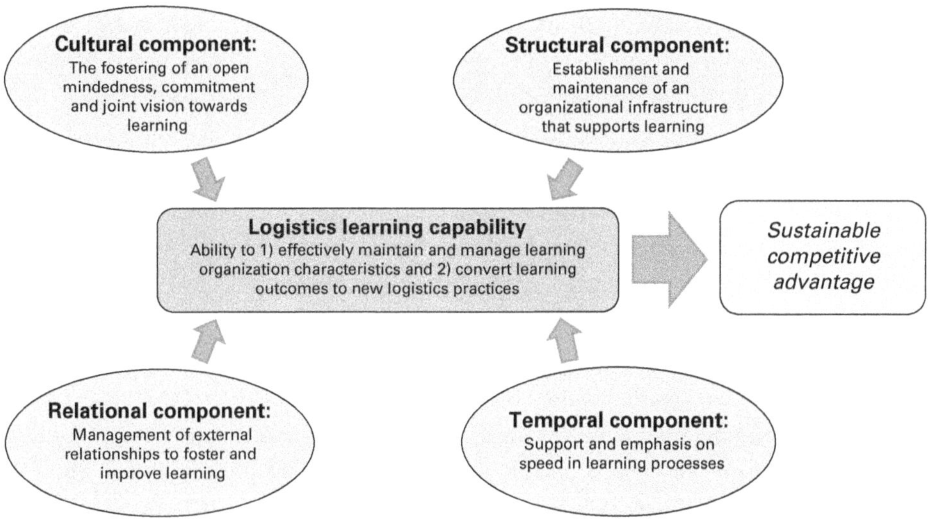

SOURCE Adapted from Esper et al (2007); Sandberg (2015); Sandberg and Abrahamsson (2022)

logistics learning, as well as the actual development of, for example, new activities and processes that take place as a result of the learning conditions. In this chapter, these two topics are targeted in one section each.

5.3.1 Logistics learning components

To achieve an efficient and effective logistics learning, Esper et al (2007) suggested that there is a need for management to nurture the following four 'learning components'; the cultural, relational, structural and temporal components (see Figure 5.2). While the learning processes of an absorptive capacity described above illustrate the inherent processes of *how* an organization learns, these four learning components describe the contextual *conditions* for favourable logistics learning.

The *cultural component* primarily revolves around the company's attitude towards learning. An appropriate learning culture is important for the propensity among employees to question and challenge prevailing rules and norms. For this, an open mindedness towards new ways of working, and a commitment to learning, i.e. the willingness to learn, are here important building blocks. Furthermore, shared vision and goals in the learning unit, be it a function, company or supply chain, are essential in order to direct and concentrate learning efforts. By doing that, synergies in the learning processes can be achieved as well as a momentum of change in a specific direction. The cultural component should be seen as a starting point for the other three learning components.

The *structural component* mainly refers to the establishment and maintenance of an appropriate infrastructure for learning within and across organizations. Such a structure is characterized by information sharing between employees and different parts throughout the supply chain. Some suggestions for structural elements that can be launched deliberately to support organizational learning include targeted, specific training initiatives, job rotations, cross-functional teams with boundary-spanning objectives, follow-up and evaluation work, mentorship programs, IT systems for information support, etc. (Esper et al, 2007). Meanwhile these suggestions are launched and facilitated in a top-down approach; an appropriate learning infrastructure also allows for more decentralized initiatives to be taken, fostering flexibility and adaptability and the emergence of more local learning infrastructures.

The *relational component* focuses on relationships with other actors in the supply chain as an important source for organizational learning. Because of the boundary-spanning nature of logistics, and as pointed out in conjunction with, for instance, the relational view (Chapter 3), the existence of IDCs (Chapter 4) or absorptive and desorptive capabilities, logistics development naturally broadens the resource base from the individual company to also include external resources in the supply chain network. Organizational learning is an essential ingredient when accessing these resources and for the surrounding relationships. From a learning perspective, it becomes particularly important to foster and maintain good relationships with those actors in the supply chain with the greatest potential for future learning. This is an important criterion to keep in mind for relationship management in the supply chain, for instance in conjunction with the selection of logistics service provider. A selection of a logistics service provider cannot only be based on the offered price, quality of services, service levels, capacity and equipment, but also what potential for mutual future organizational learning there is. Such 'soft' factors are of course harder to assess and weigh into the decision but are nonetheless valid points to consider.

Finally, the *temporal component*, emphasizing speed in the organizational learning processes, is another important component. In essence, this includes a more rapid learning transition throughout various learning processes, both from individuals to organizations, and between organizations. For instance, the temporal component illustrates the need to quickly transfer new knowledge through the absorptive capacity processes of acquisition, assimilation, transformation and exploitation. The strategic importance of the temporal component cannot be overstated. In fact, in a dynamic and volatile business environment it is relevant not only to have organizational learning in place. In addition, as the temporal component highlights, the speed of learning, and by extension change, must also be taken into consideration.

REAL-WORLD EXAMPLE The components of H&M's logistics learning capability

The rapidly changing competitive landscape of retail fashion (see also the example of H&M's dynamic capabilities for logistics flexibility, Chapter 4) highlights the need for organizational learning to maintain a high pace of development of supply chain practices. Considering H&M's supply chain development practices and related organizational functions such as logistics, purchasing, IT, business development and sales, these can be further outlined by Esper et al's (2007) four components of a logistics learning capability.

Despite H&M's legacy and large-scale, global and complex operations, an often-emphasized aspect of the *cultural component* of H&M's logistics learning capability is entrepreneurial spirit. Typical values mentioned among H&M employees are for instance simplicity, belief in people, continuous improvement, high ambitions and solution orientation. In line with these values, H&M has a strong focus on end customer satisfaction as a main guiding principle for logistics development. The more traditional logistics values of cost efficiency and environmental performance (e.g. reduction of CO_2 emissions in transportations) are often considered as mandatory requirements, whereas customer satisfaction is what really drives development. An explanation for the focus on end customer satisfaction is the relatively comprehensive managerial attention given to logistics and supply chain development. The managerial attention typically accelerates more cross-functional, holistic targets in which customer satisfaction becomes a natural, key deliverable.

The *structural component* of H&M's logistics learning capability is characterized by cross-functional development projects. In general, this enables a wider scope for logistics development, in which logistics and supply chain operations become part of larger business objectives that go beyond operational cost efficiencies and inventory reductions. Of particular importance here are the boundaries and collaboration between logistics and IT functions. In order to launch and maintain cross-functional development projects, formal coordination among projects is a prerequisite. Controlled top-down by management, a portfolio of projects is managed, including the initiation, maintenance as well as termination of individual projects.

Given the emphasis on the inclusion of logistics development practices into a larger business objective (customer satisfaction), the *relational component* at H&M targets intra- as well as interorganizational relationships for improved learning. In particular, this often results in intense relationship management and knowledge exchange between the logistics department, IT, production offices and sales organization. This interaction is present not only at a top management level, but also at an operational level. In general, interaction and mutual learning at this 'grassroots level', for instance in the form of cross-boundary development projects, are generally stressed as important occasions for learning and sharing experiences within the company.

Finally, the *temporal component* of H&M's logistics learning capability is mainly fostered by the multiple, co-existing approaches for knowledge gathering as well as information sharing in conjunction with logistics learning. For instance, considering communication channels between different development projects these span from very simple, personal communication via telephone and email, to formal instruction videos and training activities. Interestingly, another feature of the temporal component acknowledged by H&M is the importance of having a joint, basic knowledge and understanding of a topic among employees. In many cases, the pace of learning can be drastically improved when such a joint, initial knowledge has been established.

SOURCE Sandberg et al (2022), www.hm.com; author's research notes

5.3.2 *Contemporary logistics development practices*

The second part of Esper et al's (2007) definition of a logistics learning capability revolves around the actual processes for how to exploit the new, acquired knowledge when strategizing and transforming the underlying resource base to leverage logistics as a sustainable competitive advantage.

In a more traditional approach, these processes, i.e. the conversion of new knowledge into new logistics management strategies, tactics and operations as outlined by Esper et al (2007), are often viewed as relatively well-structured, rigid and lengthy top-down processes. Clear phases are expected to be distinguished, typically ranging from analysis, via implementation and change, to evaluation. However, in reality, given the increasingly volatile and rapidly changing competitive landscape, development through these kinds of processes has become challenging.

As an alternative, in a response to this challenge, logistics development practices today increasingly rely on experience-based learning, often in the form of short-term, more local experiments or test pilots. Such practices are close to the concept of experiential learning as outlined in organizational learning theory (e.g. Huber, 1991). Experiential learning can be described as a holistic approach in which experiences, perceptions, cognition and behaviour influence the learning outcome (McCarthy, 2010). It includes a wide range of practices such as formal experiments but also more cultural, tacit experience learning approaches through knowledge sharing and other informal interactions among employees, etc. (Huber, 1991). Experience-based learning outcomes typically emerge in fast, often more tacit iterations, in which efficient and effective alignment between different organizational levels (ranging from individuals to supply chains) is decisive. From a practical point of view, these processes are often described as 'learning by doing' (McCarthy, 2010), or 'test and learn' (Sandberg and Abrahamsson, 2011) that can be more or less deliberate and planned.

Overall, as learning under such circumstances relies less on straightforward, sequential activity processes that are easy to distinguish and manage separately from each other, this poses new challenges for how to manage logistics development. In order to better understand the managerial challenges related to this type of learning, the concept of experimental logistics development (ELD) was elaborated by Sandberg and Abrahamsson (2022), and defined as: 'A customer-oriented test-and-learn approach, financed and supported by top management, aiming at fast and systematic development and implementation of new logistics practices across functions, where existing physical logistics resources are boosted by new technologies' (Sandberg and Abrahamsson, 2022, p. 13).

There are three features that are of particular importance for the management of ELD practices (Sandberg and Abrahamsson, 2022):

Fast, locally launched test pilots: A main feature of ELD practices is the central role of fast, locally launched test pilots. Within the scope of these, 'semi-finished' solutions can be tested to extract learnings in a controlled and limited scale. These tests mainly utilize existing resources and capabilities within the organization or at partners, in order to avoid initial time-consuming start-up challenges related to, for instance, external coordination of resources or access to competencies. The test pilots are typically driven by passionate individuals with clear mandates, capable of rapidly advancing them, and extract experiences and knowledge from them. IT applications and support may here be a crucial component but may not necessarily be included in the initial phases of a pilot. Rather, during later stages, when appropriate, and once a proof of concept of the pilot has been achieved, IT support may be utilized.

Cross-functionality: Another feature of ELD is the emphasis and significance of forums for joint planning and evaluations across functions. Efficient and effective logistics development practices require continuous dialogue and inputs from various organizational departments like marketing, sales, production and IT. Understanding the performance and objectives from different functions and operations, as well as interacting with test pilots and projects outside the scope of logistics, is essential for achieving an overall success in logistics development. Furthermore, as a result of the cross-functionality of logistics development, ownership and responsibility for a test pilot or project may be switched between functions over time.

Systematic governance and evaluation: Finally, management of ELD requires a systematic governance and evaluation of these cross-functional tests and projects, especially when parallel, overlapping projects are occurring. Prioritization and effective coordination of these projects, supervised by top management, is necessary, along with clear communication about their initiation, maintenance and termination. In particular, a systematic approach when eliminating or closing down projects is essential to ensure long term organizational learning and knowledge dissemination. Development sometimes occurs alongside regular operations but always under controlled conditions, ensuring integration with existing operations and projects. Finally, successful projects and tests must be scaled up with proper internal ownership and clear mandates.

5.4 Summary

This chapter presented some of the fundamental premises of logistics development, including systems thinking, economies of scale, scope and integration, and the design and use of key performance indicators, KPIs.

Systems thinking is an important starting point for logistics development and is based on the idea of considering an entity (e.g. a company, process, warehouse or a supply chain) as a system-of-systems, in which resources and objectives in a number of more narrow systems can be combined and understood to be subsystems of a more holistic, larger system. A systems thinking acknowledges the importance of having the ability to zoom in and improve specific details and parts of the system, as well as zoom out in order to 'get the full picture' of the larger, surrounding system-of-systems. A swift and smooth change between different system levels is key for successful logistics development practices. *Economies of scale, scope and integration* are three financial logics that can be seen as guiding principles for how to understand what constitutes efficient and effective logistics practices.

A third fundamental premise for logistics development is the *design and use of KPIs*. Appropriate and purposeful KPIs enable organizations to identify areas for improvement, make informed decisions, and track progress throughout development and implementation processes of various kinds. KPIs are also needed for the alignment between operational logistics practices on the one hand, and the overall business strategy on the other. One way to structure and categorize KPIs is the SCOR model, that includes KPIs in the six main processes of plan, source, make, deliver, return and enable.

'Behind the scenes' of these fundamentals of logistics development stands organizational learning, an essential ingredient for logistics development as well as strategizing in general. Organizational learning revolves around a number of coupled processes that include how knowledge is discovered, interpreted, expressed, formalized and transformed across various organizational levels, ranging from individuals to interorganizational supply chains. Absorptive and desorptive capacities and their various subprocesses are here presented as two main capabilities for organizational learning at an interorganizational level. In a logistics setting, grounded in the absorptive capacity concept, a logistics learning capability has been proposed. This capability covers both the conditions, or antecedents, to learning, as well as the actual development of, for example, new activities and processes that take place as a result of the learning conditions.

Finally, this chapter highlights that contemporary logistics development practices tend to rely less on well-structured, rigid and lengthy top-down development processes. Instead they are grounded in experience-based learning, often in the form of short-term, more local experiments or test pilots. Overall, such ELD practices are characterized by fast, locally launched test pilots, cross-functionality, and systematic governance and evaluation.

End-of-chapter questions

Discussion questions

1 Why is systems thinking often argued to be a fundamental prerequisite to logistics and supply chain management practices?

2 What are the common denominators between organizational learning and the dynamic capabilities perspective?

3 Why do you think ELD practices are becoming increasingly important in contemporary logistics development practices? When is it especially important?

Study questions

1 What does a supply chain orientation mean?

2 Explain briefly the financial logics of economies of scale, scope and integration.

3 What is the SCOR model?

4 Explain the processes of organizational learning that may occur between companies.

5 What is a logistics learning capability?

6 Explain the concept of experimental logistics development.

References

Caplice, C and Sheffi, Y (1994) A review and evaluation of logistics metrics, *International Journal of Logistics Management*, 5(2), 11–28

Caplice, C and Sheffi, Y (1995) A review and evaluation of logistics performance measurement systems, *International Journal of Logistics Management*, 6(1), 61–74

Crossan, M, Lane, H and White, R (1999) An organizational learning framework: From intuition to institution, *Academy of Management Review*, 24(3), 522–537, doi.org/10.5465/amr.1999.2202135 (archived at https://perma.cc/3R87-ZH8R)

Esper, T, Fugate, B and Davis-Sramek, B (2007) Logistics learning capability: Sustaining the competitive advantage gained through logistics leverage, *Journal of Business Logistics*, 28(2), 57–81

Hedberg, B (1981) How organizations learn and unlearn. In P C Nystrom and W H Starbuck (eds), *Handbook of Organizational Design*, 3–27, Oxford University Press, New York

Huber, G P (1991) Organizational learning: The contributing processes and the literatures, *Organization Science*, 2(1), 88–115, doi.org/10.1287/orsc.2.1.88 (archived at https://perma.cc/LQB7-YGSU)

Kaplan, R and Norton, D (1996) *The Balanced Scorecard: Translating strategy to action*, Harvard Business Publishing, Boston

Lichtenthaler, U and Lichtenthaler, E (2009) A capability-based framework for open innovation: Complementing absorptive capacity, *Journal of Management Studies*, 46(8), 1315–1338

McCarthy, M (2010) Experiential learning theory: From theory to practice, *Journal of Business & Economics Research*, 8(5), 131–140

Mentzer, J T, DeWitt, W, Keebler, J S, Min, S, Nix, N W, Smith, C D and Zacharia, Z G (2001) Defining supply chain management, *Journal of Business Logistics*, 22(2), 1–25

Panzar, J C and Willig, R D (1981) Economies of scope, *AEA Papers and Proceedings*, 71(2), 268–272

Sandberg, E (2015) *Logistik och Strategi: För lönsamhet och tillväxt*, Studentlitteratur, Lund

Sandberg, E and Abrahamsson M (2011) Logistics capabilities for a sustainable competitive advantage, *International Journal of Logistics: Research and Applications*, 14(1), 61–75

Sandberg, E and Abrahamsson, M (2022) Exploring organizational learning and experimental logistics development at the global fashion retailer H&M, *Global Business & Organizational Excellence*, 41(2), 6–20, doi.org/10.1002/joe.22143 (archived at https://perma.cc/CHA9-RJUV)

Sandberg, E, Abrahamsson, M, Björkman, M and Sondell, M (2022) *Dynamiska förmågor i handelns logistiksystem: För ökad grad av innovation och flexibilitet*, Forskningsrapport, 8, Handelsrådet, handelsradet.se/app/uploads/2019/11/Rapport-2022_82.pdf (archived at https://perma.cc/8LVK-MEF7)

Senge, P M (2006) *The Fifth Discipline: The art and practice of the learning organization*, rev. edition, Currency Doubleday, London

Zahra, S A and George, G (2002) Absorptive capacity: A review, reconceptualization, and extension, *Academy of Management Review*, 27(2), 185–203

Managing paradoxes

06

As was pointed out in the previous chapter, a key feature that characterizes logistics development is the focus on how to combine various organizational building blocks such as resources, competencies, relationships, strategies, values, beliefs and personnel, both within and between companies. Grounded in systems thinking, at the very heart of strategic logistics management is the need to constantly manage competing interests and goals that arise among these building blocks. In particular, this becomes evident in environments characterized by complex supply chain structures with many independent stakeholders, and when there is need for rapid change and scarcity of resources that forces involved organizations to make prioritizations of their businesses. Under such circumstances, which is indeed often the case in contemporary logistics practices, interest conflicts have a tendency to come up to the surface.

A premise of this chapter is that a crucial task for strategic logistics management is to consider these conflicts of interest in a more structured and comprehensive manner than what has usually been emphasized in a logistics context. Overall, analyses that take an 'on the one hand – on the other hand' perspective are becoming increasingly important, as is the ability to handle multiple extremes at the same time and to utilize various tensions for strategizing and strategic development purposes. In order to do so, the paradox theory, originating from organizational theory, provides a fruitful foundation for further exploration of how to manage – and also utilize – conflict of interests. In essence, paradox theory informs researchers as well as practitioners on how to identify and understand various conflicts, and subsequently, how to manage them.

Section 6.1 introduces paradoxical thinking as a lens for how to understand the nature of conflicts of interest. Thereafter, as a means to enable a more structured identification and explication of paradoxes in a logistics and supply chain context, four classes of paradoxes are presented in section 6.2. Finally, in section 6.3 strategies for how to handle these paradoxes are discussed by providing approaches for navigating the complex and often contradictory interests faced by logistics management. Section 6.4 summarizes the chapter.

6.1 Paradoxical thinking

Paradox theory has its roots in earlier schools of thought within organizational theory. Somewhat simplified, the focus of organizational research has undergone three different stages (Sandberg, 2015). In early research, attempts were made to answer the question of whether the argument A or B was the most effective way to organize a company. The next generation of researchers developed contingency theory in the 1960s, which sought to answer the question: Under what conditions is A or B the most important argument to consider for the effectiveness of the organization? Against this backdrop, paradox theory began to develop during the 1980s. In line with a dynamic mindset, proponents of paradox theory argued that the main question, instead of choosing an argument, is often about being able to cope with, and consider, both A and B simultaneously. In such a perspective, the interdependency as well as the contradiction between A and B are acknowledged, seen as 'two sides of the same coin' (Lewis, 2000, p. 761). When looking at just one side of the coin this argument seems perfectly logical, but is challenged when looking at the other side, representing an equally relevant and logical argument. In line with this, one of the most common definitions of a paradox is: 'contradictory yet interrelated elements that exist simultaneously and persist over time' (Smith and Lewis, 2011, p. 382).

In a logistics and SCM context, the reasoning around conflicts of competing goals and interests has historically often been limited to trade-offs, in particular in conjunction with performance measurements such as costs, lead times and service. A typical trade-off involves a situation where prioritizing one aspect inevitably leads to a reduction in another. Dealing with trade-offs therefore to a large extent revolves around decision-making where advantages and disadvantages for the competing sides are put forward. The task is to, preferably by quantification of, for instance, included costs and service performance, make a choice and 'optimize' the end result so that the interest conflict can be resolved and eliminated.

However, in line with the definition of a paradox above, a key conclusion from recent years of logistics research is that not all interest conflicts can – or should – be treated as trade-offs that are going to be resolved and eliminated. Neither are all interest conflicts about performance, but include other types of contradictions. When managing internal resource developments, supply chain relationships and cross-functional activities, opposing arguments related to, for instance, efficiency and flexibility, global integration and local responsiveness, and standardization and customization become evident. These types of conflicts can typically not be resolved in a straightforward way by just 'sacrificing' the advantages of one of the sides. Instead, involved arguments from both sides of the conflict must be continually addressed, indicating the need to embrace, and confront the arguments simultaneously. As indicated in the definition above, such a reasoning acknowledges that some interest conflicts 'persist over time' – and should do so. In essence, managing a paradox means a move from an 'either/or' choice to a 'both/and' perspective.

In the logistics and SCM context, the need for an extension of managing conflicts beyond a management approach based on trade-offs is becoming increasingly clear, not least when considered from a dynamic capabilities perspective. The creation, extension and modification of a resource base to achieve an evolutionary fitness is intrinsically related with how to address inherent underlying interest conflicts. For instance, to cope with competing interests related to low cost and environmental performance, dynamic capabilities of sensing, seizing and reconfiguring have to be able to bring about changes in the resource base that balance and allow for acceptable performance related to both costs and environmental performance. This might be done by pushing the productivity frontier, as was discussed in Chapter 4.

Paradoxes should here not primarily be seen as something negative that need to be eliminated. Rather, they should instead be recognized and considered in the light of the company's need for change and renewal. The competing arguments that underscore the paradox can be seen as a catalyst for development and change, pushing the company towards, or beyond, the existing productivity frontier. A metaphor can be made here, in which an organization with inherent paradoxes may be seen as a somewhat uncomfortable chair that is used in a situation when you need to stay alert and develop. To sit still in the chair for a long time is difficult, which means that you have to continuously update and change how you are seated. In contrast, if the paradoxes are removed, you encounter a chair that is more comfortable for the moment, but with less opportunities for keeping you alert and pushing you for change.

Paradox theory can be considered as a meta-theory (Schad et al, 2016), in which terminology sometimes is confusing. In fact, discussed in the paradox theory is not only paradoxes that are not possible to be resolved (in line with the definition above), but also various other interest conflicts that are 'non-paradoxical', i.e. they should from a managerial perspective be settled. For instance, as was outlined above, *trade-offs* belong to this latter category. Another type of interest conflict that is expected to be settled is a *dilemma*, which refers to a situation in which a difficult 'either/or' choice must be made between two or more alternatives, often equally undesirable (Smith and Lewis, 2011). In contrast to trade-offs, a dilemma is often less possible to quantify, and includes other types of more difficult, ethical or moral considerations. In a logistics setting for instance, the design for global sourcing may encounter dilemmas when establishing production in developing countries with low wages. Is such an establishment to be considered as positive or negative for the population in the country? Does the establishment bring new jobs and incomes, or is it rather exploitation of cheap labour?

It should be noted that the delineation between these concepts, and whether they are really possible to settle or not, is not entirely clear, and different stakeholders in a system may perceive the conflict differently. Regardless of whether one has a narrow view of paradoxes or a more comprehensive one, paradox theory compared with logistics literature provides a broader and more structured picture of interest conflicts. In the next section, four classes of paradoxes are presented that together give a thematic overview of possible paradoxes.

6.2 Classes of paradoxes: a framework

A major contribution from paradox theory that simplifies and systematizes the identification of paradoxes is the framework that was first presented by researchers Wendy Smith and Marianne Lewis (Smith and Lewis, 2011, based on their earlier work in Lewis, 2000 and Luscher and Lewis, 2008), which categorizes paradoxes into the four classes of performing, belonging, organizing and learning. Figure 6.1 shows these four classes and four strategies for how to manage them, which is further elaborated in section 6.3 below.

6.1.1 Performing

Performing paradoxes arise from the fact that organizational units (e.g. supply chains, companies or functions) may have several goals and objectives simultaneously that sometimes compete with each other. Furthermore, performing paradoxes may also arise due to the fact that different units have different goals and objectives that contradict each other. In both these cases, the performing paradoxes revolve around the three sustainability dimensions of economic, environmental and social performance, and occur both within and between these dimensions. In essence, paradox theory recognizes that the triple bottom-line perspective, as today often emphasized in strategic logistics management, may sometimes (but not always) come with contradictory goals and objectives related to these dimensions. Indeed, these may be experienced within the same organizational unit (such as a logistics function) as well as between units (e.g. companies in a supply chain).

Performing paradoxes also occur as a result of tensions between short-term and long-term objectives. The need for immediate results, such as economic profitability and efficiency in the near future, must be balanced against the necessity to invest in long-term development and innovation initiatives to ensure these objectives also in a long-term scenario. This paradox is often manifested in decisions regarding resource

Figure 6.1 Four classes of paradoxes

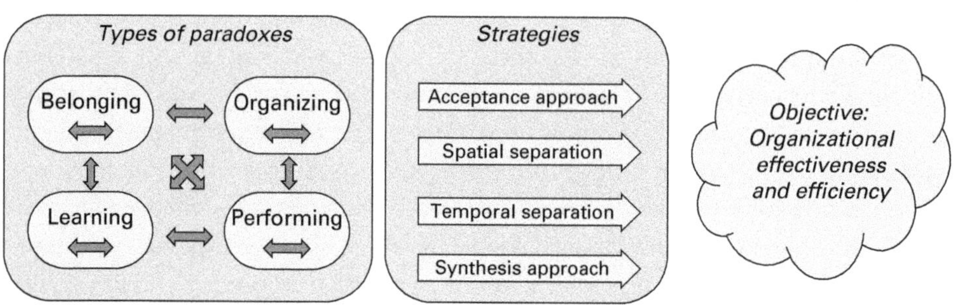

SOURCE Adapted from Smith and Lewis (2011)

allocation, where immediate gains might conflict with future opportunities. A contemporary example of this is that of logistics service providers that are facing the paradox of cost-optimization of the currently often fossil-based transportation fleet while customers and consumers increasingly also demand sustainable delivery modes that are based on electric vehicles. These are currently often more expensive than fossil-based ones, but may soon be necessary. Thus, balancing this paradox requires strategic investments that consider both immediate operational costs and long-term environmental performance.

6.1.2 Belonging

Belonging paradoxes are a result of competing values, beliefs and norms between different organizational units and/or different hierarchical levels in an organization. On the one hand it could be argued that there is a need to harmonize these aspects in order to structure and maintain an overarching strategic focus and vision of the organization. However, 'one size does not fit all', and there is also a need to maintain specific identities and culture that foster purposeful innovation and development at different units and levels of the organization. Conducting this act of balance requires leadership that is able to recognize the values, beliefs and norms present at different units and levels, and at the same time keep unity and standardization of the entire organization in mind.

From a strategic logistics management perspective, typical organizational levels relevant for conflicts related to belonging span from functions, companies, to supply chains. From an individual's perspective, that exists and operates at all these levels simultaneously, there is often a constant loyalty conflict that must be dealt with (Pålsson and Sandberg, 2020). For instance, different ethical considerations and cultural norms can cause various interest conflicts, not the least in larger, geographically spread, organizations.

Another often discussed belonging paradox in strategic logistics management is that of competing values with respect to environmental performance. As often claimed, there is not one single development path ahead, i.e. environmental sustainability can be acknowledged and addressed in multiple ways. These different development paths may of course not always contradict each other (in fact, they may sometimes reinforce each other), but can be subject to belonging tensions. One example is the global vs the local environmental ambitions. A company's headquarters in a Western country may have high environmental ambitions and priority of using renewable energy sources, which may not always be the most relevant environmental objective in a developing country setting. A local subsidiary in such a setting may have more pressing environmental issues, such as water scarcity or air pollution, which is prioritized over the use of renewable energy sources. This is why guidelines and policies for sustainability practices must be outlined in such a way so that a clear joint vision of the company is achieved; meanwhile the vision leaves room for level-specific creativity and initiatives within these boundaries.

6.1.3 Organizing

Organizing paradoxes revolve around competing organizational design logics that occur both within and between organizations. When designing organizational building blocks such as processes, activities and functions, conflicts related to the objectives of centralization versus decentralization, collaboration versus competition, standardization versus customization and control versus flexibility may come to the surface and stand in conflict to each other. As for the other paradox classes, organizing paradoxes may also be found at an interorganizational level, hence with a crucial role for supply chain design and collaboration.

At the core of organizing paradoxes is to understand and balance advantages as well as disadvantages of different organizational structures and processes, and what outcomes they have for business strategy short term as well as long term. In a logistics and supply chain management context one of the most significant organizing paradoxes is that between centralization and decentralization, which may be described in several dimensions, each presented as a 'degree of…'. The extremes at each dimension come with advantages and/or disadvantages. For instance, the *degree of physical centralization* concerns to what extent logistics activities are located to the same geographical place. A central warehouse here provides opportunities for economies of scale and scope, but may also result in longer distribution lead times and worsened market presence. Conversely, these disadvantages could be avoided in a decentralized logistics structure. *Degree of standardization* describes to what extent goals, rules, routines and procedures are streamlined and followed across the organization (no matter where they are physically conducted). A high degree of standardization creates opportunities for predictability and resource planning, but may jeopardize a company's ability to be flexible and adjust to specific (local) customer demands. *Degree of centralized decision-making* describes to what extent decisions related to logistics are taken centrally, often by top management. If top management takes an active role this provides a 'proximity to the top' for logistics (Chow et al, 1995) and a place on top management's agenda, which provides opportunities for investments and managerial attention. On the other hand, local autonomy in the organization typically decreases, which may hamper local bottom-up initiatives and developments. Finally, another example of dimension is that of *the degree of knowledge and expertise concentration*. In organizations with a high concentration, the main knowledge and expertise are consolidated to a central point in the organization such as a development centre or specialized team. These concentrations often facilitate efficient and effective analysis of current developments of, for example, customers and technologies, but may be less efficient to sense emergent, local development patterns until later on when new knowledge is more established.

Another often highlighted organizing paradox is that between collaboration and competition, not the least between companies at the same supply chain tier in a supply chain network. Whereas collaboration between independent companies can be seen as a major tool for joint improvements and innovations that is beneficial for both parties, competition is at the same time a strong driving force for development and innovation. In practice, a combination of collaboration and competition, i.e. coopetition, may be seen in the use of third-party logistics providers, where competitors use the same providers and by that indirectly contribute to each other's performance and ability to create necessary economies of scale and scope. In a similar vein, the relationship among fashion retailers is often characterized by fierce competition in the linear supply chains, while many of the circular supply chains are characterized by collaboration and knowledge exchange. Such collaboration is generally accepted among fashion retailers and considered as a means to accelerate the entire industry's efforts towards improved circularity performance.

6.1.4 Learning

Learning paradoxes deal with the tension between exploiting existing knowledge and exploring new knowledge. In the very centre of these paradoxes stands the existing knowledge that results in efficient and 'comfortable', well-known practices and routines, which is challenged by new knowledge that may lead to new, more unknown practices and experiences. These may come with higher uncertainty, costs and risks, but also innovation and quantum leap improvements of various kinds. In essence, a learning paradox means to continuously build on, but also to a certain extent neglect, past knowledge and experiences to create something new. It is about finding the right balance between maintaining order and routine while being open to transformation and innovation (Smith and Lewis, 2011).

Learning paradoxes in a logistics and SCM context are often geared towards the conflict between incremental and radical developments. Considering the development process for picking and packing in a central warehouse, existing operational procedures that are well-known for employees as well as management often offer opportunities for smooth dialogue and consensus on how these could be improved. However, due to the close alignment of the existing knowledge base, thinking 'outside the box' is sparse in such a development process and with moderate improvements as a result. In contrast, when new, more radical ideas are introduced, often in conjunction with new technology, there is often a greater potential for larger improvements. However, for this to happen, there is a need to reevaluate and challenge old truths and behaviours. New facts must be brought to the surface that support the new ideas, and the results of such an analysis are not always evident to all involved people.

Finally, as indicated in Figure 6.1, it should be noted that paradoxes not only occur within each of these four classes, but also in between. The relationships between the paradox categories must therefore also be acknowledged. In fact, it may be counterproductive to strategize around each paradox class individually as this risks establishing new silos where competing interests between the classes are neglected.

Examples of paradoxes in global purchasing practices with respect to the four types

During the past decade, the author has conducted a number of research projects on the global sourcing practices of several Swedish brick and mortar retail companies, from which a variety of paradoxes arise.

	Examples from retailers' global sourcing
Performing	Global purchasing practices in retail are typcially organized and evaluated based on several criteria that can be more or less contradictory. The most significant KPIs include, but are not limited to, product price, transportation costs, total logistics costs, lead times, availability, and quality. Over the last decade, KPIs related to environmental impact, and CSR (Corporate Social Responsibility) have gained considerably more attention. Even though all these KPIs are not contradictory, there are obvious risks that some of them are competing with each other.
Belonging	In conjunction with global sourcing practices, individual stores and their managers may find themselves in loyalty conflicts, as what is best for the individual store does not always align with what is best for the store chain or the corporation as a whole. This is most characteristic for buying groups where each store constitutes an own, individual company with its own strategies and goals. Typical areas where loyalty is tested include assortment strategies, and participation and timing of product campaigns.
Organizing	In global purchasing a crucial paradox is that between control and flexibility. For instance, there is a need to create long - term supplier contracts to secure predictability and stable access to products and/or production capacity. Meanwhile, too long contracts may hamper the ability to develop and arrange new, better agreements. Perhaps this paradox becomes most clear when considering the role of a local purchasing office through which control (of local suppliers) as well as flexibility (in terms of ability to rapidly adjust supplier relationships) should be achieved.
Learning	For successful long-term learning and development in conjunction with purchasing in retail companies long-term supplier relationships with personal bonds and trust is pivotal, not the least in cases of smaller purchasing quantities where buying power based on volumes is less likely to be utilized. However, at the same time learning and developments of products are often shaped by new supplier relationships, where innovation and new ideas come into play. The act of balance between old and new supplier relationships is therefore crucial for many global purchasing organizations.

6.3 Strategies for managing paradoxes

Although a systematic classification of paradoxes into various types provides support for bringing up competing interests on the managerial agenda, it is also necessary to cope with them, i.e. there must be strategies in place for how to manage them. These strategies are typically individually developed to fit the specific context where the paradoxes arise, and there is hence no straightforward manual on how to develop these strategies or their actual content. However, earlier research (e.g. Hahn et al, 2015; Poole and van de Ven, 1989; Schad et al, 2016) has proposed a number of generic approaches for how to respond to and manage paradoxical tensions over time. Together, these provide an overview of available strategies for how to manage paradoxes.

Acceptance is an approach where the paradox is identified and made visible, but when there is no attempt to influence or resolve the paradox. Instead, learning how to 'live with it' (Poole and van de Ven, 1989) is emphasized, which not the least includes to utilize the inherent capacity of a paradox to foster innovation and development by explicitly addressing both underlying arguments of the paradox. Thus, an acceptance approach embraces the idea that a great deal can be learned from each argument when posed against each other, even if they are incompatible.

A common example of an acceptance approach can be seen when considering the organizing paradox that concerns an organizational design that fosters both efficient and effective flows of materials. Efficiency objectives related to resource utilization (e.g. full truck loads in transportations and utilization rate in machineries) are here important, but equally valid are also objectives related to effectiveness (e.g. responsiveness, customer satisfaction, etc.).

Both these arguments must be taken into consideration when designing a supply chain, and in order to keep awareness of both these objectives, various key performance indicators, KPIs, of these are often applied, even though they may be contradictory. Typically, these figures create an awareness that these conflicting interests exist, without the company necessarily making any changes. Instead, the plurality of KPIs is considered a valid tool for innovation along parallel development paths.

Spatial separation includes a division of the arguments in a paradox, so that different parts or levels of the organization (or supply chain) are consciously governed to support one of the arguments each. By doing this, the two arguments of the paradox are allowed to exist and be developed in parallel, without too much interference and conflict. This gives a possibility for long-term planning of a business where each part of the organization is given the freedom to focus on one side of the argument. An example of spatial separation related to learning paradoxes, is that of establishing separate development projects that are organized in parallel with the ordinary organization. This may, for instance, occur in ELD practices, as was presented in Chapter 5. This separation may foster new innovative thinking in the project where new practices are explored and befriended; meanwhile the ordinary organization may continue as before, based on existing knowledge and experiences.

It should be noted that a separation strategy also comes with challenges. When organizationally separating arguments of a paradox, there is always a risk of power imbalances where one argument of the paradox begins to dominate. For instance, if organizationally separating environmental and economic objectives of supply chain development, there is an obvious risk that the development towards environmental objectives, that are in general more difficult to measure and quantify, may be less prioritized than the economic ones.

Temporal separation is another strategy for splitting the different arguments in a paradox. In this approach, one argument of the paradox is allowed to dominate the company and its development in the short-term perspective at the cost of the other. The other argument is, however, still acknowledged and is planned to be prioritized in the long-term perspective. In a warehouse management environment, for instance, a temporal separation approach may be seen in conjunction with larger implementation projects of new technology or working processes. Short term, the managerial priority is often to learn new ways to work and operate (i.e. exploration of new working routines), whereas the long-term objective is to improve performance in terms of efficiency and effectiveness of the warehouse performance (exploitation of existing working routines). In addition to a short- vs long-term perspective, a temporal separation approach can also be based on a development where the arguments in the paradox are prioritized back and forth over time. In such an approach, the timing and decision-making around when to switch the dominating argument becomes critical (Schad et al, 2016).

Finally, a *synthesis* approach revolves around finding new ways to combine the arguments of the paradox in new, innovative ways or introduce new perspectives that eliminate the opposition between the arguments. As was pointed out above, dynamic capabilities that bring the company towards, or beyond, the productivity frontier could here be considered as a key to unlock paths ahead towards a synthesis. The development of chambres separées as applied by suppliers in the automotive industry is one example of a synthesis approach for how to resolve the organizing paradox of competition vs collaboration among customers to the suppliers. In such an organizational set up, product development at the supplier aimed to several competing customers' products can be organized in such a way that the unique characteristics of each customer's end product can be maintained, whereas economies of scale and scope, as well as learnings across different customers' products, can at the same time be achieved in the development processes. Another common approach for synthesis of performing paradoxes may, for instance, involve the merge and combination of different KPIs in order to optimize various conflicting interests and create an acceptable path forward. An essential ingredient when doing this is the ability to articulate a clear vision that encompasses both arguments in the paradox.

Finally, it should be noted that the above presented approaches may be applied in combination. For example, in reality a combination of spatial and temporal approaches can be launched to manage a paradox, in which one side of the argument is exploited by one part of the organization (such as a specific department) in the short-term perspective, which is thereafter, in the longer-term perspective, replaced by efforts made in another part of the organization that supports the other argument in the paradox. Another common combination of the approaches is to initially apply an acceptance approach to learn about and understand the arguments inherent in the paradox and their outcomes. Later on, one of the three other approaches can be applied.

In conjunction with the application of these approaches, it is also important to note that paradoxes can be nested, and influence each other in various, sometimes unpredictable ways. For instance, an organizing paradox of standardization vs customization in a warehouse operations setting may be dealt with by introducing an automation solution that enables mass-customization. However, this in turn can result in a learning paradox related to the use of the new technology. Therefore, to conclude this chapter, paradoxical thinking that acknowledges competing interests across logistics activities and processes in the entire supply chain should be a continuous lens for managing paradoxes.

REAL-WORLD EXAMPLE Strategies for managing paradoxes in global food packaging supply chains

Packaging plays a fundamental role for efficient and effective food supply chain operations, both within and between companies. The packaging system typically includes the following items, which must each be able to fulfil a number of functional requirements:

- primary packaging (i.e. the consumer and sales packaging of an individual product)
- secondary packaging (for a number of individual products such as trays or paperboard cartons)
- tertiary packaging (for a number of secondary packages, e.g. a pallet)

These include, for instance, issues related to protection, unitization, communication, ability to track and trace, promotional activities, etc. From a paradox perspective, the existence of multiple requirements and the fact that several, independent supply chain members are involved in the handling of the products along the supply chain, means that a number of interest conflicts must be acknowledged and managed.

In a study on food packaging in Swedish supply chains, the author of this book and his colleague professor Henrik Pålsson identified a number of paradoxes as well as suggested strategies for how to cope with these.

In the study, *performance paradoxes* were identified that span the intra- as well as interorganizational (i.e. supply chain) levels. In different ways, within and between the case companies, attributes such as the creation of efficiencies related to transportation, production and handling, the costs of packaging materials, product protection, and end user friendliness were identified.

For instance, a common paradox was that between having (enough) materials for protection of the product on the one hand, and the requirements of cost reduction (when less materials means less costs) on the other. In order to cope with these conflicts of interest, an initial strategy among many of the case companies turned out to be an *acceptance* strategy, in which the conflicts were acknowledged. Supported by various KPIs in the supply chain (e.g. durability of the products when at shelf, costs for transportation and handling, share of damaged goods, etc.) *spatial separation* strategies could also be a possibility, where for instance a company could have different demands and expectations on its KPIs between commodities and premium products. Furthermore, a *synthesis* strategy in the form of a weighted KPI index was also suggested. With such a weighted index, different packaging performance objectives could systematically be combined and managed over time.

The case companies and their packaging system also had many *organizing paradoxes*. In particular, the different logics of (1) being responsive towards changes in customer requirements of the packaging and (2) being cost efficient in terms of providing a limited, standardized range of different packaging to enhance economies of scale and scope, were identified. A *spatial separation* strategy was here suggested, in which a company could work very closely with some customers to develop and innovate new packaging in a project format, whereas the majority of customers were to be targeted with more standardized, cost-efficient packaging solutions. Another organizing paradox was identified between the objectives of joint planning and design of a suitable packaging system at a supply chain level on the one hand, and the fact that individual companies are involved in several different supply chains on the other. To handle this conflict, in particular among smaller, less-powerful companies, an *acceptance strategy* was often identified. In some cases, though, *spatial separation* could also be a viable way forward, where individual companies were to handle packaging matters differently in their various supply chains.

Belonging paradoxes mainly surfaced around how to define environmentally friendly packaging and cost-efficient packaging among various organizational levels, ranging from individuals to the supply chain. For instance, what defines environmentally friendly packaging could be based on the type and the amount of packaging materials used. Alternatively, a broader definition could guide the values and beliefs regarding environmental performance, in which, for example CO_2 emissions from involved transports and effects on product waste are also included.

To manage these different views, an *acceptance* strategy was suggested as a means to make people in the organization aware of the various ways to understand and measure environmental performance, and by that commence efficient and effective development and improvement processes. *Spatial* as well as *temporal separation* strategies were also considered as a means to facilitate the co-existence of different packaging solutions at different organizational levels and give these different emphasis at different points in time.

Learning paradoxes were mainly a result of contradictions between incremental development processes that are mainly relying upon existing packaging knowledge on the one hand, and more radical, fast-paced development practices, where new knowledge is an important ingredient, on the other. In order to manage this paradox, *spatial separation* was considered, in which different organizational units (or companies in the supply chain) were to be given different learning approaches. Whereas some units could lean towards more incremental, stable development and learning processes, other units could be managed towards more rapid, quantum leap improvement steps.

SOURCE Pålsson and Sandberg (2022)

6.4 Summary

Grounded in systems thinking, at the very heart of strategic logistics management is the need to constantly manage competing interests and goals that arise within and between companies in a supply chain. The existence of these conflicts of interest is a well-known fact in a logistics management context, typically addressed as trade-offs. This chapter has introduced paradox theory as a lens for a further, more thorough exploration of conflicts of interest in a logistics and SCM context. In essence, paradox theory informs researchers as well as practitioners on how to identify and understand various conflicts, and subsequently, how to manage them.

Paradoxical thinking embraces the idea that conflicts of interest are not necessarily something negative that needs to be eliminated. Rather, they can be viewed as catalysts for development and change, pushing a company towards, or beyond, the existing productivity frontier. When dealing with the arguments in a paradox, a 'both/and' perspective rather than an 'either/or' perspective should hence be adopted.

This chapter presented a framework with four classes of paradoxes. *Performing paradoxes* arise from the fact that organizational units may have several goals and objectives simultaneously that sometimes compete with each other. *Belonging paradoxes* are due to competing values, beliefs and norms between different organizational units and/or different hierarchical levels in an organization. *Organizing paradoxes* revolve around competing organizational design logics that occur both within and between organizations, for example centralization vs decentralization.

Finally, *learning paradoxes* concern the tension between exploiting existing knowledge and exploring new knowledge.

This chapter also presented four generic strategies for how to respond to and manage paradoxes. And the *acceptance* approach identifies and makes the paradox visible, but does not make any attempt to influence the paradox. *Spatial separation* aims at dividing the arguments in a paradox, so that different parts or levels of the organization (or supply chain) are consciously governed to support one of the arguments each. *Temporal separation* includes a separation of the arguments of a paradox in time, when the two arguments are allowed to dominate the company at different periods of time. Finally, a *synthesis* approach revolves around finding new ways for how to combine the arguments of the paradox in new, innovative ways or introduce new perspectives that eliminate the opposition between the arguments.

End-of-chapter questions

Discussion questions

1 Provide examples of trade-offs that are commonly discussed in a logistics and supply chain management context.

2 For each paradox class of performing, belonging, organizing and learning provide examples of paradoxes from different organizations. Are there any major contextual differences between the examples (e.g. industry, size of company) and how can these differences be further described?

Study questions

1 What is the difference between a trade-off and a paradox?

2 How can paradoxes be considered as something positive?

3 Explain the four strategies of acceptance, spatial separation, temporal separation and synthesis for managing paradoxes.

References

Chow, G, Heaver, T D and Henriksson, L E (1995) Strategy, structure, and performance: A framework for logistics research, *Logistics & Transportation Review*, 31, 285–309

Hahn, T, Pinkse, J, Preuss, L and Figge, F (2015) Tensions in corporate sustainability: Towards an integrative framework, *Journal of Business Ethics*, 127(2), 297–316

Lewis, M W (2000) Exploring paradox: Toward a more exploring comprehensive guide, *Academy of Management Review*, 25(4), 760–776

Luscher, L and Lewis, M (2008) Organizational change and managerial sensemaking: Working through paradox, *Academy of Management Journal*, 51(2), 221–240

Pålsson, H and Sandberg, E (2020) Paradoxes in supply chains: A conceptual framework for packed products, *International Journal of Logistics Management*, 31(3), 423–442

Pålsson, H and Sandberg, E (2022) Packaging paradoxes in food supply chains: Exploring characteristics, underlying reasons and management strategies, *International Journal of Physical Distribution & Logistics Management*, 52(11), 25–52, doi.org/10.1108/IJPDLM-09-2019-0270 (archived at https://perma.cc/3TWF-BTS8)

Poole, M S and van de Ven, A (1989) Using paradox to build management and organizational theory, *Academy of Management Review*, 14(4), 562–578

Sandberg, E (2015) *Logistik och Strategi: För lönsamhet och tillväxt*, Studentlitteratur, Lund

Schad, J, Lewis, M W, Raisch, S and Smith, W K (2016) Paradox research in management science: Looking back to move forward, *Academy of Management*, 10(1), 5–64

Smith, W K and Lewis, M W (2011) Toward a theory of paradox: A dynamic equilibrium model of organizing, *Academy of Management Review*, 36(2), 381–403

Managing supply chain resilience 07

In line with the megatrends outlined in Chapter 1, the current business landscape is increasingly marked by an unpredictable and highly competitive nature, in which complexity has escalated. This complexity typically stems from various interdependencies, outsourcing and specialized roles, and limited transparency and visibility along the supply chain tiers. In addition, supply chains are exposed to a number of environmental uncertainties and disturbances, including geopolitical turbulence, natural disasters and a growing emphasis on regulatory factors. As a result of these developments, companies and their supply chains increasingly become vulnerable to various disruptions and shocks. The outbreak of the Covid-19 pandemic in 2020 is one example of such a disruption that has had a significant impact on logistics and supply chain operations worldwide.

To cope with the vulnerability, logistics scholars as well as practitioners have since the beginning of the 2000s acknowledged supply chain resilience (SCR) as a major managerial priority. From a strategic management perspective, supply chain resilience can be considered as a dynamic capability to ensure continuous operations, respond to customer demands and, at the end of the day, maintain a sustainable competitive advantage. One of the most prominent definitions of supply chain resilience was made by Ponomarov and Holcomb (2009): 'The adaptive capability of the supply chain to prepare for unexpected events, respond to disruptions, and recover from them by maintaining continuity of operations at the desired level of connectedness and control over structure and function' (Ponomarov and Holcomb, 2009, p. 131).

This section first scrutinizes and classifies the reasons why supply chain resilience is required, i.e. supply chain disruptions (section 7.1). Thereafter, the characteristics of supply chain resilience are elaborated (section 7.2) and its different phases examined from a longitudinal perspective (section 7.3). Finally, supply chain resilience strategy themes for how to cope with disruptions are presented (section 7.4).

7.1 Supply chain disruptions

The reason why supply chain resilience is required is due to the existence of various disruptions that impact the performance of the supply chain. Such a supply chain disruption is an unintended, unwanted triggering event that influences the supply chain performance negatively, i.e. there is a negative deviation from the normal state of performance. Other similar, overlapping terms are shocks, glitches, disturbances, failures, accidents, disasters, catastrophes or crises.

7.1.1 Types of disruptions

Supply chain disruptions can be categorized in many ways depending on the purpose. For instance, they may be classified based on the extent they influence supply chain performance, ranging from a relatively small, often local impact to a large impact that may be decisive for the survival of the company and even its supply chain. Another common classification is based on where they occur, for example whether they are external or internal to the supply chain. Well-known disruptions *external* to the supply chain include for instance natural disasters such as earthquakes and bad harvests, man-made disasters such as terrorism, pandemics, uncertainties in end consumer demand, and geopolitical instabilities such as war. Disruptions *internal* to the supply chain include a number of events that are more directly concerned with the supply chain such as supplier quality problems, machine breakdown in production and transportation delays. Internal disruptions can further be classified into disruptions internal to an organization (company level), and those that are external to the organization, but in the organization's supply chain (supply chain level). Based on this classification, Figure 7.1 shows examples of supply chain disruptions.

The various supply chain disruptions listed in Figure 7.1 may influence the supply chain negatively in many different ways, for instance causing shortages of the following (Olivares-Aguila and Vital-Soto, 2021):

- lack of money
- lack of employees
- lack of production
- lack of material
- lack of supply
- lack of demand
- lack of transportation
- lack of information
- lack of communication

Figure 7.1 Examples of supply chain disruptions

Types of supply chain disruptions

Company level

- Production facility failure
- Product quality problems
- Safety incidents
- Theft or vandalism
- IT system breakdown
- Unexpected shortage of labour

Supply chain level

- Customs delays
- Communication failure
- Supply chain fraud
- Partner bankruptcy or insolvency
- Unanticipated or volatile demand
- Strikes in e.g. ports or production
- Capacity shortages in production and warehouse
- Fire and other catastrophic events

Environment

- Natural disasters
- Unanticipated end consumer demand and requirements
- Geopolitical instability
- Regulatory and legal changes
- Pandemics
- Disruptive shifts in technology
- Infrastructure breakdowns of electricity, energy, fuel, water, IT, etc.

SOURCE Adapted from Ho et al (2015); Shekarian and Mellat Parast (2021); Christopher and Peck (2004); and Behdani et al (2012)

Given the supply chain perspective and the fact that a supply chain consists of interdependent organizational entities, processes and activities, the consequences of a disruption somewhere in the supply chain may be cascaded and have an impact also at other parts of the supply chain. For instance, the Tohoku earthquake in Japan in 2011 led to damage of the nuclear plant in Fukushima and major losses of production capacity in the surrounding area. The earthquake also caused a tsunami and a number of fires that led to even further damage of production as well as infrastructure. As a domino-effect, the resulting production shortages had in turn a negative impact in many supply chains all around the world with an estimated economic total damage of more than US$195 billion (Pettit et al, 2013).

The phenomenon of how a disruption and its consequences are propagated in a supply chain is labelled the ripple effect. A ripple effect is created in cases when the consequences of a disruption cannot be fully absorbed directly in the surrounding part of the supply chain where it first occurred. The consequences of the cascading effects may be of various types and very difficult to foresee. As in the case of the Tohoku earthquake they may lead to damage of production capacity, which in turn can cause supply shortages at retailers. This may in turn lead to reduced sales volumes, scarcity and higher prices in the end market. In addition, from a more long-term perspective, a reduced production capacity may cause loss of job opportunities and other structural changes in the supply chain such as change of supplier base, legal challenges due to geographical changes, lack of knowledge and experience, etc.

Another way to classify supply chain disruptions is based on the fact that disruptions may be more or less known in terms of their likelihood of occurrence and their impact on supply chain performance. In practice, they range from those that are well known and easy to predict, to those that are difficult to predict, both when it comes to likelihood of occurrence as well as their consequences. As a means to better

Figure 7.2 Types and examples of disruptions based on whether their likelihood of occurrence and impact on performance is known or unknown

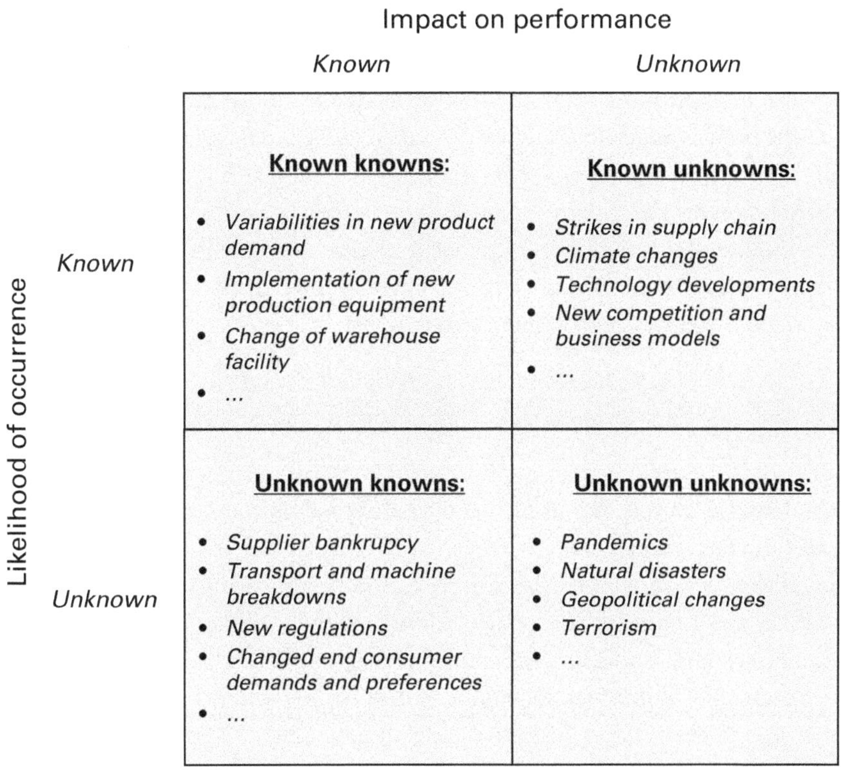

understand various types of disruptions, it may be insightful to elaborate on what is known, and what is not known, i.e. unknown, with respect to likelihood of occurrence and impact on performance (see Figure 7.2).

The *known knowns* quadrant typically represents disruptions that are well known and often recurrent, which means that there may be experience related to these events from the past. The frequency of these disruptions might also be known. Thus, they are in general more measurable and are often referred to in relation to risk. Risk is a vast construct with various underlying meanings and concepts and can be discussed and associated with both negative and positive opportunities. Taking this broad, neutral understanding, March and Shapira (1987) defined risk as the 'variation in the distribution of possible outcomes, their likelihoods and their subjective values' (p. 1404). In decision-making theory, more 'risky' alternatives typically mean higher variation of the possible outcomes, i.e. higher possible losses as well as gains. However, from a managerial point of view, the dangers and negative outcomes often dominate the understanding of risk, i.e. *the losses* associated with possible outcomes are often focused on, rather than *the range* of possible outcomes (Peck, 2006).

When risk, and the management of the risk, i.e. risk management, is associated with a negative outcome, it may be difficult to conceptually distinguish it from resilience. In practice these concepts are often overlapping and even used interchangeably. However, one approach for doing such a distinction, and as a clarification for how the terms are referred to in this textbook, would be to consider risk to be concerned with disruptions in the known knowns quadrant. In such a case, coping with disruptions in this quadrant could be described as risk management, which typically includes various measures for understanding and mitigating a negative impact on performance.

In the known knowns quadrant, when a disruption's likelihood of occurrence as well as its impact on performance is fairly well known, it is possible for the risk to be quantified, for instance in economic terms, as:

Risk = likelihood of a disruption to occur ×
the financial impact on supply chain performance if it occurs

Examples of disruptions in this quadrant can be those related to variabilities in new product demand, launch and implementation of new production equipment, change of warehouse facility, etc.

The *known unknowns* are disruptions that occur repetitiously and there is a fairly known likelihood of their occurrence. However, their impact on the supply chain performance is more difficult to foresee. This may be due to the unpredictable nature of the disruption, for instance when the disruption is not a direct threat in itself, but when ripple effects are. For instance, the consequences of a strike in a production facility may be difficult to evaluate for a retailer situated a number of supply chain tiers away from the production facility. Another example is climate change that is well known but may still be difficult to relate to an individual organization's supply chain.

The *unknown knowns* are disruptions that are often easy to understand in terms of their consequences but are less possible to predict in terms of their likelihood of occurrence. The likelihood of occurrence may be difficult to interpret due to a number of reasons such as a lack of adequate competence and/or knowledge in the organization about the disruption and the circumstances around its occurrence. For instance, a company may have limited knowledge on geopolitical situations in a region where it is not operating, which means that disruptions that stem from this region may be difficult to predict. Examples of unknown knowns disruptions include supplier bankruptcy, various breakdowns in the supply chain in terms of machinery and transports, changed end consumer demands, and new regulations.

Finally, the *unknown unknowns* are the truly unexpected disruptions sometimes called the black swan events. Other names are macro-risks, unpredictable disruptions, tsunamis, dragon kings, perfect storms, mega-crises, super disruptions, deep disruptions and so on (Olivares-Aguila and Vital-Soto, 2021). These terms have in common a unique nature and are hence difficult to foresee and to evaluate consequences in a more structured manner. Proactive cautions may be taken but are often general. For instance, a dormant crisis management team may be installed, but without specific instructions as the organization and the team cannot foresee the nature of the disruption and its consequences. Examples of well-known black swan events are the outbreak of the Covid-19 pandemic in 2020, the terrorist attack of 9/11 in 2001, the tsunami in 2004, the Russia-Ukraine war in 2022, etc.

7.1.2 Techniques and tools for enhancing knowledge on disruptions

To enhance knowledge with respect to likelihood of occurrence as well as the impact on supply chain performance, i.e. go from 'unknown' to 'known', and subsequently develop strategies for how to cope with disruptions, there exist a number of analytical tools and techniques that are applicable in the different four quadrants shown in Figure 7.2. In a risk management context, i.e. disruptions in the known knowns quadrant, a vast range of suggested techniques and methods exist for how to estimate and ultimately even quantify risks, i.e. likelihood of occurrence as well as supply chain performance impact. For likelihood estimations historical data and frequencies (of, e.g. breakdowns) could be used as an input, together with expert estimates based on, for instance, the Delhi method. In a similar vein, when it comes to the impact on supply chain performance, the Analytic Hierarchy Process (AHP) has been suggested as a means to evaluate the impact of multiple factors in a structured manner. Other related methods include expert opinions and quantitative simulation methods.

In the other quadrants similar approaches, but with less focus on quantification, have been suggested. Here for instance the PESTLE framework (Political, Economic, Sociological, Technological, Legal and Environmental) could be used to structure and enhance understanding of various disruptions' likelihoods of occurrence. Other tools for estimations of likelihood of occurrence, their impact on performance as well as development of resilience strategies, may include process charts, stress tests, brainstorming, anticipatory failure determination, SWOT analysis (Strengths, Weaknesses, Opportunities and Threats), simulations and scenario planning, etc. In general, to enhance knowledge, these techniques and tools may be applied internally at an organization but can also be jointly applied in collaboration with supply chain partners.

In recent years, digitalization has also enabled improved opportunities for understanding disruptions and how to cope with them. For instance, the use of Internet of Things and blockchain technologies offer many opportunities for increased visibility throughout the supply chain network, which enables improved monitoring and analysis of various kinds of potential as well as actual disruptions. In a similar vein, digitalization provides opportunities for predictive analytics with Artificial Intelligence, AI. With AI-based tools companies can enhance more detailed proactive contingency plans related to not only internally oriented disruptions such as supply shortages and demand fluctuations, but also external ones such as geopolitical events. Related to this, the application of digital supply chain twins (see Chapter 8) can offer new approaches for real-time simulations of material flows and provide new insights into the consequences of various disruptions in the supply chain.

7.2 Characteristics of supply chain resilience

The concept of resilience originates from the ecology professor, C. S. Holling (1973), who argued that a system's properties of resilience and stability is crucial. Holling (1973) pointed out that resilience of an ecological system refers to its ability to absorb various disturbances and maintain the relationships among the system's entities, whereas the concept of stability refers to the capacity of the system to return to an equilibrium state after a temporary disturbance. The faster the system is able to return to the equilibrium state, the greater is its stability (Ponomarov and Holcomb, 2009).

In addition to ecology, resilience is also a well-known concept in other streams of literature, such as sociology, psychology and economy. Inspired by these streams of literature, resilience in a logistics and SCM context has since the beginning of the 2000s also received tremendous recognition along with related terms such as risk and robustness. It was based on these other literature streams that Ponomarov and Holcomb (2009) provided their definition of supply chain resilience (see the introduction to this chapter).

In essence, supply chain resilience refers to the ability of a supply chain to cope with disruptions, before, during and after they occur. There are four inherent system characteristics that become crucial for doing this (Fiksel, 2003). Inspired by resilience in an ecological setting, these features together allow an overall description of the nature of supply chain resilience. *Diversity* enables a system, such as a supply chain, to find new, alternative routes ahead more easily in case of a disruption. Diversity could in a supply chain setting include multiple product configurations, business strategies as well as knowledge bases. *Efficiency* in terms of resource utilization enables the system to sustain value delivery in turbulent times and may be a driver for innovation and new thinking that is required in conjunction with disruptions.

Adaptability is a key priority for a system's ability to not only bounce back to an original state, but sometimes also to find a new, possible and/or more advantageous way forward. For this, organizational learning and logistics development as were outlined in Chapter 5 are key ingredients. Finally, *cohesion*, i.e. the existence of unifying forces among system entities (such as functions or companies), enables improved power to respond to disruptions and adopt the system. In practice, cohesion could for instance enable supply chain transparency and improved collaboration.

Analogous to, and as was described already in Holling's (1973) reasoning, a main feature of supply chain resilience is the ability of a system, such as a supply chain, to 'bounce back' after a disruption, i.e. return to the state prior to the disruption. For instance, a key priority in case of a factory fire is often to rebuild the factory in order to restore the manufacturing capacity. However, as was indicated in the adaptability feature above, supply chain resilience also covers occasions when it is not possible for a system to bounce back to the previous position, as this original state may no longer be possible or desired. In the case of a fire in the factory, customers may swiftly change supplier and it may therefore not make sense to rebuild the factory with the same features and at the same place as previously. Thus, resilience could also be understood as an ability to adapt to a completely new state or equilibrium in a supply chain environment that has significantly been changed.

Extending this reasoning further, it could be argued that in today's volatile and turbulent business environment there are multiple disruptions that occur on a more or less continuous basis. In fact, it may not be meaningful to discuss a single disruption and the recovery from that disruption separately. A system that is possible to be controlled and kept in a fairly stable state simply does not exist in most real existing supply chains. The meaning of 'coping' with supply chain disruptions instead becomes the ability of the supply chain to continuously adapt to new states, which at the moment is the best-known alternative (Ivanov, 2024). In such an environment, supply chain resilience will predominantly not be about selecting among a number of pre-existing potential responses that seek to establish an equilibrium state. Rather, it will be about being regenerative and supply chain resilience will be similar to a dynamic capability, focused on the creation, extension and modification of the resource base to cope with the disruption.

7.3 Phases of supply chain resilience

Resilience is often described in phases; before, during and after a disruption. Figure 7.3 shows how supply chain resilience can be understood from a longitudinal perspective based on proactive strategies conducted before the disruption, and reactive strategies that take place after the disruption.

7.3.1 Proactive strategies

Proactive strategies can be described as measures that can be undertaken in the supply chain to either (1) avoid performance loss, i.e. improve robustness of the supply chain, or (2) reduce the performance loss. Proactive strategies include the processes

Figure 7.3 A longitudinal perspective on supply chain resilience

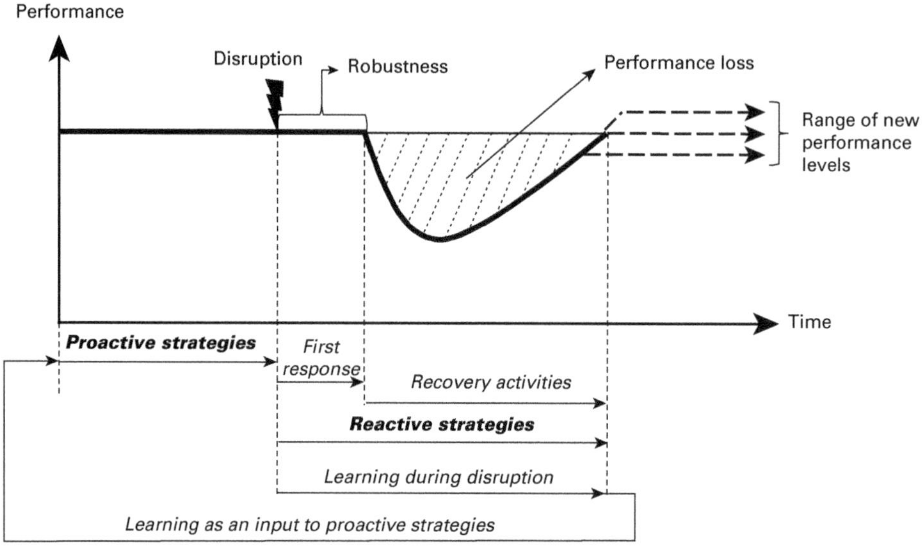

SOURCE Adapted from Ivanov (2024); Tukamuhabwa et al (2015); Bedhani et al (2012); Sheffi and Rice (2005)

of *identification of potential disruptions*, and, if possible, their *assessment* in terms of likelihood of occurrence and potential impact (see also Figure 7.4). To support these processes various tools and techniques can be exploited as were elaborated above.

Furthermore, proactive strategies are also concerned with the identification as well as implementation of *contingency plans and measures* for how to cope with potential disruptions. These measures often involve efforts and investments related to organizational changes aiming at strengthening performance in case a disruption occurs. In contrast to reactive strategies these undertakings are more generic, aiming at preparedness against a wide range of potential disruptions. Proactive strategies also tend to be implemented in such a way so that synergies with other business objectives can be achieved. For instance, a strategy of dual or multiple sourcing may be due not only to resilience, but also for cost efficiency reasons. Thus, proactive strategies tend to be embedded in other business initiatives and development projects. For this to happen proactive reasoning and awareness of potential disruptions must be part of the organizational culture. Proactive resilience strategies are, therefore, just as dynamic capabilities, something that can be deliberately developed and maintained by management.

Another dimension of proactive strategies concerns the continuous *monitoring* of those potential disruptions known to the company. An early detection of a disruption is often key to enhancing successful reactive strategies. Monitoring may include a wide scope of activities with an internal as well as external focus in the supply chain, as well as informal and formal structures. In general, collaboration and visibility are key ingredients for monitoring, along with an organizational disruption awareness, which in turn, again, requires managerial knowledge and attention.

7.3.2 Reactive strategies

Reactive strategies can be divided into two different phases, including a first response (after the occurrence of the disruption), and subsequent recovery strategies. Reactive strategies during the first response phase (see Figure 7.3) are typically concerned with the *disruption detection* and the first, *initial measures* taken to deal with the disruption. Overall, the objective of these efforts is to enhance robustness of the system, which can be described as the ability of a system to maintain its functioning and performance when a disruption occurs, and by that minimizing or even avoiding performance loss. In a supply chain with several interdependent entities, reactive strategies during the first response phase are typically dependent upon other parts of the supply chain in order to achieve robustness. If the ripple effect can be 'absorbed' or coped with before it reaches the actual part of the supply chain, robustness may be more easily accomplished there. First response strategies are therefore dependent upon, and should be coordinated with, resilience strategies in other parts of the supply chain. It is also important to align various first response strategies with each other. For instance, a buffer stock of a Product A can be seen as a strategy to enhance robustness of a particular part of the supply chain to cover supply shortages. However, if Product B is also required for the supply chain's functionality, a buffer stock of Product B may also be required.

Another feature of strategies in the first response phase is that they often include a continuation of the proactive strategies, for example activating measures that aim to reduce the forthcoming, expected consequences for the system. If, for instance, a redundant extra production-capacity has been ensured as a proactive strategy (see the supply chain resilience strategies below), the first response strategy will be about the timely and swift utilization of this capacity. In practice, proactive and reactive strategies are hence often closely intertwined, and it may sometimes be difficult to clearly distinguish between their proactive and reactive elements.

Sometime after the disruption an impact on performance may be more or less unavoidable, and except for first response phase strategies there may also be a need to deploy *recovery activities* that aim to reduce the performance loss in conjunction with the disruption. As indicated in Figure 7.3, this is a combination of reducing the impact, i.e. 'severeness' of the disruption, and the duration in time when the disruption has an impact. Together, the dashed area in Figure 7.3, sometimes called the 'resilience triangle', represents the most common way for how to – at least on a conceptual level – measure the performance loss (Tukamuhabwa et al, 2015). As further highlighted in the figure, it is also worth noting that the actual performance level may not always bounce back to the original level of performance, but will in a regenerative manner develop into the 'best possible' state.

Overall, reactive strategies are often characterized by a crisis awareness among employees as well as management that functions as a major driver for innovation and new ways for responding to the disruption. *Learning* is here a crucial aspect both during, and after, a disruption. Especially in times of major disruptions, such as the outbreak of the Covid-19 crisis in 2020, learning to find new ways to operate the supply chain, in combination with strong leadership, rapid decision-making and collaboration across functions as well as organizational borders is essential. For instance, the Covid-19 outbreak caused requirements on swift change in market channels from physical stores to e-commerce. Also, already established omnichannel companies were faced with a significant increase of e-commerce business. To cope with the significantly changed volumes in the different market channels, learning and finding new ways to cope with picking and packing capacity as well as delivery services were needed with extremely short notice.

7.3.3 The interplay between proactive and reactive strategies

For an efficient and effective supply chain resilience to be achieved, a combination of proactive and reactive strategies is in reality often sought for, not least for economic reasons. On the one hand, proactive strategies, i.e. measures undertaken in a preventative purpose, are needed in order to prepare for a smooth and swift handling of disruptions when they occur. Neglecting proactive strategies may result in larger performance losses.

On the other hand, however, proactive strategies may be costly and tend to be generic, sometimes with limited and blunted ability to handle a specific disruption. Furthermore, no organization is able to completely avoid disruptions and their consequences on the supply chain performance. Therefore, reactive strategies are equally important for an efficient and effective supply chain resilience. Designing supply chain strategies hence becomes an act of balance between proactive and reactive ones, where the optimization of total costs for conducting these strategies plays a decisive role.

Finally, it may be worth noting that proactive strategies and reactive strategies target *potential* disruptions as well as *actual* disruptions. Managing supply chain resilience hence incorporates two separate cycles as illustrated in Figure 7.4. As shown in this figure the left circle for managing potential disruptions plays a key role for establishing an understanding of potential disruptions and proactive measures that can be taken. The proactive cycle of managing potential disruptions is directly linked to the actual management of a specific disruption in the process of monitoring. From the right-hand cycle, which is concerned with the management of a specific disruption that has occurred, learning is highlighted as a key outcome. This learning, as is also illustrated in Figure 7.3, is important during the actual disruption, but is also crucial for improving the management of potential, future disruptions.

Figure 7.4 The cycles for managing potential and actual disruptions

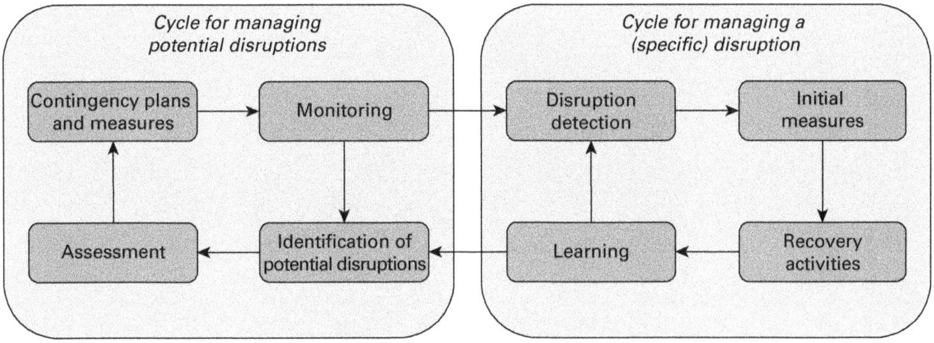

SOURCE Adapted from Behdani et al (2012)

7.4 Supply chain resilience strategies

In addition to a longitudinal process perspective based on proactive and reactive strategies, it is also possible to distinguish strategies based on their content, i.e. how an improved resilience is to be achieved. These strategies, sometimes also labelled elements or capabilities, may include proactive as well as reactive elements, and can be measured and evaluated in different ways. While there exists a wide range of individual organizational approaches for how to enhance resilience, literature tends to summarize these strategies into the four main themes of flexibility, agility, redundancy and collaboration (Tukamuhabwa et al, 2015; Shekarian and Mellat Parast, 2021), see Figure 7.5. Together, these themes span the existing research on resilience strategies although they are also overlapping. Thus, in practice, a launched real existing strategy may include several of these themes.

7.4.1 Flexibility

At an overall level, flexibility can be described as an ability that is concerned with an organizational entity's (e.g. a function, a company or a supply chain) response to long-term and/or fundamental changes in the supply chain by adjusting the configuration of the supply chain. It can be described along the two dimensions of range flexibility and response flexibility (Slack, 1987) that are concerned with the possible amount of alternative configurations and the efficiency of the change process. In a logistics context, logistics range flexibility can be defined as 'the number of potential states it is possible to achieve in the physical supply and distribution and related purchasing and demand functions' (Sandberg, 2021, p. 704).

Figure 7.5 Four overlapping themes in supply chain resilience strategies

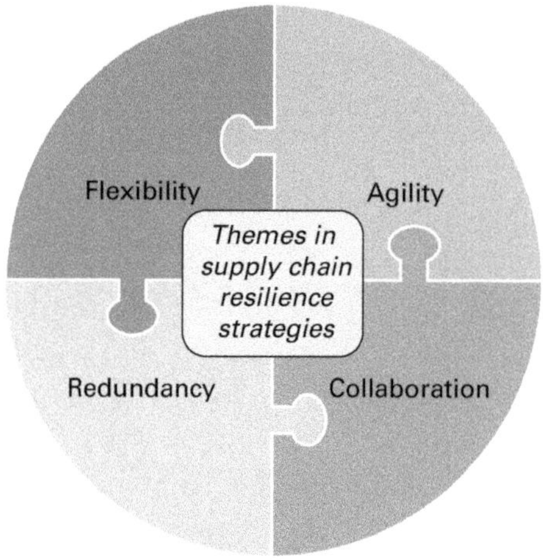

In turn, logistics response flexibility is defined as 'the ease (measured in logistics performance indicators such as costs, speed, service, environmental impact, etc.) with which changes can be made within the logistics flexibility range' (Sandberg, 2021, p. 704). Together, these two flexibility types capture the ability to develop alternative options as well as the ability of efficiently achieving a new state in response to a disruption. These matters of variety as well as speed are both crucial elements for supply chain resilience and hence, in practice, organizations may launch strategies that contain elements from both flexibility dimensions. In terms of performance measurement, metrics for flexibility strategies can be mirrored in two dimensions, including, for example lead times in conjunction with changes of supply chain structure, response time in case of a disruption (related to response flexibility), and number of viable alternative actions that can be undertaken in case of a disruption, diversity in skills, knowledge and capacities, etc. (range flexibility).

There are several more tangible strategies that are based on flexibility, including:

- *Dual sourcing*, in which the introduction of two or several (i.e. a multiple sourcing strategy) suppliers can reduce vulnerability related to supply. Another option for a more flexible supplier base is flexible contracts in terms of capacity to enhance potential variety in volumes as well as delivery timing.
- *Postponement*, in which the final configuration of products are delayed, i.e. a manufacturing postponement, or the physical distribution is delayed, i.e. logistics postponement. These delays offer less uncertainty when matching supply and actual demand.
- *Flexible manufacturing*, in which different types of products are made possible to be produced in the same manufacturing process and facility. This corresponds well to the overall dimension of range flexibility.

- *Flexible transportation*, in which several modes of transportation such as air, sea and railway are utilized. A flexible transportation strategy could also include collaboration with multiple logistics providers and use of several geographically distributed routes as a preparation for a bottleneck somewhere.

7.4.2 Agility

The strategy theme of agility overlaps to a large extent with flexibility but is more geared towards responding to changes in the marketplace, in particular changes in demand. In a broader sense, an agility strategy concerns the efficient, effective and swift response towards both changes in volumes and variety (Christopher, 2016). A similar overlapping term with the same main message is responsiveness defined as 'the ability to respond and adapt time-effectively based on the ability to "read" and understand actual market signals' (Catalan and Kotzab, 2003, p. 677).

The changes in demand that the agile strategy should handle can include relatively expected events that can even be quantified, i.e. disruptions that can be placed in the known knowns quadrant in Figure 7.2, but also the more unknown unknowns that are due to market changes. In this category, for instance, the demand changes during the Covid-19 outbreak of protection masks can be placed.

In terms of performance measurement, agility strategies tend to be measured on their capacity to fulfil customer demands, for example captured in metrics such as delivery lead times, product availability, inventory turnover and demand forecast accuracy. Some of the more prominent examples of agile strategies include the following:

- *Demand management*, in which (if possible) customer preferences during a shortage of a product are manipulated through, for instance, changed prices and offerings of alternative products. Another similar strategy would be to shift demand to another point of time. For instance, in case of shortage, offer the customer a discount if the purchase can be delayed.
- *Activity synchronization through information sharing*, in which a company can improve its agility together with, or based on, the supplier performance. Information sharing upstream often plays a significant role for a reduction of throughput time, which in turn could enhance a swifter response to demand changes in the marketplace. Synchronization and information sharing with suppliers may also be a relevant strategy in case of product quality issues, facilitating a faster response.
- *Market orientation*, in which market sensing activities are launched to enable adequate and prompt indication of market changes such as demands and trends. Utilization of point-of-sales data could here be a useful measure. In case of a multinational business, another critical factor may be to have the ability of understanding and adopting the diverse cultural settings in different marketplaces.

7.4.3 Redundancy

In a broad sense, strategies related to redundancy aim to provide additional resources, production capacity or inventory across the supply chain to maintain and manage the performance during a disruption. Surge capacities of various kinds could here be used as a buffer or 'shock absorbers' (Hohenstein et al, 2015) against disruptions to enhance robustness (i.e. avoidance of performance loss) as well as efficient recovery (minimizing the performance loss). Performance measurements for redundancy include metrics that deal with various capacities in the supply chain, for example inventory levels, total production capacity, warehouse storing capacity, etc.

More specific examples of redundancy strategies include:

- *Use of buffer stock*, in which extra stock enables a capacity to ensure robustness in case of supplier shortages and/or increase in demand.
- *Back-up production capacity*, in which for instance extra production capacity can be utilized, if necessary, for example due to shortage of the ordinary production capacity or increased demand. The back-up production capacity can be organized internally at an organization or somewhere else in the supply chain through a contractual agreement, for instance at a supplier. A well-known example of a company that has this strategy is the Spanish fast fashion retailer Zara, which has contracted capacity at a number of external manufacturers that enables production at short notice.
- *Extra transportation and storing capacity*: Except for extra production capacity, the same reasoning is also possible for other types of capacities, such as transportation or storing capacities throughout the supply chain.

7.4.4 Collaboration

A fourth, somewhat more generic strategy theme that in practice is often combined with the other three themes is collaboration. In line with SCM philosophy, collaboration among included supply chain members fosters information sharing and coordination of processes and activities, which is fundamental to the efficient and effective management of disruptions. Furthermore, collaboration based on trust, joint risk sharing and planning typically reduces potential barriers to supply chain resilience and offers a ground for new innovative supply chain design solutions that are able to cope with disruptions in more efficient and effective ways.

A particularly important dimension of a collaboration strategy is visibility, which plays a crucial role both in proactive as well as reactive strategies. Visibility refers to the ability of a company to observe activities taking place throughout the company's supply chain. For instance, visibility in a supply chain, throughout the different supply chain tiers, is a major enabler for assessment and proactive decision-making to avoid or reduce impact from disruptions, as well as early discovery when a disruption occurs. Overall, visibility through collaboration enables access to information that supports effective and efficient operations to better cope with supply chain disruptions.

Performance measurement related to collaboration covers a broad range of aspects related to supply chain relationships. Examples of more detailed metrics include number of suppliers and customers, joint goals and visions, frequency of information sharing, level of formal collaboration agreements, etc. Examples of collaboration strategies include:

- *Joint supply chain planning and forecasting*, in which redundancy as well as flexibility can be achieved at the lowest possible costs. This joint planning is also an effective measure to learning across company borders on current supply chain structures and potential disruptions and their impact.
- *Risk and resource sharing*, in which supply chain members jointly design the supply chain in order to improve its efficiency and effectiveness in case of a disruption.
- *Supplier development*, in which companies consciously incentivize their suppliers to conduct various measures to improve supply chain resilience, for instance including financial investments, learning and organizational changes.
- *Establishment of public-private partnerships*, in which supply chain members create contact, understanding and trust with public authorities. Such partnerships can for instance include joint sharing of risks and rewards in investments and preparation plans in case of a disruption.

As was mentioned above, the four presented strategy themes could be considered as overlapping, both in their content and occurrence in time (i.e. they could be deployed before as well as after a disruption). They may also reinforce each other, for example an agility-oriented strategy of market orientation may enable an improved redundancy-strategy of buffer stock. In a similar vein, a postponement strategy could be facilitated by a joint planning and forecasting strategy.

However, due to the overlap, as well as positive synergies there may also be interest conflicts among the themes that must be dealt with. For instance, the often-long-term collaboration strategies may sometimes conflict with flexibility objectives, as the long-term perspective of collaboration may hinder a flexible sourcing solution with new suppliers. In a similar vein, the use of extensive buffer stock as a redundancy strategy may obstruct an agility-based strategy aiming at a rapid response to new market requirements (e.g. demand for new type of products).

To avoid suboptimizations and counterproductive strategy themes, it is essential to deal with them in a comprehensive manner. For this, both when it comes to synergies and conflicts among the themes, as well as their relationships to other objectives beyond resilience, systems thinking as was outlined in Chapter 5 is here a crucial prerequisite for discovering, evaluating and understanding these relationships.

REAL-WORLD EXAMPLE Supply chain resilience strategies at Procter & Gamble

Procter & Gamble (P&G) offers a portfolio of different consumer products related to daily-use cleaning, health and hygiene needs, offered through a number of well-known brands such as Pampers (nappies), Ariel (laundry products), Always (feminine care pads), Braun (grooming), Gillette (razors and skin care) etc. To master their extensive global production and sales operations, supply chain management is a key component in the overall business strategy of the company, and their excellence in this area has been widely acknowledged among practitioners, for example through the analyst firm Gartner's prestigious annual ranking of the top 25 global supply chains.

One of the reasons for P&G's successful supply chain performance is their continuous struggles towards finding a balance between cost efficiency in the global supply chain and production operations on the one hand, and resilience on the other. At a more detailed level, P&G has adopted a number of supply chain resilience strategies that include the themes of flexibility, agility, redundancy and collaboration. Some of the most prominent examples of SCR strategies at P&G are the following:

Continuity plans: For a long time, and part of their act of balance between supply chain efficiency and resilience, P&G has developed hundreds of detailed continuity plans. Part of this is the '90/50 plans' in the production, with the objective to find out solutions for how to remain at 90 per cent of throughput during a crisis in a production facility with only 50 per cent of the manpower. These back-up plans have also been stress-tested in order to get to know the consequences of a disruption better. Another result of the continuity plans and the stress tests is an improved knowledge about the most important nodes in the supply chain network that are to be prioritized during a disruption. In particular, the existence of continuity plans includes elements of *flexibility* as well as *agility*.

Visibility: Another crucial SCR strategy at P&G is visibility, typically enhanced by means of adopting advanced technologies for information sharing and real-time transparency in the supply chain. Since the 1990s, P&G has worked systematically to explore and understand how various potential supply chain disruptions such as an earthquake would impact the supply chain performance and for this, visibility is pivotal. Together with the continuity plans, these proactive analyses mean that P&G has a relatively well-developed ability to predict supply chain disruptions and create swift responses, i.e. *agility* is here a key component. For instance, during the Covid-19 pandemic, P&G could, thanks to their supply chain visibility, quickly reduce the number of stock-keeping units, SKUs, and by that simplify their supply chain operations and prioritize the most urgent needs towards customers.

Supplier relationship management: Another key SCR strategy at P&G is to invest heavily in building strong relationships with suppliers. Many of the more important suppliers to P&G are to be considered as long-term partners where transparency and joint innovation are key ingredients. Price and cost efficiency is also recognized as a factor in these relationships, but are accompanied by a more strategic win-win thinking. From a resilience perspective, these strong supplier relationships enable a mutual understanding in the supply chain, which is important in times of turbulence and crisis. For instance, during the Covid-19 pandemic the close boundaries to suppliers could be utilized to cope with rapidly changing demands and lack of products and resources. *Collaboration* is hence a key aspect in conjunction with P&G's supplier relationship management. It also includes possibilities for *agility*, *flexibility* as well as *redundancy*.

SOURCE us.pg.com; EY (2022)

7.5 Summary

This chapter presented the fundamentals of supply chain resilience, a key managerial priority in the contemporary business landscape. In essence, supply chain resilience refers to the ability of a supply chain to cope with disruptions, before, during and after they occur. A disruption is here understood as an unintended, unwanted triggering event that influences the supply chain performance negatively, i.e. there is a negative deviation from the normal state of performance. Such disruption can be classified with respect to their occurrence internal to a company (e.g. production facility failure), in the supply chain (e.g. customs delays) or external to the supply chain (e.g. natural disasters). Disruptions may also be classified based upon whether the likelihood of occurrence is known or not, and, whether their impact on supply chain performance is known or not. Together, the disruptions hence cover 'known knowns' disruptions that can be handled by means of risk management, to 'unknown unknowns', the latter often referred to as 'black swan events'. Depending on their characteristics, several different techniques and tools exist for enhancing knowledge on disruptions, including quantitative as well as more qualitative ones.

Resilience is often described in phases; before, during and after a disruption. Accordingly, strategies for how to cope with the disruptions, i.e. supply chain resilience strategies, cover both proactive and reactive ones. *Proactive* strategies include the processes of identification of potential disruptions, and, if possible, their assessment in terms of likelihood of occurrence and potential impact. They also include contingency plans and measures for how to cope with potential disruptions, and the continuous monitoring of potential disruptions. In turn, *reactive* resilience strategies include processes for disruption detection and the first, initial measures taken to deal with the disruption. At a later stage they also include recovery activities that aim to reduce the performance loss in conjunction with the disruption, and learning to enhance future supply chain resilience strategies. Learning is here considered as a crucial aspect both during, and after, a disruption.

As well as a longitudinal process perspective based on proactive and reactive strategies, it is also possible to distinguish supply chain resilience strategies based on their content, i.e. how an improved resilience is to be achieved. These strategies tend to be summarized by the four main themes of flexibility, agility, redundancy and collaboration. *Flexibility* is concerned with the response to long-term and/or fundamental changes in the supply chain by adjusting the configuration of the supply chain, and can be further described along the two dimensions of range and response flexibility. *Agility* overlaps with flexibility, but is more geared towards responding to changes in the marketplace, in particular changes in demand. *Redundancy* aims to provide some kind of overcapacity in the form of resources, production capacity or inventory across the supply chain to maintain and manage the performance during a disruption. Finally, *collaboration* based on trust, joint risk sharing and planning reduces potential barriers to supply chain resilience and offers a ground for new innovative supply chain design solutions that are able to cope with disruptions in more efficient and effective ways.

End-of-chapter questions

Discussion questions

1. Elaborate on how the effects of a major supply chain disruption, such as an earthquake or a global pandemic, can be cascaded throughout a supply chain.
2. Why is it difficult to foresee the 'unknown unknowns' disruptions, i.e. so-called black swan events?
3. Why is it important to have both proactive and reactive supply chain resilience strategies?
4. How can improved collaboration foster and strengthen supply chain resilience?

Study questions

1. What is a supply chain disruption?
2. What does the ripple effect mean?
3. Explain the processes that underscore proactive and reactive supply chain resilience strategies.
4. Explain the four overlapping themes inherent in supply chain resilience strategies.

References

Behdani, B, Adhitya, A, Lukszo, Z and Srinivasan, R (2012) How to handle disruptions in supply chains: An integrated framework and a review of literature, *SSRN Electronic Journal.*

Catalan, M and Kotzab, H (2003) Assessing the responsiveness in the Danish mobile phone supply chain, *International Journal of Physical Distribution & Logistics Management*, 33(8), 668–685

Christopher, M (2016) *Logistics and Supply Chain Management: Creating value-adding networks*, 5th edition, Pearson Education Limited, Harlow

Christopher, M and Peck H (2004) Building the resilient supply chain, *International Journal of Logistics Management,* 15(2), 1–14

EY (2022) How P&G's supply chain excellence positioned it to prosper in disruption, https://assets.ey.com/content/dam/ey-sites/ey-com/en_gl/topics/alliances/ey-pg-supply-chain-excellence-000421-22gbl.pdf (archived at https://perma.cc/7FAX-EHT6)

Fiksel, J (2003) Designing resilient, sustainable systems, *Environmental Science & Technology*, 37(23), 5330–5339

Ho, W, Zheng, T, Yildiz, H and Talluri, S (2015) Supply chain risk management: A literature review, *International Journal of Production Research*, 53(16), 5031–5069

Hohenstein, N, Feisel, E, Hartmann, E and Giunipero, L (2015) Research on the phenomenon of supply chain resilience, *International Journal of Physical Distribution & Logistics Management*, 45(12), 90–117

Holling, C S (1973) Resilience and stability of ecological systems, *Annual Review of Ecology and Systematics*, 4, 1–23

Ivanov, D (2024) Two views of supply chain resilience, *International Journal of Production Research*, 62(11), 4031–4045

March, J G and Shapira, Z (1987) Managerial perspectives on risk and risk taking, *Management Science*, 33(11), 1404–1418

Olivares-Aguila, J and Vital-Soto, A (2021) Supply chain resilience roadmaps for major disruptions, *Logistics*, 5(4), 78

Peck, H (2006) Reconciling supply chain vulnerability, risk and supply chain management, *International Journal of Logistics: Research and Applications*, 9(2), 127–142

Pettit, T J, Croxton, K L and Fiksel, J (2013) Ensuring supply chain resilience: Development and implementation of an assessment tool, *Journal of Business Logistics*, 34(1), 46–76

Ponomarov, S Y and Holcomb, M C (2009) Understanding the concept of supply chain resilience, *International Journal of Logistics Management*, 20(1), 124–143

Sandberg, E (2021) Dynamic capabilities for the creation of logistics flexibility: A conceptual framework, *International Journal of Logistics Management*, 32(2), 696–714

Sheffi, Y and Rice, J B, Jr (2005) A supply chain view of the resilient enterprise, *MIT Sloan Management Review*, 47(1), 41–48

Shekarian, M and Mellat Parast, M (2021) An integrative approach to supply chain disruption risk and resilience management: A literature review, *International Journal of Logistics Research and Applications*, 24(5), 427–455

Slack, N (1987) The flexibility of manufacturing systems, *International Journal of Operations and Production Management*, 7(4), 35–45

Tukamuhabwa, B R, Stevenson, M, Busby, J and Zorzini, M (2015) Supply chain resilience: Definition, review and theoretical foundations for further study, *International Journal of Production Research*, 53(18), 5592–5623

Managing logistics-based business models 08

A logistics-based business model can be considered as a structured approach for explaining how strategic logistics management of a company should be operationalized and, ultimately, contribute to the company's sustainable competitive advantage. Paradoxically companies are, the more rapid change and development required, in need of more rigid, thought-through understanding of their businesses, underlying structures and logics. For this, a business model perspective as will be outlined in this chapter often works as an excellent lens. In fact, research has shown that companies that deliberately engage in their business models are financially more successful than other companies (Wirtz et al, 2016).

Section 8.1 introduces the content of an overall business model perspective and how a business model can be further delineated into various components. Thereafter section 8.2 elaborates the elements critical for a logistics-based business model as a means to further outline how the strategic role of logistics management can be understood. Finally, some key aspects related to business model innovation, i.e. the change of the business model, are presented in section 8.3. The chapter is summarized in section 8.4.

8.1 A business model perspective

The concept of business models has become a popular means to describe and communicate a company's strategy and activities among practitioners as well as academic scholars. In its simplest form, a business model can be understood as an operationalization and description of how a company can exploit business opportunities, enhance value creation and appropriation, and, ultimately, contribute to a company's sustainable competitive advantage. In relation to the first part of this book, it can be seen as a further extension and operationalization of the strategic management perspectives that were outlined previously.

Figure 8.1 The scope of a business model

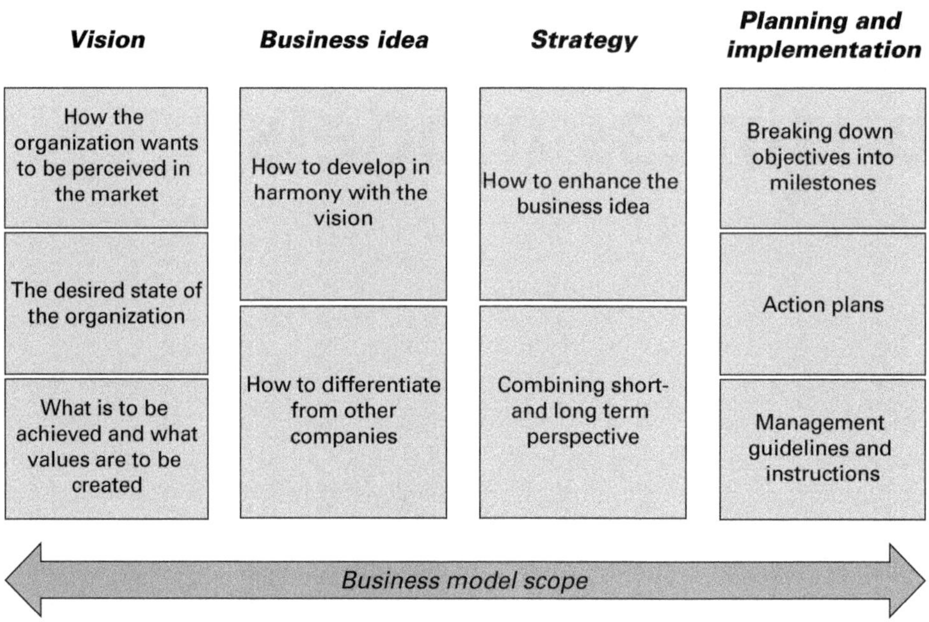

SOURCE Adapted from Sandberg and Abrahamsson (2019)

Drawing on these theoretical groundings, the scope of the business model concept ranges from a company vision to the planning and implementation of actual undertakings for the fulfilment of that vision (see Figure 8.1). A business model is hence not only a description of a '*what*' when it comes to company vision, business ideas and strategies, but explains also '*how*' these are to be implemented and fulfilled by means of the organization's structure, processes and systems.

The business model concept has been widely acknowledged in academia as well as in practice, and numerous different interpretations and definitions exist. The concept has also undergone a development from being a more technology-oriented concept, to an organizational one, and also, more recently, a concept within the realms of strategic management (Wirtz et al, 2016). Although intrinsically integrated, two major streams for how to understand business models have occurred in research, taking a stance in the value concept and the activity system. Combining these two streams of literature, this book defines a business model as follows:

> **A business model** explains how a company's strategic intentions should be operationalized in terms of the value proposed, created, delivered and appropriated. It includes detailed descriptions and principles of the company's offering, its position in the external environment, and how the operational platform in terms of activities, resources and capabilities internal as well as external to the company should be organized.

In the following, these two streams of literature for how to understand the business model concept are outlined.

8.1.1 Business models and the value concept

From a value concept point of view, a business model is in its simplest form about understanding what customers want, providing products or services that deliver on those requirements, and benefitting from this, thus ensuring profitability. A business model should therefore be able to provide a detailed description on the following four value components (e.g. Chesbrough, 2010; Amit and Zott, 2012):

1. The *value proposition*, describing the benefits offered to customers in terms of products and services the business model is about to deliver. Accordingly, key for value proposition is to identify customer needs and customer problems that can be solved in order to enhance customer experiences.
2. The *value creation*, describing the actors and their activities involved for producing the value.
3. The *value delivery*, describing how the value is attained and absorbed by the customers.
4. The *value appropriation*, describing how the value created is to be captured by the company, i.e. the 'money-making logic' of the company.

In practice, these four components may be difficult to deal with separately, and their consistency is vital. For instance, the effectiveness of the value proposition depends on how, by whom, and to whom the value is created and delivered. Furthermore, a value proposition and subsequent value creation, delivery and appropriation are often described in terms of economic shareholder value and customer value, but other types of values such as environmental and social values may also be created and delivered. In order to fully comprehend the different value components and how they are aligned, it is therefore necessary to describe these components from a triple bottom-line perspective.

In addition, as discussed in Chapter 2, the phenomenon of value co-creation between a supplier and customer means that the customer may also blur the lines between the various value components. In particular, the value creation and value delivery could overlap in reality. For instance, in IKEA's business model when the final assembly of the products is conducted by the customers, it may be difficult to distinguish between the value creation process and the value delivery process.

8.1.2 Business models and the activity system

Except for understanding and describing a business model by means of the value concept, another approach is to target the *activity system* (see Chapter 2) that underscores the business model. The activity system, i.e. a set of interdependent activities (internal as well as external to a focal company), is what enables the value creation and appropriation, and understanding the activities involved, how and by whom they are performed, and when, can here serve as a fruitful foundation when describing a business model.

Similar to the value concept a business model based on an activity system logic is often described to consist of a number of components that together constitute the business model. Although consistency among the different components is essential, such a division is sometimes useful, not the least for analytical and communication purposes. Perhaps the most famous classification of business model components is that included in the Swiss business model expert Alexander Osterwalder's business model canvas (Osterwalder et al, 2005) that includes the following nine building blocks:

1 Customer segment(s): what customers are targeted.
2 Value proposition: the type and content of the value(s) delivered to the customers.
3 Channel(s): how the value proposition reaches the customers.
4 Customer relationships: type and content of relationship with each targeted customer segment.
5 Revenue streams: how the company can get paid and earn money.
6 Key resources: resources involved for the realization of the value proposition.
7 Key activities: activities involved for the realization of the value proposition.
8 Key partnerships: collaboration and external actors required.
9 Cost structure: the cost drivers and expenses in relation to the activities and resources involved.

The classification of building blocks may, however, differ depending on the purpose of the business model description. A more generic classification that is more directly linked to the strategic management perspectives outlined earlier in this book is to consider a business model that contains the following three generic components:

1 The company's *external environment* is based on an operationalization of the thoughts from a market positioning perspective (Chapter 2) and includes primarily how the company is positioned with respect to Porter's five competitive forces (threat of new entrants, threat of substitutes, bargaining power of customers and suppliers, and rivalry among existing competitors), as well as choice of generic strategy (cost leadership, differentiation and focus) the company relies upon to achieve the (favourable) position.
2 The company's *operational platform* has its roots in the resource-based perspective (Chapter 3) and dynamic capabilities perspective (Chapter 4) and targets how

involved activities, resources and capabilities (internal as well as external to the company) are organized, managed and exploited to achieve the company's position and offering.

3 The company's *offering* details the actual customer offering, in particular how the offering satisfies customer needs and thereby creates value. The offering here includes, as well as the product or service itself, additional services, in which logistics typically often has a crucial role.

8.1.3 The business model as a management tool

From a more practitioner point of view, a business model can be seen as a comprehensive management tool for communication as well as strategic decision-making. A business model represents a *tool for communication* of a company's strategic intentions and their operationalization that can enhance understanding, coordination and commitment across all functions and organizational levels. From an internal point of view, addressing questions such as those presented in Figure 8.2 helps to ensure that employees understand how their roles contribute to the overall competitive structure

Figure 8.2 Examples of questions to be answered by a business model

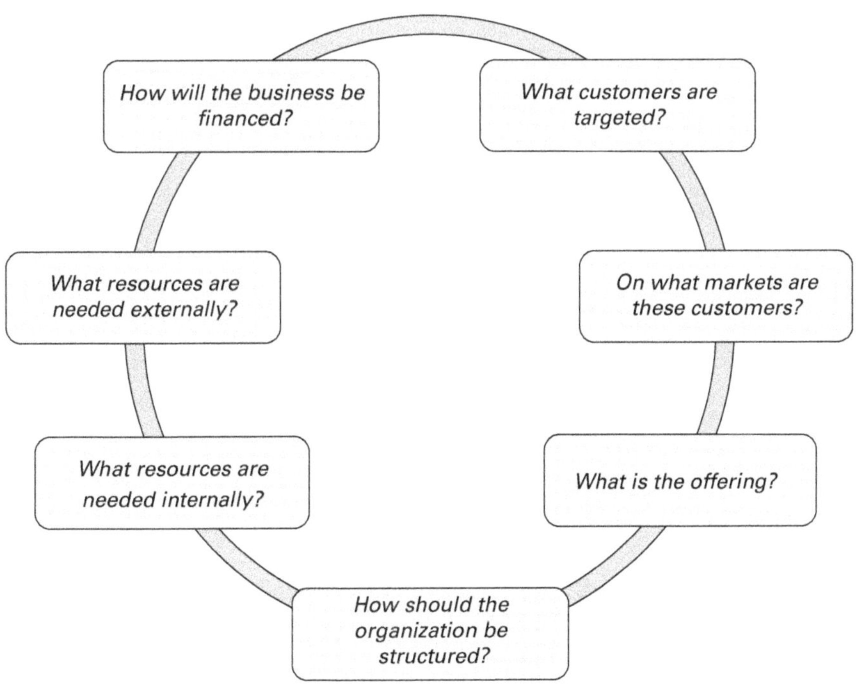

SOURCE Adapted from Sandberg and Abrahamsson (2019)

of the company, and to trigger an alignment of efforts towards shared goals and objectives.

A business model has also shown to be an effective means for communication towards external stakeholders such as customers, suppliers and investors. From an SCM point of view, a business model and its explication of a company's strategic intentions and how they are going to be achieved, offers a valuable starting point for improved coordination and partnering in a supply chain. For investors, the business model concept provides a structured analytical lens for improved understanding of what constitutes a company's sustainable competitive advantage. In particular, the money-making logic can here be scrutinized in conjunction with the activities and resources that underscore this logic.

Explicating a company's strategic intentions and their operationalization in a business model, for instance by addressing the questions shown in Figure 8.2, also serves as a *tool for decision-making*. In particular, it helps managers and executives to evaluate how new initiatives, products or organizational changes might impact the overall business performance and therefore lead to more informed decisions that are consistent with the company's strategic intentions. For instance, evaluation and subsequent decisions with respect to revenue streams, effective resource allocations, investment priorities and risk management can be helped by a business model approach.

8.1.4 Alignment and strategic fit

Although a business model can be described, evaluated and communicated in terms of its inherent components for analytical purposes, a requirement for a successful business model is the alignment between its different parts. In line with a systems thinking as described in Chapter 5, the components of a business model should support and strengthen each other, i.e. there is a need for a strategic fit between the different components to make them aim at the same goals and objectives. For instance, for an e-commerce retailer in the pharmacy industry with limited possibilities to influence and differentiate the actual products sold, a vital part of an offering component may be fast and reliable last-mile deliveries - this can be a major competitive weapon that creates additional value for customers vis-à-vis pharmacies that are based on sales via physical stores. For the operational platform component it is therefore necessary to design and prioritize appropriate activities and resources needed for these last-mile deliveries.

Alignment between the different parts of a company and its environment, including vertical (e.g. consistency between the various management levels in an organization ranging from top management to individual functions) as well as horizontal (e.g. between different functions) alignment, has been discussed extensively in strategic management research and is older than the business model concept. Prominent in this research stream is how a company's strategy and structure interact. For example, Chandler's (1962) book *Strategy and Structure: Chapters in the history of the industrial enterprise*, is a commonly referenced source when discussing whether the strategy should precede the creation of structure (i.e. the company's organization) or vice versa (i.e. that the structure guides the development of the strategy). Exactly how this matching, interaction or reinforcement should occur is, of course, different from case to case. Within organizational theory, various types of fit have been proposed to better analyse the interaction. This includes for instance the fit between different organizational units, the fit between organizational units and processes, as well as the fit between different processes. Grounded in the market positioning perspective and the activity system a strategic fit among activities can also be discussed. Porter (1996) outlined three types of strategic fit among activities that can also be used as a classification of how various types of fit among the business model components can be understood:

- *Simple consistency* between activities and overall business strategy, i.e. all activities (or components in a business model context) contribute to, and are fixed towards achieving the same overarching strategic intentions of the company, for example a low-cost position on the market, organic geographical expansion into new markets, or vertical supplier integration as a means to improve upstream coordination in the supply chain.
- *Reinforcing activities*, where the strategic intentions are achieved by the creation of synergies between different activities. The successful combination of activities is here a central objective. For instance, the installation of technical equipment such as RFID tags (Radio Frequency Identification) may need to be complemented with new working routines and processes in order to reap the benefits from the technology.
- *Optimization of effort*, in which coordination of different activities (in terms of how they are designed and managed) and information sharing enables an improved achievement of the strategic intentions. This type of strategic fit may be similar to the reinforcing activities, but takes a stance in the total efforts of how value is created in the larger activity system. In a logistics context, a transportation planning that enables a combination of last-mile deliveries and pick-up of returns is an example of such a focus on the total effort. Another one could be an improved product design that is based on modularization, which enables, among other things, smoother repair and recycling processes.

8.2 A logistics-based business model

Given the definition of a business model it can be difficult to clearly distinguish a logistics-based business model from a generic one – when and how does a business model qualify to become 'logistics-based'? A simple answer is that a logistics-based business model is pertinent for logistics-oriented companies (such as Amazon, exemplified in Chapter 1), i.e. for companies in which logistics is relevant on the business strategy level and plays a role for the company's sustainable competitive advantage. In such cases, no matter how the business model is further described, the logistics content in the business model components becomes crucial for their functionality and contribution of fulfilling the company's strategic intentions (e.g. Sandberg, 2013; Sandberg and Abrahamsson, 2019). In particular, a logistics-based business model draws managerial attention to the following six elements: supply chain position, how logistics augments the offering, resources, activities, organization and performance measurement (see Figure 8.3). In this chapter, these six elements are further elaborated as a means to demonstrate the strategic role of logistics in a business model context.

8.2.1 Supply chain position

In a logistics-based business model a company's position in the supply chain is essential for achieving and upholding a favourable position in the market. Many companies with a logistics-based business model can therefore be described as channel captains with an exceptionally good control and understanding of their supply chain

Figure 8.3 The business model content and six logistics management related elements

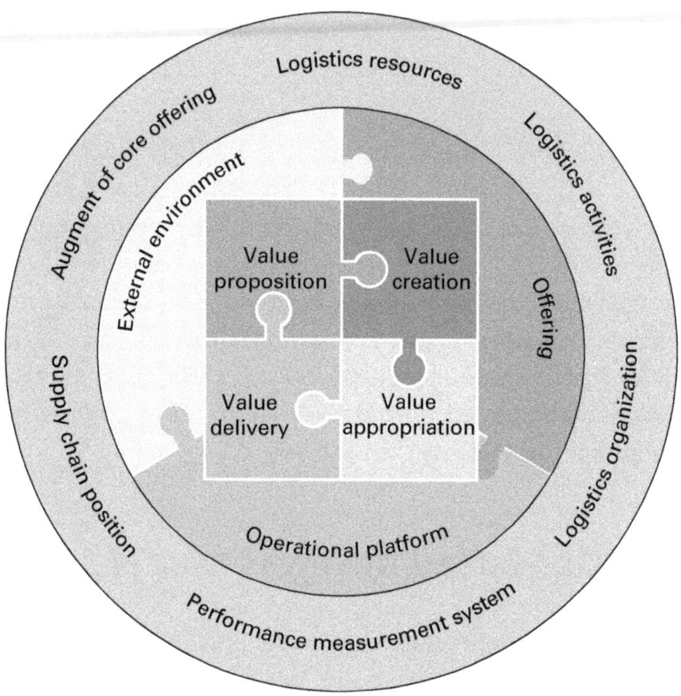

network. In line with theory on IDCs (see Chapter 4) a channel captain typically is in possession of orchestration capabilities (exploitative and/or firm-based) that coordinate resources and relationships along the supply chain to fulfil the individual company's as well as the supply chain's strategic intentions. Questions regarding organizational belongings and ownership are here less important, instead it is the design of the supply chain as a whole that matters for the business model. The channel captain is also expected, in order to be able to create and maintain an effective and efficient supply chain, to develop and manage appropriate relationships towards other supply chain members, ranging from transaction-based arms-length agreements to long-term, collaborative ones. The management of these, including segmentation and a continuous update of the relationship portfolio, is thus another crucial part of a logistics-based business model.

Fundamental for a company's supply chain position is other supply chain members' dependency on the channel captain, which can for example be due to the possession of valuable resources such as expertise, customer relationships, patents or a size that enables economies of scale, etc. In other words, a channel captain typically has some form of power advantage over other supply chain members, and from a business model perspective it is important to understand what underlines this power. Power, in particular in a logistics management context, can sometimes be seen as something negative and in conflict with a traditional SCM philosophy, where mutual win-win thinking and equal collaboration are often advocated. However, power can also be seen as an important enabler and driving force for an orchestration and successful development of the supply chain. Thus, a channel captain who bases the development of the supply chain on a power advantage does not necessarily have to be negative. On the contrary, without a power imbalance in the supply chain, development and change may be difficult to achieve to the extent required.

REAL-WORLD EXAMPLE IKEA's supply chain position

The Swedish furniture retailer IKEA is an example of a company that can be considered as a channel captain. IKEA's business model is mainly known for being grounded in a clear cost leadership strategy with the sale of 'flat packs' – a nowadays well-known concept among consumers around the world that makes the customers part of the value chain during the final assembly of the product. IKEA is a global company with some 470 physical stores mainly located in Europe, North America and Asia, accompanied by a growing online sales business. The supply chain by IKEA mainly covers the processes of design, manufacturing, distribution and sales, and is complex with its own as well as outsourced manufacturing and a franchise-system for the stores. In total, the global supply chain of IKEA sources from 55 countries, from around 1,500 suppliers for home furnishing, transport, logistics and distribution services, components and food.

To excel in their cost leadership strategy, the orchestration of this supply chain network is pivotal, and new goals for efficiency improvements are continuously set and pursued by the organization. As pointed out by IKEA's former CEO Anders Dahlvig, the company's success is largely based on its ability to control and coordinate the entire chain, from raw material access to the point where products are sold.

An important aspect of IKEA's cost control is that it extends far beyond the company's own borders. A prerequisite for this is systems thinking, process orientation and transparency that span across the entire supply chain's functions and operations. Standardization of processes, joint forecasts, and comparable KPIs are some of the key parameters required for this. Another important aspect for achieving cost control along the supply chain is the fact that IKEA itself owns all product rights, which gives them greater flexibility regarding, for example, changing suppliers and product specifications.

Except for keeping track on costs, supply chain control is also increasingly addressed as a key matter for ensuring sustainability performance. For IKEA as the channel captain with the overall responsibility for the sourcing of raw material, expertise in wood and forestry is a crucial factor. With more than 1,000 home furnishing suppliers and an extensive amount of sub-suppliers to these, and the fact that IKEA's products today include wood material sourced from more than 50 different markets, means that IKEA is in need of in-depth knowledge on the global wood industry and how it works. For this, IKEA employs a team of some 40 wood supply and forestry experts that work closely together with suppliers to ensure sustainable sourcing practices around the world.

SOURCE www.ikea.com; Statista (2024); Sandberg (2015)

8.2.2 Augment of the core offering

Central for a company's offering is that it satisfies customer needs and thereby creates value for the customers. Not only does a physical core product or service (e.g. a repair) create value, but also the surrounding services that augment the core offering. In fact, these services can be what really provides an opportunity for a company to differentiate itself from competitors. Consider for instance the example of the e-commerce pharmacy retailer as mentioned above. Pharmacy products are to a large extent standardized commodity products which means that fast and reliable last-mile deliveries, in particular the value delivery component, represent a crucial augment of the core offering.

In a logistics-based business model context it is vital to design and manage more specific, logistics services (such as last-mile deliveries or returns) that can be adapted and individualized to fulfil specific customer needs, and at the same time enhance an overall logistics design that is standardized and modularized in order to maintain cost efficiencies. To manage this act of balance, clarifications are required regarding which customer segment(s) are to be targeted by the services, and how the logistics operations should be internally organized to satisfy as many customers as possible in a rational manner. For this, an in-depth analysis of customer requirements within different segments is required, as well as an internal ability to modularize the logistics operations and offering in a simple way, so that more customers can be reached with relatively few standardized activities and processes.

Another feature of how logistics services can augment the core offering in a successful logistics-based business model is that it often (but not always) can offer the customer both service and cost advantages. In the value proposition this is primarily expressed by a strong focus on the shortening of various lead times throughout the order and delivery process. By reducing lead times, service elements such as delivery reliability can typically be improved; meanwhile the customers' inventory carrying costs can be kept low. On a more general note, different types of uncertainties for the customers and in the supply chain can be reduced, which has positive effects on both service and cost performance.

An additional important aspect for how the core offering can be augmented by logistics is the ability to rapidly adapt to new customer requirements in terms of the surrounding services. This may include new delivery points (to the customer), or new reporting routines on information regarding CO_2 emissions. In order to meet these requirements, organizational speed when it comes to, for example decision-making and managerial competencies in logistics, is required.

8.2.3 Logistics resources

The logistics resources that underpin the supply chain position as well as the offering are another crucial element in a logistics-based business model. Logistics resources should here be broadly defined and described in line with the definitions outlined in Chapter 3 of this book (see e.g. the definition provided in section 3.1), hence including a wide range of different resources, for example physical assets, knowledge, relationships, capabilities etc.

In order to better understand the role of logistics resources in the context of a logistics-based business model, an analysis based on the VRIO-variables suggested in RBV (see Chapter 3) could provide a useful ground. As such, in a logistics-based business model there should be logistics resources that are valuable, rare and difficult to imitate – otherwise there is reason to doubt whether the strategic intentions of the company can be achieved by means of a logistics-based business model.

From a business model perspective, perhaps the hardest criteria to fulfil is to have resources that are sufficiently rare and difficult to imitate. Many business models that indeed are logistics-intensive, such as e-commerce with last-mile deliveries or a manufacturing company with an extensive global distribution network, may not always fulfil these criteria. This is especially true for companies that have outsourced parts of their logistics to a third-party logistics provider offering a standard setup that is essentially available to all companies in the market. Thus, a business model with a vast amount of logistics content does not automatically qualify as a logistics-based business model.

An analysis based on the VRIO criteria does not only provide an understanding for the strategic relevance of resources, but can also be a useful lens for a further understanding of how the resources are aligned with the other business model components. For instance, involved resources can shed light on the potential for augmenting the core offering in terms of, for example, external relationships and collaborations available, access to storing and transportation capacities, etc. Understanding the strategic relevance of the resources in a business model can also provide insights about the logistics organization in terms of, for example, division of responsibility and governance of the resources.

8.2.4 Logistics activities

Logistics activities is another fundamental element of a logistics-based business model. Similar to the logistics resources included in a logistics-based business model, the activities often constitute the direct foundation for the company's value creation and delivery and are instrumental for how to augment the core offering. Focusing on these often operational activities is also what distinguishes a business model from a business idea or strategy in a more general sense – operational activities explains the *how* in a business model. The logistics activities in a logistics-based business model can typically be described as:

- Well-motivated and logical, i.e. it is easy to understand their rationale and why they are performed. This creates clarity in the organization as well as a solid foundation for improvement work.
- Standardized, so that they can easily be combined and function in various processes.

Except for these simple characteristics, it is also relevant to consider how digitalization can enhance the logistics activities involved in the business model. Digitalization has had a profound impact on activities and performance, and it can be considered as one of the main tools for how to realize the vision of SCO and SCM (see Chapter 1), hence it is of instrumental importance to a logistics-based business model. Digitalization offers completely new opportunities to gather information and, with this information as a starting point, it offers new opportunities to control, monitor, plan and manage logistics activities – often in real-time. Digitalization is hence a technical enabler for a more proactive management of logistics throughout the entire supply chain that enables remarkable opportunities for the value proposition, creation, delivery as well as appropriation point of view. Some examples of advanced technologies that can be leveraged in a logistics-based business model are:

- Internet of Things (IoT) devices: IoT devices, such as sensors and RFID tags, enable the monitoring of the condition and location of physical objects (trucks, products, machines etc.) throughout the supply chain and managing them in real-time. Advantages include improved resource utilization, enhanced reliability and information to customers, such as real-time updates to customers.
- Artificial Intelligence (AI) and Machine Learning (ML): The use of AI and ML in conjunction with logistics activities potentials predictive analytics of various kinds, which means new opportunities in a long row of different logistics domains such as demand forecasting and route planning. The benefits include, for instance, reduced costs, and the ability to anticipate and meet customer demands more accurately.
- Blockchain technology: The blockchain technology offers a new, distributed way to store information on transactions of goods throughout a supply chain in real-time. The distributed storing of this information improves the transparency of a supply chain, meanwhile fraud and false information regarding the products can be inhibited. Thus, the advantages are mainly related to enhanced security, reduced fraud and improved trust among supply chain partners.
- Digital twins: Digital twins can be described as virtual replications of physical things that can be used for various simulation and tests. In a logistics context, digital twins of warehouses, transportation vehicles or entire supply chains can be created to simulate and optimize logistics activities. The benefits are mainly due to cost savings and improved planning opportunities.

8.2.5 Logistics organization

The logistics organization, including the supply chain structure where the company operates, is another element of significant importance in a logistics-based business model. In particular, it plays a vital role for the supply chain position and the inherent logistics resources and activities in the business model. Although there is no typical standard solution for how the organization is to be designed, some recurrent themes of a logistics organization in a logistics business model are the following (Sandberg, 2013; Sandberg et al, 2011; Sandberg and Abrahamsson, 2019):

- Decision-making in the logistics organization is largely centralized and, in line with the strategic relevance of logistics in a logistics-based business model, an important task for the company's top management.
- The physical resources and activities do, however, not need to be centralized. For example, different warehouse locations may exist for different markets, and

different logistics processes may be adapted for different customers. In fact, in order to, for instance, leverage on a combination of the logistics strategies lean and agile (see Chapter 1), or combine a cost leadership strategy with a differentiation strategy (see Chapter 2), such a physical decentralization may be advantageous or even necessary.

- There are clear interfaces between organizational units, meaning it is predictable and clear what falls under the responsibility of each department, function or team. This facilitates communication and collaboration between different units and an efficient and effective development of operations.
- The degree of integration between different units and companies along the supply chain is often high and is characterized by openness and transparency, even if this integration does not necessarily need to be based on collaborative win-win thinking as outlined in the traditional SCM philosophy.
- Responsibilities and questions regarding division of organizational control in the physical flow are determined based on what is considered an effective and efficient flow of goods. As an example, in logistics development projects a priority is first given to the design of activities and processes. Thereafter, the question of responsibilities and organizational belongings is focused.

8.2.6 Performance measurement system (PMS)

Finally, another important element of a logistics-based business model is the existence of a PMS that is capable of measuring and following up the logistics performance targeted by the business model. It acts as a compass that guides and aligns the business model performance with the strategic intentions of the company. A more thorough presentation of PMS and evaluation criteria for what constitutes a good PMS were outlined in Chapter 5 of this book.

In line with the message of that chapter, a recurrent theme and feature of a PMS in the context of a business model is that it measures the 'how' of the business model, such as the operationalization of the strategic intentions, at various organizational levels. The focus here is to capture the performance at various levels in order to align them. In line with the descriptions of the other elements above, organizational borders here are typically of less concern, rather it is the 'total' performance of the business model that counts. It is especially crucial for the PMS to capture performance related to the costs and revenue streams in the business model.

The importance of a PMS can also be understood from a broader perspective, where it is an essential foundation for the development and improvement of the business model. Important areas to be considered in this development, and hence crucial for the PMS to capture, are the costs and revenue streams, but also customer demands on logistics services provided, in particular trends and changes in these demands. As such, the PMS could function as an important input to business model innovation, which is discussed in the following section.

8.3 Business model innovation

Business model innovation occurs when companies develop their existing business models or introduce new ones and can be seen as a necessity in a dynamic and changing environment. As argued in the dynamic capabilities perspective in Chapter 4, with rapidly changing customer requirements and technology advancements there is a need to continuously create, extend and modify the company's resource base. In a business model context this means that there is a need for having an ability to innovate the business model. If not, there is an obvious risk that the existing business model may become a burden for the company, where old behaviours, mindsets and relationships are reinforced and cemented.

Although often overlapping in reality, business model innovation can come from an activity system perspective and can take place in three ways (Amit and Zott, 2012):

1. Adding novel activities to the business model's activity system. In a logistics context, for instance, a third-party logistics provider with a business model based on storing and transportation services can add assembly services to the offering.
2. Linking the existing activities in novel ways. For instance, when a company combines existing last-mile deliveries with returns and pick-up services (i.e. first-mile deliveries).
3. Changing the governance of the activities involved in the business model. For example, a company with warehouse operations may outsource these to a third-party logistics provider and by that change the cost structure of the business model's operational platform.

The changes can occur in either deliberate or emergent development processes. In a *deliberate change process*, the alternation of the business model occurs in a conscious, explicit and systematic way. It can be considered as a rational problem-solving process that typically includes the phases of anticipating the future, generating alternatives and implementing plans based on the various business model components. As part of a deliberate change process, a focus is naturally placed on how various types of barriers to business model change can be removed. According to Professor Henry Chesbrough (2010), there are two general types of barriers, obstruction and confusion, which need to be overcome:

- Obstruction to change of the business model is primarily due to a reluctance to change internally within the company. A new business model design can challenge the existing logics for the various value components, i.e. there could be a paradox between current value components and the future ones, which may obstruct development and initiatives for change. A current business model may also represent a more convenient way of working and a well-established mental logic, whereas a new business model may result in a need to step outside the 'comfort zone' of employees. In a logistics context, for instance, an electrification of a third-party logistics provider's transport fleet may challenge the current operating margins due to higher investment costs, and hence obstruct the development of new greener transportation offerings. In addition, electrification may require new knowledge in conjunction with, for example route planning, which may lead to a reluctance towards change among employees.

- Confusion, in turn, arises when there is no clear, obvious path of development for the company. That is, in cases where there is a lack of new thinking in strategy and innovation and one simply does not know how the business model should be changed. This is why, for instance, the dynamic capability of sensing (see Chapter 4) plays a vital role for identification of new business opportunities. A common example in a logistics context for avoiding confusion is to better understand the role logistics has for augmenting the core offering in the business model – this is a crucial input for business model innovation.

In an *emergent change process*, business model innovation can be seen as a continuous, mainly reactive, alignment to the company's business environment. It is seen as an evolutionary process with an emphasis on learning, in which the business model changes as the employees and the company learn new things. The emergent change process view has many similarities with the ELD practices as were outlined in Chapter 5. In fact, the three main features of ELD practices, i.e. the launch of test pilots, cross-functionality and systematic governance and evaluation, are all crucial cornerstones of an emergent approach of business model innovation in a logistics context.

As for ELD practices, and as is the case in both deliberate and emergent business model innovation processes, the role of top management is fundamental. The actual role and governance from top management do, however, differ between a deliberate and an emergent business model innovation process. In a deliberate process, top management are typically in charge of and play an active role for the formulation as well as subsequent implementation of the new business model content, as well as overcoming the various barriers along the way. For instance, outlining the future strategic agenda of the company is typically a main ingredient for overcoming barriers related to obstruction as well as confusion in deliberate business model innovation settings. In emergent innovation processes, this type of clarification also becomes a key task for top managers but does not necessarily mean that top managers should take an active role in the innovation. Rather, top management often has a role of facilitator of various more incremental development initiatives taken in various parts of the company.

The actual management of the business model innovation also depends on its scope. For instance, while sometimes only minor, gradual changes in an individual business model component are required, at other times a completely new business model may be necessary, which demands entirely different capabilities within the company. For example, characteristics such as organizational governance and formal control become important for smaller changes, while attributes related to entrepreneurship and innovation become more important for larger changes.

8.4 Summary

This chapter has outlined the fundamentals of business models, in particular logistics-based business models. A logistics-based business model can be considered as a structured approach for explaining how strategic logistics management of a company should be operationalized and, ultimately, contributes to the company's sustainable competitive advantage. It hence covers both the fundamental question of *what* strategic intentions a company has as well as *how* these are going to be implemented. In relation to the first part of this book, it can be seen as a further extension and operationalization of the strategic management perspectives that were outlined there.

Although intrinsically integrated, two major streams for how to understand business models have occurred in research, taking a stance in the *value concept* and the *activity system*. The value concept can be further detailed into the four components of value proposition, value creation, value delivery and value appropriation. From an activity system perspective, another way of describing the content of a business model is to describe it in the three generic components of the external environment, the operational platform and the offering. Independent from whether the business model is described based on the value concept or the activity system, a business model can be seen as a comprehensive management tool for communication as well as strategic decision-making.

A crucial aspect for a successful business model is the requirement for alignment between different components included in the business model. In line with a systems thinking, the components of a business model should support and strengthen each other, i.e. there is a need for a strategic fit between the different components to make them aim at the same goals and objectives.

This chapter also discusses the existence of logistics-based business models. In practice it can be difficult to clearly distinguish a logistics-based business model from a generic one. This chapter takes the stance that a logistics-based business model becomes pertinent in those companies where logistics is relevant on a business strategy level and plays a role for the company's sustainable competitive advantage. In particular, a logistics-based business model draws managerial attention to the six elements of supply chain position, how logistics augments the offering, resources, activities, organization and performance measurement.

Finally, this chapter also presented some of the key messages in business model innovation literature. Business model innovation occurs when companies develop their existing business models or introduce new ones, and is considered as a necessity in a dynamic, changing environment. Business model innovation can occur in deliberate as well as emergent change processes. In both these processes top management plays important, but different, roles.

End-of-chapter questions

Discussion questions

1 Based on a company you are familiar with, explain its business model components of external environment, operational platform and offering.

2 Discuss and provide examples of how the six elements of a logistics-based business model are linked to and may support the offering component of a company's business model.

3 How can dynamic capabilities be used to enhance business model innovation?

Study questions

1 Explain the essence of a business model.

2 How can a business model be used as a management tool?

3 What is the difference between a business model and a logistics-based business model?

4 What are the elements that become especially critical in a logistics-based business model?

5 What does business model innovation mean and why is it important?

References

Amit, R and Zott, C (2012) Creating value through business model innovation, *MIT Sloan Management Review*, 53(3), 40–50

Chandler, A (1962) *Strategy and Structure: Chapters in the history of the industrial enterprise*, MIT Press, Cambridge

Chesbrough, H (2010) Business model innovation: Opportunities and barriers, *Long Range Planning*, 43(2–3), 354–363

Osterwalder, A, Pigneur, Y and Tucci, C (2005) Clarifying business models: Origins, present, and future of the concept, *Communications of AIS*, 16, 1–25

Porter, M (1996) What is strategy? *Harvard Business Review*, 74(6), 61–78

Sandberg, E (2013) Understanding logistics-based competition in retail: A business model approach, *International Journal of Retail and Distribution Management*, 41(3), 176–188

Sandberg, E (2015) *Logistik och Strategi: För lönsamhet och tillväxt*, Studentlitteratur, Lund

Sandberg, E and Abrahamsson, M (2019) *Logistikdriven Affärsutveckling*, Studentlitteratur, Lund

Sandberg, E, Abrahamsson, M and Kihlén T (2011) Characteristics of a logistics-based business model, *Journal of Marketing Channels*, 18(2), 123–145

Statista (2024) Statistics report about IKEA, www.statista.com/study/20967/ikea-statista-dossier/ (archived at https://perma.cc/7FHY-ZJQ4)

Wirtz, J, Göttel, V and Daiser, P (2016) Business model innovation: Development, concept and future research directions, *Journal of Business Models*, 4(1), 1–28

Managing circular supply chains 09

In line with society's overall sustainability focus, the concept of Circular Economy (CE) has gained increased attraction among academics as well as industry practitioners, and is considered a major route ahead towards globally sustainable and fair businesses with an end to the depletion of natural resources and the accumulation of waste.

So far the development of CE practices has mainly been driven by various technology developments, new circular business models (CBMs) and circular product design aspects. As will be discussed in this chapter, managing circular supply chains is another key ingredient for the realization of CE, ensuring that waste is minimized, resources are used efficiently, and the value of products and materials is maximized throughout their entire life cycle. In total, about 100 billion tonnes of materials are entering the global economy every year (World Bank, 2022) and professionals in logistics and SCM with their overview of sourcing, transportation, handling and transformation of these materials, are in pole position for the creation of more CE practices. For this to happen, however, there is a need to extend the traditional scope of forward, linear supply chains and also create and manage the reverse, circular ones.

From a strategic point of view the development of CE practices comes with many challenges for logistics management but also many business opportunities for economic, environmental as well as social value creation. For those companies that are able to master the circular supply chains and create these values, CE constitutes a major possibility for strategizing and, at the end of the day, enhances a sustainable competitive advantage.

Another theme in this textbook is therefore managing circular supply chains. Section 9.1 first introduces the concept of CE and motivates the drivers for CE practices. It also presents a number of circular principles, the various R-principles, that lay the foundation for a number of circular supply chains, and explains a number of overall strategies for how to enhance CE practices. Different categories of circular business models are also covered. Section 9.2 continues with a presentation of circular supply chains, including a definition of circular SCM and the strategic relevance of this concept. Finally, Section 9.3 covers the main logistics management implications of circular SCM.

9.1 Circular economy extends the scope of logistics management

The concept of circular economy – sometimes also referred to as a strategy, model or philosophy – aims to replace the traditional, linear take-make-use-dispose business practices with circular ones that are instead guided by a make-remake-use-return logic (Parida et al, 2019). In essence, what *enters* the network of supply chains, i.e. primary virgin materials, should be kept to a minimum, as well as the generation of waste, i.e. what *leaves* the supply chain network (to either incineration or landfill). In order to enhance this another key objective of CE is to retain the highest possible value of the products and materials already in the network.

The ambitions of CE include both biological as well as non-biological (technical) materials, although these two types of materials are fundamentally different from each other in terms of how they are circulated. In short, biological materials such as food, cotton and wood are regenerative in the sense that they are biodegradable and can be returned to the biosphere with processes of composting or anaerobic digestion. In contrast, non-biological, technical materials from the subsurface such as metals, minerals and man-made compounds (e.g. polymers or alloys) are not biodegradable and hence need to be circulated in restorative processes, for instance by repairing or recycling activities.

9.1.1 Drivers for CE

The underlying ideas to the concept of CE are not new and have for a long time been advocated in various streams of literature such as industrial ecology, economics, management and corporate sustainability. However, for a number of reasons they are now brought forward more intensively than ever (see Figure 9.1).

Due to the global growth of population and economic progress, many industries have faced an increased *resource scarcity*. The scarcity, and the volatile prices and general risk of raw material shortages that are related to this scarcity, has led to increased cost for supply of virgin raw materials and hence alternative supply strategies based on CE practices have become more economically feasible. Another aspect is the vulnerability of global trade and the fact that various supply chain disruptions (see also Chapter 7) may cause local or regional scarcity. In contrast, CE can sometimes provide and facilitate a supply of raw material closer to the production and end markets. In general, to tackle the resource scarcity, efforts towards waste minimization and resource efficiency, i.e. the very essence of CE practices, become attractive paths ahead when strategizing.

Figure 9.1 Drivers for CE practices

Legal requirements and societal objectives are other drivers for the development towards CE. Driven mainly by environmental concerns, but also social and economic ones, individual governments as well as other multinational authorities have embraced the concept of CE. In Europe, for instance, the European Commission has launched the Circular Economy Action Plan (CEAP), being one of the main building blocks in the European Green Deal, i.e. Europe's agenda for achieving sustainable growth. Other worldwide organizations such as the United Nations and the World Economic Forum (WEF) play crucial roles in promoting CE through various global initiatives, research and investments. Furthermore, non-governmental organizations such as the Ellen MacArthur Foundation are pivotal in advocating CE practices. Overall, the efforts and interests from these various societal institutions have resulted in many legal regulations, policies, supportive activities and standards with an impact on the emergent CE.

Immense *technology developments* of various kinds have further accelerated the development towards CE practices. Innovations and developments regarding materials and new production processes have facilitated a product design that supports durability as well as repair, disassembly and recycling practices. Increased digitalization has also broken new grounds for CE practices. For instance, appropriate tracking and tracing of products and materials have been facilitated that enables smoother use of secondary, non-virgin, raw materials; digital platforms have enabled a matching of supply and demand of products and materials within as well as across supply chains and industries, etc. Furthermore, technology developments have also facilitated measurements of, for example environmental impacts of CE practices, which have further improved these.

Finally, the concept of CE has also been promoted by *consumer demands and expectations*. Environmental concerns and awareness among consumers have led to a shift in market demand towards more sustainable and ethically produced goods and services and for this the concept of CE comes with many new business opportunities. New circular business models (CBMs) have been launched that are able to align with the consumer demand and expectations on environmental and social sustainability performance, and at the same time offer consumers new values based on differentiated, unique offerings and customization. In line with this, many CBMs are also enabling improved brand image and reputation values which further boost the development towards increased CE practices.

9.1.2 The R-principles

The concept of CE can be further explained by addressing a number of circular principles that all start with the letter R. From the initial 3R-framework that was targeting reduce, reuse and recycling, academic scholars have extended and further finetuned these principles, and there is now a 9R-framework proposed with, in total, 10 principles

Table 9.1 The R-principles

Smarter product use and manufacture	R0 Refuse	Avoid to use or produce, or replace by a different product
	R1 Rethink	Expand the use of the product, e.g. encourage multi-functionality
	R2 Reduce	Increase resource efficiency in product manufacture and/or the use phase
Extend lifespan of products and its parts	R3 Reuse	Change ownership of products and continue to use, e.g. through secondhand sales
	R4 Repair	Maintenance of defective product in order to regain its original function
	R5 Refurbish	Restore and upgrade old products, e.g. by replacing components in the product
	R6 Remanufacture	Use parts of discarded goods in new products with the same function
	R7 Repurpose	Use discarded products or their parts in new products with a different function
Useful application of materials	R8 Recycle	Process (e.g. shredding or melting) waste materials to new materials with lower, the same, or higher value
	R9 Recover	Incineration of material to extract energy

SOURCE Adapted from Kircherr et al (2017); Potting et al (2017); Ludeke-Freund et al (2018)

(see Table 9.1). Altogether, these principles capture the CE concept's focus on *smarter product use and manufacture* (Refuse, Rethink and Reduce), *extending the lifespan of products and their parts* (Reuse, Repair, Refurbish, Remanufacture and Repurpose) and *useful application of materials* (Recycle and Recover).

Inspired by the R-principles, an overall illustration of various circular supply chains and how these are related to the linear one, can be depicted as in Figure 9.2.

As shown in Figure 9.2 various circular flows stimulate the CE objectives of waste minimization, resource efficiency and value retainment within the same, original supply chain (R3–R8). Altogether these principles lay the foundation for a *closed loop supply chain*, which brings back products and materials from different downstream supply chain tiers to upstream tiers in the same supply chain. Typical examples are consumer-used products that are brought back into the supply chain by second-hand sales, or waste materials from manufacturers that are brought back as raw material into the production again.

As a guidance for retaining as much value as possible in this closed loop supply chain context it could be argued, as a rule of thumb, that the larger scope of the flow

Figure 9.2 The R-principles and the various circular supply chains

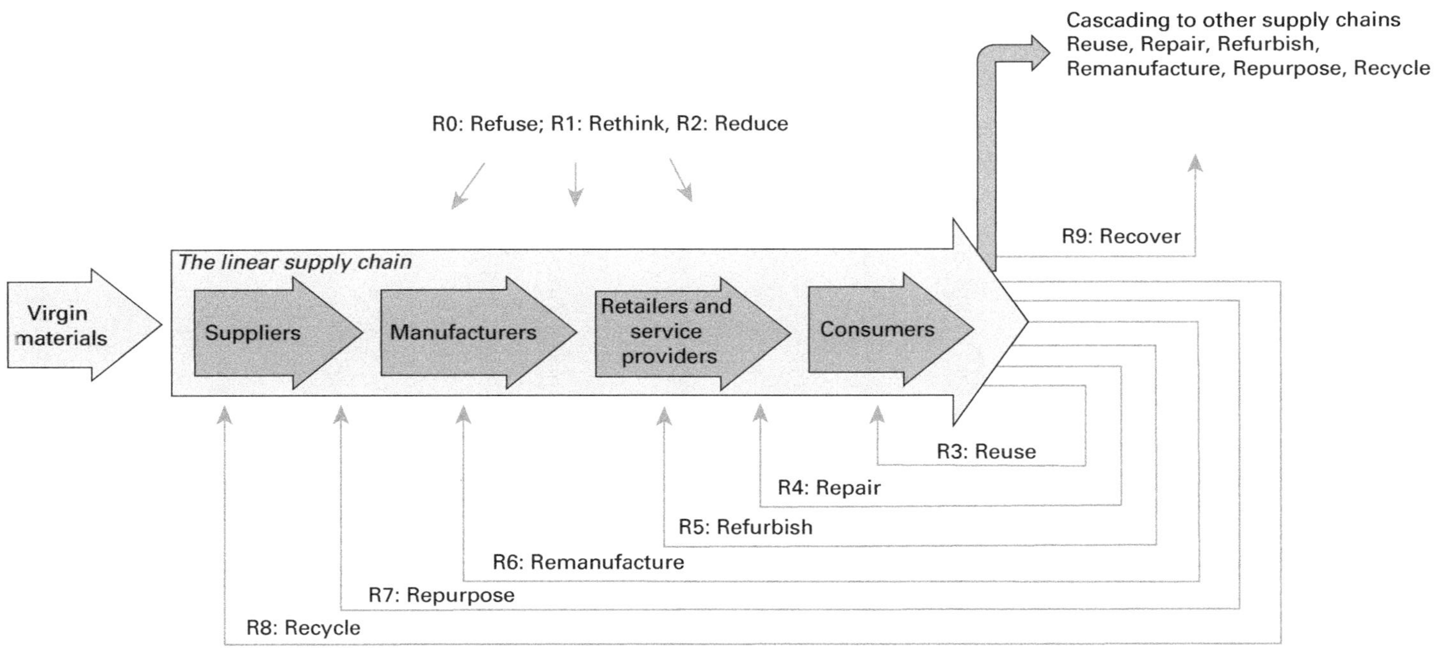

created by an R-principle, the more amount of time, energy, money, resources and other efforts will be required to put the material back into the linear supply chain again. It is therefore often better to preserve the shape and energy of the original product or material as long as possible by keeping various material flows as tight as possible, i.e. 'smaller' supply chain loops are to be preferred over the larger ones. This means that reuse options should be prioritized above repair options, repair options over refurbishment, and so on.

To further boost waste minimization and resource efficiency the R-principles may also be realized through forward, *open loop supply chains*, in which products and materials (often by-products or waste) are brought into other supply chains than the original one. Such *cascaded supply chains* may be in the same industry but can also stretch across industry borders. Examples of such cascaded supply chains are, for instance, that of food waste that become various animal feed products and used clothing that becomes cleaning wipes.

In comparison to closed loop supply chains, open loop supply chains offer new, more comprehensive opportunities for how to achieve the overall CE objectives. Cascaded supply chains may innovate and support other supply chains, improving overall economic, environmental as well as social value creation. An extension of the supply chain network, however, also comes with many challenges. In particular, for logistics management and other functions involved in the design of CE practices, decision-making regarding *how* and *where* used product or materials should be brought back into the linear supply chain(s) for optimal valorisation requires managerial attention.

9.1.3 Strategies for enhancing CE

To further bring forward the CE objectives and guide the design of R-principles and their related circular supply chains, three overall strategies have been suggested in literature: slowing, closing and narrowing material flows (Bocken et al, 2016).

Slowing material flows includes various initiatives for extending the product life cycles of products as a means to reduce the need for replacing them with new ones. A key here is durable product design that enables an initial long life of the product, but also life extension practices such as Reuse, Repair, Refurbish, Remanufacture and Repurpose (see Figure 9.2). From a logistics management perspective, the slowing strategy implies fewer activities when it comes to transportation and delivery of new products and materials. On the other hand, a slowing strategy accelerates the need for collection, sorting and activities in conjunction with the various life extension practices, i.e. 'service logistics'. A key task related to this is for instance warehouse and inventory management in order to successfully store spare parts for older products and manage the flow of returned products in an efficient and effective manner.

Closing material flows concerns the efforts of reducing waste and post-use material flows that go to incineration and/or landfill by instead recycling these materials. As for slowing, logistics management here plays a key role to enable the actual collection, sorting and further distribution into suitable circular supply chain flows. Despite the name 'closing', this task may go beyond the closed loop supply chain perspective and also include open loop supply chains where waste or by-material from one supply chain becomes input material in another. As a result, the waste products and materials must be handled in such a way that maximum value can be extracted in the new supply chain. For instance, waste products and materials may need to be kept clean during handling, storing and transportation.

Narrowing material flows refers to efforts aimed at minimizing the use of input materials in products, i.e. using fewer resources per product. Narrowing is primarily a strategy that concerns product design in the linear supply chain and could be launched independently from circular practices. In a wider sense, however, narrowing has also been suggested to include packaging and the overall use of energy throughout the entire supply chain network (circular supply chains included). From that perspective, logistics management plays an important role in terms of use of adequate packaging to reduce energy as well as materials. Energy- and resource-efficient transportations throughout the linear supply chains as well as the various circular ones also become part of a narrowing strategy that is relevant also from a logistics management point of view.

A successful implementation of the slowing, closing and narrowing strategies typically requires efforts of all members of the supply chain. While the focus has traditionally been on manufacturing companies due to their direct involvement in product design and production processes, other supply chain members such as retailers and logistics service providers play equally critical roles in the execution of the CE strategies. Given their different roles and responsibilities they may, however, approach and contribute to these strategies in different ways. Table 9.2 shows examples of how each of the three strategies can be applied by manufacturers, retailers and logistics service providers.

Manufacturing companies typically hold a key role when it comes to implementation of CE practices as these are often in charge of decisions regarding product design that is critical for the possibility of using secondary materials in the products. For instance, product design is decisive for how production processes can be conducted where virgin and secondary raw material can be combined, and the modularity of the product is decisive for the possibility to repair as well as disassemble the product. Manufacturers also play a key role for enhancing collaboration and knowledge sharing regarding the product design across the supply chain, i.e. manufacturers can play a role for driving innovation at other supply chain members with respect to circularity.

Furthermore, manufacturers can narrow the material flows by optimizing their production processes to minimize production waste and enhance resource efficiency, for instance by leveraging technologies like 3D printing and AI. From a logistics point of view, manufacturing companies also play a major role when it comes to facility location of, for example production and warehousing activities, as these decisions influence the feasibility and opportunities for efficient and effective circular supply chain practices. Factors to consider include, for instance, geographical distances and transportation costs, and national presence (due to regulations for export of waste materials).

Retailers constitute a vital link between manufacturers and consumers that have a key role in promoting and facilitating the adoption of the CE strategies. By the launch of CBMs they create and encourage consumer behaviours that support more sustainable consumption patterns that are in line with the CE strategies, for instance second-hand sales and repair services. When powerful, retailers may also have an impact on the manufacturers' decisions regarding, for example, use of secondary material and product design. In fact, in the case of private labels, retailers may have more influence on the product design than the manufacturers. Retailers can also contribute to a narrowing strategy by optimizing inventory levels and operations to reduce packaging and unnecessary transportations and handling. From a closing strategy perspective, retailers are also pivotal for encouraging consumers to participate in take-back schemes and recycling programmes. This not only helps in closing the loop by ensuring the return and proper handling of used products but also fosters a more direct relationship between consumers and the principles of circularity.

Finally, *logistics service providers* are often the operational backbone in circular supply chains, with a pivotal role for the planning and actual execution of logistics activities in the circular supply chains. For instance, when retailers and manufacturers launch new CBMs they can have significant opportunities to influence their design and success. Logistics service providers also function as intermediaries that facilitate resource pooling and the realization of necessary economies of scale and scope in the circular activities. Related to this, they may also offer specialized services related to the R-principles such as repair or disassembly that are difficult for individual manufacturers or retailers. Logistics service providers not only play an important role as intermediaries within a supply chain, but also between supply chains as well as industries, i.e. logistics service providers play an important role for the creation and functioning of open loop supply chains, which is an important component in the closing strategy.

Examining the examples from Table 9.2 further it becomes evident that the interplay and collaboration between the different types of supply chain members holds a key for the successful implementation of CE strategies. By working together, these key supply chain members can create significant environmental, economic and social values, and lay the foundation for sustainable competitive advantage.

Table 9.2 CE strategies of slowing, closing and narrowing among different categories of supply chain members

	Manufacturers	Retailers	Logistics service providers
Slowing	• Launch product design that fosters modularity and R-principles such as repair and remanufacturing • Facilitate external services based on R-principles by encouraging and sharing product and production knowledge	• Launch and promote new CBMs • Nudge consumer behaviour towards CE practices • When possible influence product design towards modularity and R-principles	• Offer reverse logistics services (e.g. collection and sorting) to facilitate the various R-flows • Provide specialized services in conjunction with the R-principles (such as repair services)
Closing	• Innovate and launch product design that facilitates use of secondary materials • Facility location to encourage recycling and waste valorization	• Source products made from secondary materials • Facilitate and nudge consumers in conjunction with product take-back schemes and recycling programs • Collaborate with recycling firms to valorize waste	• Collect and sort material waste • Organize and connect waste companies and manufacturing companies • Offer storing and distribution solutions for secondary products and materials • Provide contacts and valorization opportunities across supply chains and industries (cascading)
Narrowing	• Utilization of new technologies to reduce waste and improve resource efficiency in production	• Optimize inventory and operations to improve resource efficiency (e.g. use of packaging)	• Use of fuel-efficient vehicles and transportation route optimizations • Improve warehouse operations to reduce energy and packagings • Invest and adopt green and sustainable packaging solutions.

9.1.4 Circular business models

In order to further realize and implement the R-principles and the CE strategies of slowing, closing and narrowing in real business life, one of the most common approaches for how to do this is to innovate and launch circular business models, CBMs. As for business models in general, a CBM explains the rationale for how a company's activity system can propose, create, deliver and appropriate value. In contrast to other business models, however, CBMs set out to do this on the basis of the CE concept. At the very core of CBMs is that value proposition, creation, delivery and appropriation revolve around resource efficiency by using as little resources as long as possible, while extracting as much value as possible. In line with this – and other existing academic definitions of CBMs (e.g Bocken et al, 2016; Lewandowski, 2016; Oghazi and Mostaghel, 2018) – a CBM can be understood as:

> 'The rationale of how an organization proposes, creates, delivers, and captures value based on slowing, closing, and/or narrowing strategies in circular supply chains.'

This broad definition means that CBMs can be operated within and across 'circular supply chains', covering the various R-principles and their underlying flows within a supply chain (i.e. the closed loop supply chain) as well as the open loop supply chains. The definition also means that CBMs can take different shapes and be operated alone or in collaboration by different supply chain members such as manufacturers, retailers as well as logistics service providers.

A key objective with CBMs is to decouple value creation in terms of economic gains from the consumption of finite resources. In order to do this a design that promotes durable, modular and recyclable products plays a crucial role. Managerial attention is therefore many times given to product design issues as this becomes a fundamental enabler to many CBMs. However, in particular in cases when the design is not controlled by the owner of the CBM, the establishment and actual organization of the required circular motion (i.e. logistics) that is needed for a maximized utilization of the product also becomes a crucial component in the CBMs.

The many different business opportunities that underscore the CE and the R-principles means that an exhaustive gross list of more specific CBMs is difficult to provide. In fact, as for business models in general, the actual business model operated by a company is to be unique and designed to fit the conditions of the particular company's environment. However, some of the most prominent categories of CBMs that all require extensive involvement from logistics management include (Accenture, 2014; Ludeke-Freund et al, 2018):

Product life extension: Being perhaps the most common CBM category, the CBMs in this category are based on the provision of various services including repair, maintenance, upgrades or resell services. The key objective for the services is to prolong the product life, which can be achieved by increasing the product's value for the existing owner (e.g. through repair), and/or switching owner, for instance through second-hand sales. When providing these services, logistics management has a key role to organize the various services, not the least in cases when these are provided by specialized intermediaries such as repair firms.

Sharing platforms: These CBMs revolve around digitalization and an intensified exchange of products among product users, which can be private consumers as well as companies. Providing such an exchange service facilitates the sharing of overcapacity or underutilization and helps the owner (companies as well as private consumers) to benefit on products and assets with low utilization or ownership rates. The provision of a sharing platform typically emphasizes the role of logistics as an enabler for the smooth and convenient yet cost-efficient exchange of the products between customers. As such, these services become a crucial, integral part of the offering provided by the CBM.

Product as a service: Instead of a customer value logic based on 'buy and own', these CBMs provide *access* to the product and their functionality. Accordingly the focus becomes maximizing use value in terms of functionality and experience of the product. This is for instance the case in CBMs based on leasing, subscription or pay-per-use services. Long-lasting, robust and timeless design are often key elements in the products to be accessed. As for the sharing platforms, these services typically emphasize the role of logistics as an enabler for a convenient yet cost-efficient circular motion of the products between customers.

Recycling: These CBMs are based on a value creation logic where used materials are processed to new materials (e.g. through shredding or melting). These practices are sometimes referred to as down- and upcycling, where downcycling results in materials with lower value and upcycling in cases of higher values. Recycling CBMs could occur in the same industry, but also across industries when, for instance, textile waste become insulation material in the construction industry. As will be discussed below, when organizing these circular supply chains logistics management becomes a pivotal contributor.

9.2 Circular supply chains

As already indicated in the previous sections, for CE to be realized, the existence of efficient and effective physical flows of goods in the circular supply chains plays a decisive role. In order to embrace the circular supply chains, there is a need for a fundamental change of mindset in terms of what is the scope of SCO and SCM. In the existing supply chain relationships, the overall key question is no longer a joint plan and coordinated efforts for how to provide a successful end-product to end consumers. Instead, the key questions concern the provision of products designed for circularity while ensuring customer satisfaction and needs, and how the various circular supply chains required should be managed.

9.2.1 Circular SCM

Based on, and inspired by, previous knowledge in various academic research streams such as reverse logistics, green supply chain management and sustainable supply chain management, the adoption of the CE concept becomes most clear in what is in academic research referred to as circular supply chain management (CSCM). For the purpose of this book, and based on previous definitions of CSCM (e.g. Montag, 2023) as well as previous definitions of SCM (Mentzer et al, 2001) and sustainable SCM (Seuring and Müller, 2008), CSCM is here defined as:

> Based on the concept of CE, circular supply chain management is the systemic coordination of activities, processes and functions within and across companies to minimize waste and maximize resource efficiency of materials and products, meanwhile taking goals of economic, environmental and social performance into account.

A *systemic coordination* here typically includes the design, implementation and maintenance of various circular flows as those shown in Figure 9.2. As these flows typically stretch beyond individual organizations, a key element in CSCM – just as in SCM – is to manage relationships within and across involved supply chains. In cases of open loop supply chains these relationships may also include stakeholders in other industries where products and materials can be restored in a better way and/or waste generation avoided. In addition, the systemic coordination also includes the integration and use of primary, virgin materials and products with secondary, recovered materials and products.

To *minimize waste and maximize resource efficiency* means that when coordinating this mix of primary and secondary products and materials the secondary ones should be prioritized. In line with the R-principles, this is achieved by various means including smarter product use and manufacture, extending the lifespan of products and their parts, and a useful application of materials.

Finally, CSCM should consider *goals of economic, environmental and social performance*. CSCM practices should contribute to a company's sustainable competitive advantage, where 'sustainable' is grounded in a triple bottom-line performance. This may render paradoxes (see Chapter 6). For instance, performing paradoxes of various kinds may occur between different performance dimensions. Furthermore, belonging paradoxes can arise in the form of interest conflicts between the objectives of an individual company or supply chain on the one hand, and the interests of society on the other. A crucial task for CSCM is hence to manage these paradoxes.

9.2.2 The strategic relevance of CSCM

Managing circular supply chains efficiently and effectively may offer a sustainable competitive advantage and it is therefore important for logistics management to look beyond the linear supply chain flows and also embrace the circular ones. When mirrored in the three strategic management perspectives outlined in the first part of this book, the strategic relevance of CSCM could be motivated as follows:

From a *market positioning perspective*, the circular supply chains offer many opportunities for new types of market positions that can provide the customers with new products and services that bring customer value. For instance, in conjunction with logistics, new positions based on differentiation emerge, including an extended service offering such as take-back services and various sorting activities. In essence, the circular supply chain means an extension of the value system, which means new opportunities for unique value offerings vis-à-vis customers. The extension also opposes the risk for hypercompetition.

From a *resource-based perspective*, the resources required to carry out the activities and processes in the circular supply chains have the potential to fulfil the VRIO criteria. Value in the form of economic as well as monopolistic rents may here be created based on the circular supply chains. Some resources may be considered rare, such as larger logistics infrastructure in conjunction with collection and sorting. Resources that underpin the circular supply chains may also be imperfectly imitable for reasons such as know-how and partnerships. Finally, there is a need to have an organization in place that is able to manage and control the various circular supply chains.

From a *dynamic capabilities perspective*, it could be argued that circular supply chains, just as the linear one, are in need of continuous renewal. Indeed, creating, extending and modifying the current resource base that underscores the circular supply chains is often called for and the capabilities needed for this, i.e. dynamic capabilities, are evident. Important factors that drive this need are the rapidly changing requirements from society (e.g. in terms of new regulations) and consumers (e.g. in terms of new demands on sustainability in conjunction with products such as repair services). As for the linear supply chains, the development of new technology means that new opportunities occur, and to capture these, dynamic capabilities in conjunction with the circular supply chain operations become essential.

9.3 CSCM and the implications for logistics management

In many instances the logics and requirements on logistics management in a circular supply chain context are the same as in a linear context. However, some characteristics become more pertinent in a circular context, and render a number of implications when a linear SCM philosophy is to be replaced by a circular one. This section summarizes some of these implications.

9.3.1 First-mile logistics operations The change from the take-make-use-dispose logic to a make-remake-use-return logic means that consumers that traditionally have been situated at the 'end' of the linear, forward supply chain also become suppliers of products and materials they have previously purchased but no longer need. To take care of and bring back these products and materials into the various circular supply chains is a key task for logistics management in a circular supply chain context.

As a result, development of cost-efficient as well as convenient 'first-mile logistics' operations, i.e. the collection of these products and materials, is required. In contrast to last-mile logistics that is based on a divergent delivery logic, first-mile logistics are to be built around a convergent logic instead. Combining last-mile deliveries with first-mile pick-ups is here an opportunity to enhance transport efficiency, but comes with challenges, for instance in terms of planning and collaboration among different supply chain members.

Beyond the initial pick-up, first-mile logistics also becomes a matter of organizing and structuring the subsequent steps in the circular supply chain, including an infrastructure for warehousing of collected products and materials, and sorting operations in order to further allocate and distribute these into the various circular supply chains. In conjunction with these activities a great responsibility often falls on logistics management to initiate the secondary products or materials into the 'right' circular supply chain, i.e. the one with the most appropriate R-principle available. This includes challenges of, for instance, judging quality and value of each and every individual item, but also understanding the expected costs and environmental impact that will arise in the various circular supply chains when bringing them back to the linear supply chain.

Multidirectional flows of products and materials

Another implication stems from the emergence of multidirectional flows of products and materials throughout the supply chain structure. In particular, warehouses and their processes become the playground for this implication. Warehouses and their layouts are often primarily designed to optimize and support the linear product and material flows and not the circular ones. As a result, for instance, there may be limited space for the effective and efficient storing of waste and related sorting operations. In a similar vein, efficient and effective processes for various R-principles may also need to fit into the warehouses, such as disassembly, repair, remanufacturing, recycling etc. In contrast to the linear flows these activities tend to be more manual and time consuming. They may also require new types of competencies among employees.

Challenges can also be due to a lack of economies of scale and scope as the secondary, reverse flows contain unique products and materials that must be treated individually. Instead of handling batches of products throughout the warehouse, processes of handling and storing many circular flows require individual treatment of each and every item. For instance, in case of online second-hand fashion sales there may be a need for each item to be individually checked for quality, photographed, priced, described and stored before it can be sold again.

Increased and more complex information exchange

Another key concern related to the multidirectional flows is the fact that existing IT systems tend to have a focus on the linear flows and transactions, which means that existing systems often have limited capacity to support circular activities such as returns, pricing and production of used products or materials. New, comprehensive information exchange structures within and across the circular supply chains must therefore be established and maintained. Such a structure typically includes IT-related components such as data collection and storage solutions, data processing and analytical tools, etc. but also various interpersonal forums for knowledge sharing and decision-making. The ongoing digitalization and new technologies such as blockchain, Internet of Things and digital twins here offer many new opportunities for how to innovate and enhance these components, although most of these are still in their infancy.

Beyond supporting the circular processes, a new information exchange structure is also required to enhance the use of secondary materials in the linear supply chain. Transparency and traceability are here the key objectives for the information exchange structure. In particular, in order to provide a viable alternative to the use of primary, virgin products and materials, knowledge on *where* (in the circular supply chains) secondary, recovered products or materials are available, and *how much*, i.e. in terms of volume, is decisive. In addition, it is also important to have reliable information about, for example, material composition and quality regarding these products and materials for an optimal functioning of the linear processes such as production and retail sales. Furthermore, transparency and traceability are also decisive from an end consumer perspective. Providing details about the circular journey of a product can build customer trust and enhance the brand image in a market where sustainability is a growing concern.

REAL-WORLD EXAMPLE Supply chain transparency at Patagonia

Supply chain transparency, among supply chain members as well as towards end consumers, has increasingly been acknowledged as a source for a company's sustainable competitive advantage, not least in conjunction with social and environmental performance. End consumers and society in general are more demanding when it comes to performance of, for example, CO_2 emissions and other social matters such as fraud, animal welfare and child labour in the supply chain.

Patagonia, an American apparel retailer, has long since had a strong sustainability profile, in which logistics and supply chain performance play a crucial role. A critical aspect of Patagonia's success when it comes to sustainability is its high level of transparency towards end consumers that want to know more about the materials included in the products, from where they are sourced, how they are manufactured, etc. To meet these requirements, Patagonia has operated since 2011 a concept labelled 'Footprint Chronicles' that provides detailed information about their supply chain and their products' environmental and social impacts caused at each tier throughout the supply chain. Part of this is their materials traceability programme in which Patagonia works closely with factories, mills, spinners, processors, recyclers and farms with the objective to map the supply chain.

The programme is an important tool not only for increasing visibility towards the end consumer, but also for continuous supply chain innovation and improvement. The supply chain mapping presented in the Footprint Chronicles concept here provides in-depth insights into the supply chain performance, and constitutes a useful complement to traditional sustainability reports, code of conducts and audits.

SOURCE Bateman and Bonanni (2019), www.patagonia.com

Facility location: combining linear and circular supply chain considerations

The multidirectional flows of products and materials may not only have an impact within the existing supply chain structure but may also render a new one. In particular, the location of facilities and their geographical coverage here come into play for the creation of an economically feasible performance.

Economies of scale and scope in storing, handling and transportation are to be ensured in the linear supply chain but also in the various circular supply chains. In cases when a company wants to integrate and use the same facilities for linear and circular supply chains, it is therefore vital to not only base the location decision upon the linear supply chain operations but also include the consequences for the circular supply chain flows, taking into account economic as well as other variables.

For instance, when a company's linear supply chain structure based on warehouses with a national coverage is complemented with independent, specialized circular facilities (e.g. facilities for sorting, refurbishment or repair) these may need both larger as well as smaller geographical coverage for an optimal performance. Secondary products and materials with relatively high value (e.g. used mobile phones or precious metals) allow for longer, more costly transportation distances, even across national borders, before they are recuperated (e.g. repaired or disassembled) in a cost-efficient and cost-effective way. In contrast, products and materials with low value, such as food waste, require a more local, decentralized recuperation in order to cover the transportation costs.

Besides being a pure economic optimization problem, there are also a number of other factors that come into play. A factor that speaks for increased geographical coverage, although not economically feasible, is that specialized circular practices such as repair or recycling may only be available in a few places. For instance, the geographical cluster of Prato in Italy is a dominating hub for the recycling of wool. For many companies in the textile and fashion industry, when engaging in recycling operations of wool, it is therefore likely that Prato becomes a destination in the circular supply chain network.

There are also several factors that speak for less geographical coverage of the circular supply chains. In particular, life cycle analyses may here be considered in order to understand the environmental impact of the location decisions; even though it may be economically feasible to transport high-value secondary products and materials to distant specialized hubs for recuperation, this may be questioned from an environmental point of view. In addition, legislation and other regulations may hinder an increased geographical coverage as different countries and regions may have different legal requirements on how to, for instance, handle and/or export used materials (classified as waste).

Organizational design: new roles, responsibilities and partnerships

The involvement in CE practices and the corresponding circular supply chains also means that there is a need to reevaluate and redesign organizational roles and responsibilities within as well as across companies involved in the circular supply chains. When it comes to the internal organization, the previous natural priority given the linear supply chain must in a circular supply chain context be complemented with priorities and resources given to the organization's involvement in the circular ones. Appropriate development and management of these must be prioritized and managed individually, but also jointly, and in an integrated way with the linear supply chain practices. In particular, the latter becomes evident in the various physical nodes such as warehouses and production facilities where responsibilities, objectives and organizational requirements must be synchronized.

The involvement in circular supply chains can also cause completely new organizational roles and responsibilities for logistics management. For instance, a new role for first-mile logistics, targeting the collection and sorting of consumer-used products and materials, may be introduced. Other new organizational roles and responsibilities may be established in conjunction with the various R-principles, such as recycling and resell as a means to strengthen and prioritize these flows. In general, from an organizational point of view, a company's engagement in the various circular supply chains means that complexity in logistics flows increases and it is hence pivotal to create a new organizational design that is able to cope with, for example, competing objectives as well as limited resources, visibility, knowledge etc.

Beyond implications for the internal organizational design, CE practices can also have an impact on the external design, not least in the form of establishment and management of new partnerships. In particular, with the same logic as for the linear supply chain flows, external partnerships often provide opportunities for enhancing economies of scale and scope and/or getting access to specialization and knowledge required in conjunction with the R-principles. External partnerships are also an essential ingredient for innovation and financial risk sharing when making the investments needed for these practices.

External partnerships can occur between various supply chain members, such as for instance manufacturers, retailers and specialized service companies targeting, for example, repair or remanufacturing. Another type of supply chain member with a pivotal role for enhancing collaboration and coordination with respect to the physical flow of goods is logistics service providers. These can take an intermediary role in the various circular supply chains with a great impact on the actual design and orchestration of the circular supply chain network.

KPIs for circular supply chain practices

Closely intertwined with the organizational design is the need for re-evaluation and/or completely new KPIs that are able to capture performance in the linear as well as circular supply chains. Figure 9.3 shows examples of KPIs that attempt to capture the actual physical performance and scope of circular supply chains.

It is also pivotal to consider the already existing KPIs and their impact on CE practices. For instance, greenhouse gas emissions accounting per product item could be complemented by appropriate new KPIs that are able to capture emission reductions or emissions being avoided. This new logic for how to understand performance is crucial to CE practices as when a product's life is extended by a more durable design or repair services this means that the individual product gets associated with more emissions. If not coupled with the savings or avoided greenhouse gas emissions in the accounting system it can be difficult to motivate and incentivize CE practices.

Figure 9.3 Examples of KPIs in circular supply chains

Circular inputs
- Total weight, volume or share of circular inputs used
- Saved CO_2 emissions due to use of circular inputs
- Total costs for virgin respectively circular input materials
- ...

Process outputs
- Total weight or volume of waste generated
- Generated waste diverted from disposal for reuse, recycling or other recovery options
- Total collected weight or volume of waste
- ...

Product utilization
- Technical liftetime (product functioning time until first failure)
- Functional lifetime (time until product user requirements can no longer be met)
- Customer satisfaction with the product
- ...

Material intensity
- Total product weight or volume used against revenues
- Revenue from circular services such as repair and refurbishment
- Water or energy use in relation to revenue
- ...

SOURCE Adapted from Ellen MacArthur Foundation (2023)

9.4 Summary

The development of CE practices and their related circular supply chains provide many strategic opportunities as well as challenges. This chapter has therefore revolved around the theme of managing circular supply chains. Main drivers for CE include resource scarcity, legal requirements and societal objectives, technology developments and consumer demands and expectations.

CE aims to replace the traditional, linear take-make-use-dispose business practices with circular ones that are instead guided by a make-remake-use-return logic. Waste minimization, resource efficiency and value retainment are in this context crucial objectives. To fulfil these objectives, 10 so-called R-principles were in this chapter outlined that are of a fundamental importance to the various circular supply chains, including closed loop as well as open loop supply chains that are to be managed in a CE context.

To further bring forward the CE objectives and guide the design of R-principles and their related circular supply chains, the three strategies of slowing, narrowing and closing material flows were thereafter presented. This chapter has also emphasized that these three strategies are valid for all members of the supply chain, albeit in different ways. To demonstrate this, the chapter elaborated examples of how each of the three strategies can be applied by manufacturers, retailers and logistics service providers. Another crucial concept in conjunction with CE practices is CBMs, which was also explained and defined in this chapter. Some of the most prominent categories of CBMs that all require extensive involvement from logistics management include *product life extension, sharing platforms, product as a service* and *recycling.*

The chapter thereafter presented a definition of CSCM and explicated its strategic relevance based on the three strategic management perspectives outlined in the first part of this book.

When a linear SCM philosophy is to be replaced by a circular one this renders a number of implications for logistics management. Finally, a number of these implications were further outlined, including *first-mile logistics operations, multidirectional flows of products and materials, increased and more complex information exchange, facility location, organizational design, and KPIs for circular supply chain practices.*

End-of-chapter questions

Discussion questions

1 The book presents a number of drivers for circular economy practices. Discuss the relevance of these in different industries and contexts. Is any driver more prominent than the others, and are there any more drivers not discussed in the book?

2 Consider Table 9.2 and the circular economy strategies of slowing, closing and narrowing among manufacturers, retailers and logistics service providers. How can collaboration among these players further enhance circular economy performance?

3 Consider the different categories of circular business models presented in section 9.1.4. What are the main logistics challenges related to each of these categories?

4 The book presents a number of implications for logistics management in conjunction with CSCM practices. What new requirements do these implications bring when it comes to skills and competencies among logistics employees?

5 What are the main challenges when KPIs of circular supply chains are to be combined with KPIs for linear supply chain performance?

Study questions

1 What is the main message of the circular economy concept?

2 What do closed and open loop supply chains mean?

3 What do the circular economy strategies of slowing, narrowing and closing mean?

4 What does first-mile logistics operations mean and why is it critical in CSCM?

5 Why is transparency and traceability essential in CSCM practices?

6 Explain how the organizational design in terms of new roles, responsibilities and partnerships changes when CSCM practices are introduced as a complement to linear supply chain practices.

References

Accenture (2014) *Circular Advantage: Innovative business models and technologies to create value in a world without limits to growth*,Accenture, London

Bateman, A and Bonanni, L (2019) What supply chain transparency really means, hbr.org/2019/08/what-supply-chain-transparency-really-means (archived at https://perma.cc/45LA-M6YL)

Bocken, N, de Pauw, I, Bakker, C and van der Grinten, B (2016) Product design and business model strategies for a circular economy, *Journal of Industrial and Production Engineering*,33(5), 308–320

Ellen MacArthur Foundation (2023) Building a circular supply chain, White paper, www.ellenmacarthurfoundation.org/circular-supply-chains (archived at https://perma.cc/4G8E-76G4)

Kirchherr, J, Reike, D and Hekkert, M (2017) Conceptualizing the circular economy: An analysis of 114 definitions, *Resources, Conservation and Recycling*,127, 221–232

Lewandowski, M (2016) Designing the business models for circular economy: Towards the conceptual framework, *Sustainability*, 8(1), 43

Ludeke-Freund, F, Gold, S and Bocken, N (2018) A review and typology of circular economy business model patterns, *Journal of Industrial Ecology*, 23(1), 36–61

Mentzer, J T, DeWitt, W, Keebler, J S, Min, S, Nix, N W, Smith, C D and Zacharia, Z G (2001) Defining supply chain management, *Journal of Business Logistics*, 22(2), 1–25

Montag, L (2023) Circular economy and supply chains: Definitions, conceptualizations, and research agenda of the circular supply chain framework, *Circular Economy and Sustainability*, 3, 35–75

Oghazi, P and Mostaghel, R (2018) Circular business model challenges and lessons learned: An industrial perspective, *Sustainability*, 10(3), 739

Parida, V, Burström, T, Visnjic, I and Wincent, J (2019) Orchestrating industrial ecosystem in circular economy: A two-stage transformation model for large manufacturing companies, *Journal of Business Research,* 101, 215–225

Potting, J, Hekkert, M, Worrell, E and Hanemaaijer, A (2017) *Circular Economy: Measuring innovation in the product chain*, www.pbl.nl/uploads/default/downloads/pbl-2016-circular-economy-measuring-innovation-in-product-chains-2544.pdf (archived at https://perma.cc/T9RU-DKM7)

Seuring, S and Müller, M (2008) From a literature review to a conceptual framework for sustainable supply chain management, *Journal of Cleaner Production,* 16(15), 1699–1710

World Bank (2022) Squaring the circle: Policies from Europe's circular economy transition, Washington DC, documents1.worldbank.org/curated/en/099425006222229520/pdf/P174596025fa8105a091c50fb22f0596fd1.pdf (archived at https://perma.cc/5SHY-88T3)

GLOSSARY

Absorptive capacity is defined as 'a set of organizational routines and processes by which firms acquire, assimilate, transform, and exploit knowledge to produce a dynamic organizational capability' (Zahra and George, 2002, p. 186).

Acceptance approach is a strategy for managing paradoxes in which the paradox is identified and made visible, but when there is no attempt to influence or resolve the paradox.

Agile strategy is a logistics strategy focused on being flexible and adaptable in operations as a means to maximize customer value.

Bargaining power of customers is one of the five competitive forces presented in the market positioning perspective.

Belonging paradoxes is a paradox class that appears due to competing values, beliefs and norms between different organizational units and/or different hierarchical levels in an organization.

Bundles of resources is an expression used in the resource-based perspective that recognizes that companies can be understood and viewed as a network of intertwined resources.

Business model is a concept that explains how a company's strategic intentions should be operationalized in terms of the value proposed, created, delivered and appropriated. It includes detailed descriptions and principles of the company's offering, its position in the external environment, and how the operational platform in terms of activities, resources and capabilities, internal as well as external to the company, should be organized.

Business model innovation is the process of developing existing business models or introducing new ones.

Business strategy is in this book considered to be the strategies allocated at business unit-, corporation- and/or network-level. A business strategy seeks to design and conduct business operations in such a way so that it contributes to a company's overall sustainable competitive advantage.

Capabilities are 'complex bundles of individual skills, assets and accumulated knowledge exercised through organizational processes, that enable firms to coordinate activities and make use of their resources' (Olavarrieta and Ellinger, 1997, p. 563).

Capability hierarchy is a framework where resources and capabilities are classified into different hierarchical levels, ranging from the resources that 'here and now' constitute a sustainable competitive advantage to higher-level capabilities that create, extend and modify the existing 'here and now'-resources.

Cascading occurs when products and materials that are subject to one R-principle are redirected to another R-principle, or when materials or products are brought from one supply chain and used as input material in another.

Causally ambiguous refers to a situation when it is difficult to distinguish the exact composition of involved resources and what really is the source of a sustainable competitive advantage. It is a possible reason for why a resource is imperfectly imitable.

Circular business model can be understood as the rationale of how an organization proposes, creates, delivers and captures value based on slowing, closing and/or narrowing strategies in circular supply chains.

Circular economy (CE) is a concept that aims to replace traditional, linear take-make-use-dispose business practices with circular ones that are instead guided by a make-remake-use-return logic.

Circular supply chain management is based on the concept of CE and is the systemic coordination of activities, processes and functions within and across companies to minimize waste and maximize resource efficiency of materials and products, meanwhile taking goals of economic, environmental and social performance into account.

Closed loop supply chain includes the flow of products and materials that are circulated in the same supply chain.

Closing is a strategy for enhancing circular economy practices and concerns the efforts of reducing waste and post-use material flows that go to incineration and/or landfill by instead recycling these materials.

Co-evolving is a dynamic supply chain capability that concerns the ability of supply chain members to jointly develop and combine their resources so that a new competitive resource base can be formed.

Cost leadership is one of the three generic strategies presented in the market positioning perspective.

Cultural component is a component of a logistics learning capability that revolves around having an open mindedness, commitment and joint vision towards learning.

Customer service is 'activities between the buyer and seller that enhance or facilitate the sale or use of the seller's products or services' (CSCMP, n.d.).

Desorptive capacity is the ability of a knowledge-transmitting organization to identify knowledge transfer opportunities and subsequently transfer that knowledge to the recipient.

Differentiation is one of the three generic strategies presented in the market positioning perspective.

Dilemma is a non-paradoxical interest conflict which refers to a situation in which a difficult 'either/or' choice must be made between two or more alternatives, often equally undesirable.

Distinctive resources (or capabilities) are those resources that underscore a company's sustainable competitive advantage, i.e. they fulfil the criteria of being valuable, rare, imperfectly imitable and having an organization that is able to exploit them.

Dynamic capabilities are defined as 'the capacity of an organization to purposefully create, extend, or modify its resource base' (Helfat et al, 2007, p. 4).

Dynamic capabilities perspective is a strategic management perspective that revolves around a company's ability to create, extend and modify its resource base as a source for a sustainable competitive advantage.

Economic rents are rents that originate from a superior efficiency of a resource.

Economies of integration is a financial logic that revolves around the economic advantages that can be achieved through collaboration and coordination of resources.

Economies of scale is a financial logic that is achieved by concentrating volumes of products or services to fewer resources, and thereby increasing resource utilization. By doing this, the unit cost of a product or service can be reduced.

Economies of scope is a financial logic that is achieved when the same resources can be used for several different products, services, sales activities, customer groups etc. Compared to economies of scale that aim to reduce the cost of a product, economies of scope instead aim to lower the costs for the entire company.

Ecosystem captain is defined as a 'lead enterprise that provides coordinating mechanisms, rules, key products, intellectual property, and financial capital to create structure and momentum for the market it seeks to create' (Kay et al, 2018, p. 633).

Evolutionary fitness 'refers to how well a dynamic capability enables an organization to make a living by creating, extending, or modifying its resource base' (Helfat et al, 2007, p. 7).

Exchange value refers to the monetary value paid by a buyer to the seller.

Experiential learning is a holistic approach to learning, in which experiences, perceptions, cognition and behaviour influence the learning outcome. It includes a wide range of practices such as formal experiments but also more cultural, tacit experience learning approaches through knowledge sharing and other informal interactions among employees, etc.

Experimental logistics development (ELD) is defined as 'a customer-oriented test-and-learn approach, financed and supported by top management, aiming at fast and systematic development and implementation of new logistics practices across functions, where existing physical logistics resources are boosted by new technologies' (Sandberg and Abrahamsson, 2022, p. 13).

Exploitative IDCs are governed by an individual company and enable the company to use external resources in a way that complements its existing resources to form a sustainable competitive advantage. The beneficiary is the individual company.

Firm resource heterogeneity refers to a situation when companies do not have the same access to resources, or when resources are asymmetric, meaning they perform differently across different companies.

Firm resource immobility refers to a situation when resources are not easily transferable or moveable across companies, i.e. the resources cannot easily be acquired by a company.

Firm-based IDCs are IDCs controlled by an individual company in a network, but render benefits also to other companies in the network.

Focus is one of the three generic strategies presented in the market positioning perspective.

Glocalization a trend that revolves around the need to manage global and local supply chains and business objectives simultaneously.

Hypercompetition occurs when an entire industry develops into performing the same activities in the same way and all companies can be found at the productivity frontier.

Inside-out approach is a strategizing process that originates from an analysis of the internal conditions in a company, e.g. its resource base.

Interorganizational dynamic capabilities (IDCs) are concerned with the capacity to create, extend and modify a combination of internal and (to the company) external resources.

Key performance indicators (KPIs) are metrics that enable organizations to identify areas for improvement, make informed decisions, and track progress throughout development and implementation processes of various kinds.

Knowledge accessing is a dynamic supply chain capability that concerns the ability to know where (i.e. with whom) different types of knowledge can be accessed in a supply chain.

Lean strategy is a logistics strategy built on the idea of maximizing value for customers while eliminating various kinds of waste.

Learning paradoxes is a paradox class that arises due to tensions between exploiting existing knowledge and exploring new knowledge.

Logistics is defined as 'the process of planning, implementing, and controlling procedures for the efficient and effective transportation and storage of goods including services, and related information from the point of origin to the point of consumption for the purpose of conforming to customer requirements. This definition includes inbound, outbound, internal, and external movements' (CSCMP, n.d.).

Logistics learning capability is defined as 'the ability of a logistics organization to 1) effectively maintain and manage learning organization characteristics and 2) convert learning outcomes to new logistics management strategies, tactics, and operations in support of future development of other logistics capabilities' (Esper et al, 2007, p. 63).

Logistics management 'is that part of supply chain management that plans, implements, and controls the efficient, effective forward and reverses flow and storage of goods, services and related information between the point of origin and the point of consumption in order to meet customers' 'requirements' (CSCMP, n.d.).

Logistics-oriented companies are companies whose overall business strategies hinge upon superior logistics performance.

Logistics platform is defined as 'a homogenous part of the logistics system, which a logistics organisation centrally manages and controls, and has the power to design in a way that it is a resource base for new market positions. The logistics platform includes concepts for logistics operations, a physical structure, processes and its activities as well as the information systems needed for design, operations and reporting' (Abrahamsson, Aldin and Stahre, 2003, p. 104).

Logistics strategy is in this book considered to be a functional strategy concerned with the organization, planning and execution of logistics operations. The overall performance of a logistics strategy is often measured with respect to total costs, service and lead times.

Logistics value chain refers to that part of the larger, generic value chain that structures logistics activities.

Market positioning perspective is a strategic management perspective that revolves around how a company should position itself in the marketplace to gain a sustainable competitive advantage against its competitors.

Microfoundations are 'distinct skills, processes, procedures, organizational structures, decision rules and disciplines' (Teece, 2007, p. 1319).

Monopolistic rents are rents that originate from the possession of a unique resource that other organizations are prevented from having.

Narrowing is a strategy for enhancing circular economy practices and refers to efforts aimed at minimizing the use of input materials in products, i.e. using fewer resources per product.

Network-based IDCs are IDCs that are controlled at a network level and benefit the entire network.

Omnichannel is the seamless integration of multiple market channels, primarily sales via physical stores and online sales.

Open loop supply chain includes the flow of goods that bring products and materials from the original supply chain to a new one.

Operational effectiveness (OE) 'means performing similar activities "better" than rivals perform them. Operational effectiveness includes but is not limited to efficiency. It refers to any number of practices that allow a company to better utilize its inputs by, for example, reducing defects in products or developing better products faster. In contrast, strategic positioning means performing "different" activities from rivals or performing similar activities in "different ways"' (Porter, 1996, p. 62).

Orchestration capability is defined as 'the dynamic capability of a central actor to efficiently and effectively integrate and coordinate resources and relationships within an ecosystem to adapt to the continuously changing dynamic environment' (Shi and Shen, 2021, p. 15).

Organizing paradoxes is a paradox class that arises due to competing organizational design logics that occur both within and between organizations.

Outside-in approach is a strategizing process that originates from an analysis of the external environment of a company.

Paradox is defined as 'contradictory yet interrelated elements that exist simultaneously and persist over time' (Smith and Lewis, 2011, p. 382).

Path dependency refers to a situation when a resource is historically conditioned, and is a possible reason for why a resource is imperfectly imitable.

Performance measurement system (PMS) is a combination of individual KPIs that together cover the essential dimensions of the business to monitor, and hence provides an overview of the company's performance.

Performing paradoxes is a paradox class that arises when organizational units (e.g. supply chains, companies or functions) have several competing goals and objectives simultaneously.

Productivity frontier is a concept for describing the sum of best practices of an industry in terms of cost and value creation.

Reconfiguring capabilities is a dynamic capability class that is concerned with the long-term orchestration of resources. Their main objective is to adapt the resource base to changing customer and technology developments as well as to shape the market where the company operates.

Relational component is a component of a logistics learning capability that revolves around the management of external relationships to foster and improve learning.

Relational rent is defined 'as a supernormal profit jointly generated in an exchange relationship that cannot be generated by either firm in isolation and can only be created through the joint idiosyncratic contributions of the specific alliance partners' (Dyer and Singh, 1998, p. 662).

Relational view is a strategic management theory within the resource-based perspective that emphasizes the existence of resource-combinations across company borders that fulfil the VRIO attributes.

Rents is a term discussed in the resource-based perspective that refers to the surplus, extraordinary returns a resource can generate that are above the average profitability level of an industry.

Resource-based perspective is a strategic management perspective that revolves around the resource base and how this provides a sustainable competitive advantage.

Resource-based view of the firm (RBV) is a strategic management theory within the resource-based perspective that emphasizes superior resources as the foundation for a company's sustainable competitive advantage.

Resources are 'all assets, capabilities, organizational processes, firm attributes, information, knowledge, etc. controlled by a firm that enable the firm to conceive of and implement strategies that improve its efficiency and effectiveness' (Barney, 1991, s. 101).

Rivalry is one of the five competitive forces presented in the market positioning perspective.

R-principles are a number of approaches that aim to adopt a circular economy.

SCOR (supply chain operations reference) model is a framework that offers a structured set of KPIs which can be used for evaluation and improvement of logistics and supply chain operations.

Seizing capabilities is a dynamic capability class that revolves around the development and commercialization of new processes, products and services.

Sensing capabilities is a dynamic capability class that consists of a variety of processes aimed at discovering business opportunities and/or threats.

Slowing is a strategy for enhancing circular economy practices and includes various initiatives for extending the life cycles of products.

Socially complex refers to a situation when the superiority of a resource hinges upon individuals and personal connections, and is a possible reason for why a resource is imperfectly imitable.

Spatial separation is a strategy for managing paradoxes that revolves around a division of the arguments in the paradox, so that different parts or levels of the organization (or supply chain) are consciously governed to support one of the arguments each.

Strategic management theory includes several approaches (theories) for answering the critical question of why some companies are able to outperform others over time.

Structural component is a component of a logistics learning capability that revolves around the establishment and maintenance of an organizational infrastructure that supports learning.

Supplier's bargaining power is one of the five competitive forces presented in the market positioning perspective.

Supply chain disruption is an unintended, unwanted triggering event that influences the supply chain performance negatively, i.e. there is a negative deviation from the normal state of performance.

Supply chain management 'encompasses the planning and management of all activities involved in sourcing and procurement, conversion, and all logistics management activities. Importantly, it also includes coordination and collaboration with channel partners, which can be suppliers, intermediaries, third party service providers, and customers. In essence, supply chain management integrates supply and demand management within and across companies' (CSCMP, n.d.).

Supply chain orientation (SCO) is 'the recognition by an organization of the systemic, strategic implications of the tactical activities involved in managing the various flows in a supply chain' (Mentzer et al, 2001, p. 11).

Supply chain resilience is 'the adaptive capability of the supply chain to prepare for unexpected events, respond to disruptions, and recover from them by maintaining continuity of operations at the desired level of connectedness and control over structure and function' (Ponomarov and Holcomb, 2009, p. 131).

Supply chain resilience strategies are plans and measures undertaken to cope with supply chain disruptions and can include the themes of flexibility, agility, redundancy and collaboration.

Supportive IDCs are IDCs controlled at a network level, but rendering benefits primarily at an individual company level (among network members).

Sustainable competitive advantage is a company's overall ability to consistently outperform its competitors and can be measured, for instance, in above average profitability, company growth and customer value creation.

Synthesis approach is a strategy for managing paradoxes that revolves around finding new ways of combining the arguments of the paradox in new, innovative ways or introducing new perspectives that eliminate the opposition between the arguments.

Systems thinking is a philosophy that recognizes the existence of a 'system of systems' in which resources and objectives in a number of more narrow systems are understood to be subsystems of a more holistic, larger system.

Temporal component is a component of a logistics learning capability that revolves around the support and emphasis on speed in learning processes.

Temporal separation is a strategy for managing paradoxes in which one argument of the paradox is allowed to dominate the company and its development in the short-term perspective at the cost of the other. The other argument is, however, still acknowledged and is planned to be prioritized in the long-term perspective.

Threat of new entrants is one of the five competitive forces presented in the market positioning perspective.

Threat of substitution is one of the five competitive forces presented in the market positioning perspective.

Trade-off is a non-paradoxical interest conflict that involves a situation that requires decision-making where prioritizing one aspect inevitably leads to a reduction of priority in another.

Triple bottom line refers to an approach where economic, environmental as well as social value considerations are taken into account.

Use value, also called value-in-use, is defined as the customers' perception of a product's utility.

Value appropriation is the process of capturing a share of the value created to the customer.

Value chain is a concept associated mainly with the market positioning perspective, in which a company's activities are schematically presented into various categories of primary and supporting activities.

Value creation is a process to enhance use value for a customer.

VRIO model (Valuable, Rare, Imperfectly imitable, Organization) is a framework in the resource-based perspective that explains the attributes of a distinctive resource (or capability) that underscores a sustainable competitive advantage.

References

Abrahamsson, M, Aldin, N and Stahre, F (2003) Logistics platforms for improved strategic flexibility, *International Journal of Logistics: Research and Applications*, 6(3), 85–106

Barney, J (1991) Firm resources and sustained competitive advantage, *Journal of Management*, 17(1), 99–120

CSCMP (n.d.) Supply chain management definitions and glossary, https://cscmp.org/CSCMP/CSCMP/Educate/SCM_Definitions_and_Glossary_of_Terms.aspx (archived at https://perma.cc/686S-PSGD)

Dyer, J H and Singh, H (1998) The relational view: Cooperative strategy and sources of interorganizational competitive advantage, *Academy of Management Review*, 23(4), 660–679

Esper, T, Fugate, B and Davis-Sramek, B (2007) Logistics learning capability: Sustaining the competitive advantage gained through logistics leverage, *Journal of Business Logistics*, 28(2), 57–81

Helfat, C, Finkelstein, S, Mitchell, W, Peteraf, M A, Singh, H, Teece, D and Winter, S (2007) *Dynamic capabilities: Understanding strategic change in organizations*, Blackwell Publishing, Oxford

Kay, N, Leih, S and Teece, D (2018) The role of emergence in dynamic capabilities: A restatement of the framework and some possibilities for future research, *Long Range Planning*, 27(4), 623–638

Mentzer, J T, DeWitt, W, Keebler, J S, Min, S, Nix, N W, Smith, C D and Zacharia, Z G (2001) Defining supply chain management, *Journal of Business Logistics*, 22(2), 1–25

Olavarrieta, S and Ellinger, A (1997) Resource-based theory and strategic logistics research, *International Journal of Physical Distribution & Logistics Management*, 27(9–10), 559–587

Ponomarov, S Y and Holcomb, M C (2009) Understanding the concept of supply chain resilience, *International Journal of Logistics Management*, 20(1), 124–143

Porter, M (1996) What is strategy? *Harvard Business Review*, 74(6), 61–78

Sandberg, E and Abrahamsson, M (2022) Exploring organizational learning and experimental logistics development at the global fashion retailer H&M, *Global Business & Organizational Excellence*, 41(2), 6–20, doi.org/10.1002/joe.22143 (archived at https://perma.cc/CHA9-RJUV)

Shi, Q and Shen, L (2021) Orchestration capability: A bibliometric analysis, *Kybernetes*, 51(10), 3073–3094

Smith, W K and Lewis, M W (2011) Toward a theory of paradox: A dynamic equilibrium model of organizing, *Academy of Management Review*, 36(2), 381–403

Teece, D (2007) Explicating dynamic capabilities: The nature and microfoundations of (sustainable) enterprise performance, *Strategic Management Journal*, 28(13), 1319–1350

Zahra, S A and George, G (2002) Absorptive capacity: A review, reconceptualization, and extension, *Academy of Management Review*, 27(2), 185–203

INDEX

NB: page numbers in *italic* indicate figures or tables

Also from Kogan Page

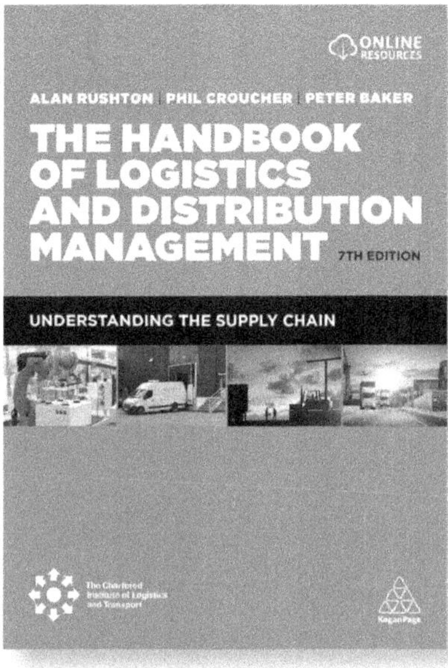

ISBN: 9781398602045

ISBN: 9780749493318

ISBN: 9780749496883

ISBN: 9781398614918